Therapeutic
Ena

Therapeutic Enactment

Restoring Vitality through Trauma Repair in Groups

Marv Westwood, PhD
University of British Columbia
Professor

Patricia Wilensky, PhD
BC School of Professional Psychology
Psychologist

Vancouver
Group Action Press

Westwood, Marv, 1944-
Therapeutic enactment : restoring vitality through trauma repair in groups / Marv Westwood, Patricia Wilensky.

Includes bibliographical references and index.
ISBN 0-9738082-0-9

1. Psychic trauma--Treatment. 2. Psychic trauma--Patients--Rehabilitation. 3. Traumatic neuroses--Patients--Rehabilitation.
4. Group psychotherapy. I. Wilensky, Patricia, 1946- II. Title.

RC489.A34W48 2005   616.85'2106   C2005-903853-5

We have changed the names of people whose experiences with Therapeutic Enactment are portrayed in this book and altered their stories to protect the privacy of the individual.

Cover photo courtesy of Digital Vision Photography/Veer Images
Book design and layout by Gray Poehnell

Printed in Canada by Hignell Book Printing, 488 Burnell Street, Winnipeg, Manitoba, R3G 2B4 Telephone 204-784-1033

For information about ordering, please visit www.ecps.educ.ubc.ca/research/mwestwood.htm

groupactionpress@telus.net

Twenty years ago, when Jenny was in her early twenties, she came home from holiday and found the body of her dead mother, who had committed suicide in the family home. She called her dad, who lived apart, but he refused to come. Jenny had to handle the police, coroner, and funeral entirely on her own. Now in her forties and the head of her department, Jenny lives alone, is estranged from her family, and drinks to ease the pain.

Ten years ago, Jack was offered a marvellous new job. He uprooted his family and travelled to a distant place to work. There he discovered his work team had wanted a different supervisor and they resented him. Suppressing his feelings of disappointment and chagrin, Jack tried to win over his work mates. After six years, though, the work environment had become toxic. Jack was depressed. Moreover, he felt hopeless and this feeling reminded him of his early years with his domineering father and alcoholic mother.

Contents

Introduction

Therapeutic Enactment is a group-based therapy that engages clients in a dynamic interpersonal and action-oriented process. We developed this therapy to help clients who have experienced trauma or psychological injury that interferes with normal healthy functioning. One of the main underlying assumptions of Therapeutic Enactment is that complex client problems require complex interventions and too often single system or theory approaches are inadequate to meet this challenge.

As a group-based intervention for trauma repair, Therapeutic Enactment involves experience of the self in group in a way that is physically, emotionally, cognitively, and spiritually embodied, so that change occurs at multiple levels within the self. These embodied experiences are enacted and reflected upon within a community; that is, the self is witnessed and affirmed within a supportive social context, rather than being affirmed within the context of a one-to-one therapist-client relationship as in other approaches to trauma repair. Our goal was to integrate several theoretical approaches into a more comprehensive method for meeting client needs. We drew from group therapy, social learning, object relations, somatic theory, narrative, and script theory (Westwood, Keats, & Wilensky, 2002). At the same time we recognized the important and contributing role of the individual system approaches that are available for our work helping clients of trauma. We believe that individual system approaches are best used in preparation and follow-up to the group intervention.

In our research while developing this method we found that clients report changes that are core to their identity. This is in contrast to other therapy methods that address symptoms of trauma but do not necessarily alter the clients' identification of themselves as victims. Through Therapeutic Enactment clients are able to release previously held trauma scripts and re-narrate a self that is more viable. They can move beyond the trauma and exist in a new way that eliminates the need for identity markers such as "survivor" or "victim". They experience repair of the trauma, allowing them to reframe a fuller sense of self and regain a sense of personal wholeness.

A Brief Overview of Therapeutic Enactment

Therapeutic Enactment allows participants to enact and reprocess a traumatic event in a safe group setting free from criticism and judgment. Safety within the group is of utmost importance. Individuals choose a traumatic event from the past, one that troubles them to the present day, a childhood event or a more recent adult wound. Assisted by two therapists, they select and plan together a specific scenario attached to the event as a basis for the enactment.

The therapists work with the clients to prepare them for working in the group by providing support to reduce their symptoms. One of the individual system approaches we use is Eye Movement Desensitization and Reprocessing (EMDR). We then work with perceptions, cognitions, behaviours in context, body sensations, emotions, and spiritual dimensions to free clients from the tormenting heightened sense of guilt and self-blame arising from the trauma. The social context in which the trauma occurred and in which the effects are lived out are enacted.

The Therapeutic Enactment process creates an interplay between the internal world and the external here and now in public, to create an "as if" scenario that truthfully reflects the participants' present needs and awareness. Enactment of the selected life scene is made possible through the process of externalizing these "internal" representations of self. In doing so clients experience increased expression and self understanding. Enacting their story is a form of "concretization" of self, events, and dynamics that previously are not in their awareness.

The witnessing circle of the group symbolically embodies the community at large, which can be particularly healing in shame-based enactments when the trauma is shared. Participants come away believing others have understood them, leading them to feel respected and affirmed—for most people a validating and desirable experience.

A reparative process is the expected outcome of Therapeutic Enactment, along with the relief of anxiety and pain. The repair of wounds to the deep inner self involves altering basic self schemas for more effective functioning. By enacting their narrative experientially in the group, clients are able to create new meaning and better ways of responding. They normally leave feeling that their energy and outlook are strengthened.

The Clients We Work With

Therapeutic Enactment is about the relief of suffering—both one's own and that of one's clients. This means confronting shame and other emotions squarely in the groups to bring about change in how participants experience, think, feel, and act. An important healing component of the enactment groups is the connection that participants make about their own and others' suffering. Many otherwise highly functioning individuals have an ambivalent relationship to their own suffering. They know that somewhere along the road they took a major blow. Their parents may have injured them deliberately or inadvertently. They may have experienced loss or neglect in early childhood. They may have suffered chronic, systemic, covert trauma throughout childhood. They may have been bullied or abused at school or work. As a result, they have developed coping strategies that have allowed them to survive, even prevail. They have made themselves strong, yet inside they feel empty and sad. They go through the motions at work or in relationships but their emotional energy and availability are low. They have lost a deep connection with self and with others that has to be re-established.

The Traumatized Client

To be traumatized means that all our assumptions about how the world works—fairness, just desserts, and even the meaning of life—are shattered (Janoff-Bulman, 1985). We experience an overwhelming sense of helplessness and even despair (Herman, 1992). Survivors of trauma often comment that the worst part of the experience is feeling out of control. They become obsessed by thoughts of "Why me?" "Why did this happen?" "What did I do to deserve or create this?" People want to deny the truth of what has happened, making minimizing statements such as "Oh, it wasn't so bad." "Other people have it worse." "They were doing the best they could." "It wasn't their fault."

Unhealed victims of trauma are prone to self-destructive, self-soothing, tension-reducing behaviours such as addiction. They over-identify with themselves as victims. They are emotionally numb. The people we have met through our therapeutic groups feel a deep split inside them. A profound disruption between self and the primary caregivers in early childhood may manifest itself later in adults who experience a split between home and work, self and others, children and parents, mind and soul, or body and spirit. This painful split makes it impossible for people who have experienced trauma to relax, to be who they really are. They feel on the threshold of something, that they could go either way. They do not feel grounded or completely committed to the task at hand. They are always ambivalent. Their relationships feel transient. Many say either that they do not yet feel grown up or that they never had a childhood.

To want to heal the split means that unhealed trauma victims must commit themselves to a process that is both a journey into their own history, as well as a journey "inward and downward", looking beneath the surface of their motivations to restore the self. It takes courage to enter into dark places in our psyche, places that hold terror and pain, without false sentimentality or pessimistic fault-finding, especially for the traumatized client. They need to reconnect with their grief in order to heal.

It is important to remember that, at some point in trauma, it may have been necessary to put grief aside in order to strengthen and survive. However, the time comes when this coping strategy works against healing. Denied grief has frozen hearts and souls. During the reparation process, intense expression of emotion wakes individuals to the fact that their hearts have been broken. It can increase their empathy and effectiveness. The archetypal psychologists, including Bly and Woodman (1998, p. 20), refer to the "crises" (wounds) in life as openings to transformation. But the transforming journey is best undertaken in the company of like-hearted travellers. Others can offer support for trauma victims on their voyage into the unknown. Others can help individuals find faith in the process, in themselves, and in our innate human ability to heal ourselves with the support of others, and as we support others to do the same.

Helping Professionals and Trauma

In addition to our usual trauma clients, a significant subgroup of clients are fellow professionals who have suffered deep-seated emotional pain—usually, though not always, originating in childhood—that may result in depression, burnout, and exhaustion. In our view the helper must be helped and returned to "whole" before they can really assist others to be healed. We wanted a method that would assist practitioners in healing their own wounds, thus freeing them to be wholeheartedly available to the needs of others. In other words, we were looking for a "practitioner heal thyself" method.

Most practitioners in the helping professions are trained to be available to their clients and to keep their own emotions and issues away from their practice. Yet they most often work alone. This leaves them, at the end of their day, with no opportunities to debrief, grieve, or decompress. Many studies have shown that professionals, particularly those who work with the victims of trauma, carry a heavy burden. They may suffer vicarious traumatization, secondary traumatization, or compassion fatigue (Figley, 1995). Trauma and burnout are common as a result of the helplessness that caregivers often feel when faced with the "unfixable suffering" of others (Plomp, 1998). The shame and distress practitioners feel because they are unable to fix such pain may not reduce their commitment to their work and clients but the personal cost gradually accumulates. It is to alleviate this distress that people come into Therapeutic Enactment groups. (Although their assumptive beliefs about the world were shattered, they can begin to trust others again through their experiences in the group.)

Both authors have worked for years with others in the "helping professions". We have watched our colleagues and students grind down with vicarious trauma that includes depression and helplessness as the consequence of years of exposure to the suffering of others. We wanted to design a way of helping practitioners revive their spirit as well as learn a new way of helping their clients. We knew that group practitioners need more tools to help the traumatized, but they also need more tools to keep themselves from going under because they feel helpless. We are both trained in group therapy, and we have worked with psychodrama and gestalt methods. We wanted a therapeutic methodology that could work in groups because we understand the value of the connection with others. Also, we wanted a method that would work with mixed groups of professionals, not solely counsellors and therapists. Participants in our groups have included physicians, lawyers, managers, social workers, nurses, the military, including veterans and returning peacekeepers, police, and fire service personnel.

Few therapeutic interventions are available to service providers struggling with the issues people in helping professions face. Finding places where we can come together for the purposes of healing is not easy. We study, we train, we work hard to facilitate positive change in our clients—and we fail. Sometimes, we do not even know whether we have succeeded or failed. When we fail we do so partly because our work lacks a necessary spirit that infuses human suffering with meaning. Therapeutic Enactment in groups has been specifically designed to address these kinds of delicate and troubling problems. What follows is an example of how this method assisted one of these high functioning professionals.

Rediscovering Emotion through Therapeutic Enactment: Kenneth's Story

One of our participants, a forty-four-year-old physician we will call Kenneth, felt burned out after twenty years of helping others. Although his patients loved him, at home he felt sad and distracted a lot of the time, skipping out on social engagements and spending weekends crashed out in front of the television. One of Kenneth's colleagues mentioned psychotherapy to him and told him about a method he had heard good things about from colleagues who had undergone it. Kenneth, out of curiosity and desperation, decided to contact the therapists and find out more. We accepted him as a client suitable for Therapeutic Enactment and encouraged him to prepare for a workshop weekend. During assessment in preparation for his enactment, Kenneth told the therapists that his most important childhood relationship was with his beloved grandfather, who died when Kenneth was ten. His parents would not allow him to attend the grandfather's funeral. Later, Kenneth's father, who had not had a warm relationship with the grandfather, refused to allow his name to be mentioned again.

Kenneth longed to say goodbye to his grandfather. "He was the most important person in my life up to then, and I never got to see him again, or touch his hand, or say how important he was to me, and how much I would miss him. For many years, I felt an ache inside, wanting to have had a final time with him, to see him. This desire never really left me because it felt so incomplete."

As therapists we helped Kenneth create a scene based on this unresolved incident. Together we decided to enact a scene in which Kenneth is a boy at his grandfather's deathbed. In this scene, he could act out what he had long wanted to say to his grandfather.

By externalizing and making concrete in the group what had been an internalized "script", Kenneth was finally able to experience and express a myriad of unexpressed feelings of grief, shame, and rage. By so doing, a block was cleared. He felt released from numbness and saw hidden things clearly. He felt free to begin uncovering other feelings and to discover new things about himself. In a role reversal, Kenneth took on the role of his grandfather and rediscovered that his grandfather loved him because he saw something in him that the little boy had yet to know. Kenneth felt good about himself simply because he believed that his grandfather believed in him. As the enactment proceeded it moved into some of Kenneth's unresolved issues about standing up to his father. Finally, Kenneth was able to express anger to his father, thus taking his place apart from him as a man.

Kenneth was surprised at the strength of his feelings about his grandfather and his ability to express them in public. He was struck by his own comfort as he settled into a supportive, loving group. In addition, he found that he was willing and able to help others as the group proceeded, by taking on roles in their families that were painful and emotionally demanding. Moreover, he found that this experience left him feeling enlivened and enthusiastic about other people and he had forgotten how much he had longed for this. In fact, Kenneth told the other participants he felt that some injured part of his inner spirit or soul had been repaired.

About this Book

This book offers the reader a therapeutic option for helping clients experiencing trauma to make significant and reparative changes, regardless of whether the trauma was relatively recent in their lives or occurred much earlier in childhood. Therapeutic Enactment has been applied successfully to all the major trauma targets such as crime, war crimes, torture, sexual abuse, and rape, as well as childhood neglect and trauma. Therapeutic Enactment is action-based, not language-dependent, and therefore is highly suited in cross-cultural contexts such as Aboriginal and other distinct cultural groups. It is also effective for both visually impaired and deaf clients and has been used in many inter disciplinary contexts, including active armed forces and mixed professional affiliations in various community settings.

Therapeutic Enactment is a deep and powerful treatment approach that helps participants move toward transformation. Isolation, shame, and grief are directly confronted. If the members can believe in the power of the group for healing then they can begin to believe in their own healing power.

Our goal, is to describe the theoretical basis, application processes, and relevant research supporting this particular group-based approach to trauma repair.

What Is Therapeutic Enactment?

CHAPTER 1

Let the young rain of tears come.
Let the calm hands of grief come.
It's not all as evil as you think.

—Rolf Jacobsen, "Sunflower"

Try to praise the mutilated world.

—Adam Zagajewski

Therapeutic Enactment is an experiential, group-based method for repairing the emotional trauma suffered in our past that still affects our present relationships, mood, and quality of life. Although it emerged out of the authors' familiarity with other group and counselling theories and methods, it is unparalleled in its emphasis on maintaining safe groups. Many participants tell us that in previous group therapies they have found the group process frightening, even abusive. Going into these groups they felt fragile or ashamed of their pain, and the group experience stirred up emotions and retraumatized them. We are extremely sensitive to this problem and constantly work to establish and re-establish feelings of safety in enactment groups. Also, unlike most groups within which individual therapy is attempted, we emphasize whole-group process, and reparation of both mind and spirit.

Often we have been asked why we call the work an enactment rather than a re-enactment. Using the *Oxford English Dictionary* as our reference, we explain that a "re-enactment" means "to act or perform again, to reproduce". This is not at all what we mean to create. We are not recalling or reproducing actual memories. Rather, we are looking more to "enact", which means "creating a public ceremony, a declaration of authority", "to implant or inspire a feeling into a person", and to "perform a public ceremony". This is what we mean by an enactment.

Therapeutic Enactment's Beginnings in Psychodrama

When we began our workshops in 1993, psychodrama was the method of practice most available to us given our emphasis on action methods to assist and bring about change. Much credit must be given to Moreno (1947) and subsequent workers in the field of psychodrama, as they showed us how to use an action-based approach that attempted to integrate several systems at one time. As teachers and researchers we were painfully aware that with psychodrama we had on our hands a method that could produce significant results but lacked a theoretical framework to which we could link practice with good research. We were actually quite cautious of psychodrama because, although an influential method of change, it had escaped rigorous examination. This led to a combined effort on our part to extend practice and initiate research to uncover and describe psychodrama's framework. We found ways to adapt the approach to produce more consistent outcomes and ensure feelings of safety among our participants.

Readers familiar with psychodrama will notice similarities and differences with the Therapeutic Enactment model. The form of the enactments does draw from dramatic methods—we use protagonists (called clients or leads here), doubles, scenes, role playing, catharsis, and directors (called therapists here). Clearly our most important difference, however, relates first to the emphasis we place on safety and group development and second on maximizing the therapeutic benefits of achieving reparation of personal trauma within the group process. The group context is as important in the change process as the enactments themselves. The authors agree with Blatner (1996), who points out that psychodrama "has a very individual focus, it is protagonist centered" (p. 11). Therapeutic Enactment practitioners, on the other hand, use the group as a critical component, involving not only those who take on roles for the lead client but also those who "witness". Witnessing helps the client be seen, which is important in situations in which repair involves having others know the story. Too often practitioners of psychodrama move too quickly into enactment without taking time to create the necessary climate of safety and control. But safety is essential so that clients are fully grounded and able to take risks based on a clear perception of trust within the group.

We developed other areas of difference from Moreno's model. We paid very careful attention to planning in advance the framework of the enactment. This planning led to highly contained enactments within the group, resulting in the restoration of the individual client's experience of self. Pre-planning includes an in-depth assessment, collection of resources, and, if possible, pre-selection of role players.

Another crucial difference from Moreno is that personal spontaneity becomes the end result of a highly successful process for the client and the group, rather than the preferred state of the client during the enactment. It is important to remember that Moreno was trying to shock the establishment steeped in neo-Freudian practices. He thus emphasized action and affect and de-emphasized cognition and understanding. This underpinned his almost religious adherence to spontaneity over thoughtful reflection and planning. For us, on the other hand, spontaneity is an outcome of successful therapeutic resolution rather than a precondition for moving into action (Black, 2002). We found that spontaneity often becomes blocked as a result of a traumatic experience and individuals require time and readiness before they can access the spontaneous part of themselves.

Several safety concerns prompted us to discourage spontaneous scene creation by the client. Without careful planning, the agreed-upon client goals tend to get lost and completion of the therapeutic repair may not be possible. Also, protecting client sovereignty has to be a major goal for therapists. Spontaneously jumping into the centre of the group without careful consideration, preparation, and resources can be an emotional response to the power of the group. However, this puts at risk the client's ultimate emotional equanimity as well as the tone of the group. We want our group members to leave the therapeutic intervention feeling better, not worse.

As a further difference from Moreno's method, we have taken similar liberties with the psychodrama phenomenon of catharsis—the sense of relief that people feel when they involuntarily release strong pent-up emotions such as grief or rage. Yalom (1998), discussing "catharsis", describes how the strong expression of emotion enhances not only the development of cohesiveness but also, with the expression of these feelings, the development of close mutual bonds. The encouragement of "emotional expressiveness" in Therapeutic Enactment is seen as the primary goal for clients as they begin to reintegrate thought, feeling, and action. Catharsis is one important form of client self-expression but it is not the end of the story. Stanislavski (1936) warned "there cannot be, under any circumstances, action which is directed immediately at the arousing of a feeling for its own sake" (p. 38). For us, catharsis is not the end goal of the enactment but the beginning of reparation and healing. Catharsis wakes individuals to the fact that their hearts have been broken. Their pain is a blessing because ultimately it helps to bring back feeling and can lead the way toward the restoration of depth and soul. Catharsis appears dramatic and certainly keeps the group on its toes. However, it tends to separate actor from audience and that is something we guard against in the structure and process of our groups.

A fourth difference from psychodrama is that, in Therapeutic Enactment, we have found follow-up of the client for several weeks with individual counselling to be essential to ensure that they are not retraumatized after the enactment and are able to integrate the reparation they achieve into their day-to-day lives. In reflecting with the therapist "after the fact", the client is able to revisit the original goals and track the changes they experience over time.

Other Theoretical Bases Underpinning Therapeutic Enactment

In developing the Therapeutic Enactment model, we draw upon several major psychological theories and practices in addition to psychodrama: group counselling theory, schema and script theory, self-psychology and object relations, gestalt therapy, and body psychotherapy. We are only going to discuss these theories very briefly. However, we have provided a list of references at the back of the book so that interested readers may investigate them further. These different theoretical perspectives provide a rationale for describing how the client may recreate an inner experience (past, present, or anticipated future event) as closely as possible through acting out or living through the event in a safe, present-centred therapeutic setting.

Group counselling theory is a major part of the Therapeutic Enactment model. We emphasize a community approach in which therapy takes place within a group context: everyone participates with routinely high commitment, involvement, and inclusion. The reparative nature of a participatory, non-judgmental work group is a central assumption of the model.

Early on we noticed that, in many groups, the work was not about the group at all. Those members who were not in the "hot seat" (Perls, 1969) were often frustrated and bored. Sometimes, they were even vicariously traumatized. What was happening was not group therapy but individual therapy in a group setting. People became observers as part of an audience, reinforcing those alienating and isolating coping mechanisms we all use when faced with the suffering of others. The group itself lost energy. In contrast, our model of Therapeutic Enactment includes a commitment to creating potent, cohesive, and safe groups. We have been influenced by the group counselling papers published by Schermer and Pines (1994) and Edelson and Berg (1999).

Schema and script theory, according to schema theorists Bruning, Schraw, and Ronning (1999), proposes that people organize knowledge into complex representations called schemata or "cognitive maps". Trauma disrupts the way an individual processes information and, even more fundamentally, disrupts the individual's attempts to repair damage and heal emotional wounds. This results in the enduring effects of the trauma. The individual feels that their life and relationships are permanently in disarray.

Schemata and scripts are highly personal and distinctive, containing the individual's emotional memories, expectations, hopes, perceptions, motivations, and action. For example, an individual might operate with an authority schema within which all men are in charge as bosses, doctors, and gods, and all women are handmaids. This schema would likely run this individual into difficulties in his male-female relationships. Therapeutic Enactment offers the possibility of restructuring such an obstructive schema and rewriting injurious nuclear scripts so that, in our example, this individual sees men and women in equal roles. New scripts and accompanying emotions are created in the process. The script is made concrete so that relationships can be seen, experienced, re-experienced, or altered. As a second example, an individual may be operating with the script: "No matter what I do now I will fail because my parents told me I would never amount to anything." During Therapeutic Enactment, they perceive that this was about their parents and not something they chose. They can decide to confront their parents and take on an altered script such as "I am a good person" and "I am lovable and competent".

Self-psychology and object relations theory involves interpersonal relationships, which are a key factor in the Therapeutic Enactment process. Kohut (1984) realized that breaks or damage in the consistency and reliability of nurture in the early years led to deficiencies in the individual's ability to form conflict-free relationships later on. According to Ford and Urban (1998), the interpersonal theories of self-psychology and object relations are concerned with how our relationships with others (whether real, imagined, past, or present) affect our overall psychological functioning. The focus is generally on early developmental experiences with primary caregivers and the internal representations of those experiences.

In Therapeutic Enactment, participants are able to overcome dissociated and depersonalizing defences left over from childhood because the therapist holds the client safely in the group. What this means is that the therapist reintroduces projected material back to the client in conscious and deliberate measures. New experiences allow understanding of old notions of the self to be discarded or renewed. For instance, asking a client to take on the role of a neglectful or cold parent can be very demanding yet yield sudden empathic shifts in the client's sense of self. In one Therapeutic Enactment, a client who described a cold and distant mother and who thought of herself as self-contained and unemotional realized during the enactment that, in fact, she was "the passionate one" in the family and had felt disdained for this. She had suppressed her "emotionality" in order to fit in and had grown to believe that this was her true personality. At the end, she said: "I feel loved [by her family of choice]. I don't have to close off."

Also, we have been influenced by Winnicott's (1965, p. 51) descriptions of "play" and "creativity". Understanding and interpretation take second place to the state when "the patient surprises himself or herself" at play. People are unable to play because they are crippled by shame. The enactment group can provide a restorative setting to get back in touch with their own creative inner self. Self-psychology aims for the development of an inner strength in the person, free from compulsive, self-defeating patterns of childishly dependent or ambivalent relationships. This is something we strive for consciously in the enactment groups.

Gestalt therapy theory (Perls, 1969) offers a variety of techniques that are helpful in moving clients into action rather than remaining solely at the level of thinking, reasoning, and talking. When clients experience awareness of bodily sensations, energy levels, hesitations, and tone of voice in the present moment, these are called gestalts or wholes and are ways of looking at and constructing reality. Personal integration is facilitated by linking what they are thinking to what they are doing and feeling. Reclaiming disowned parts of the self occurs when the therapist first helps to increase the client's awareness and then explores this material with the client. For example, the therapist may say to the client as they proceed through the scenario: "What are you aware of right now?" A common reply might be: "I am aware that I thought I would be angry but I feel really sad and this surprises me." One of the main tenets of gestalt therapy is that once individuals have their awareness changed, then they are free to choose their actions. Like many of these early therapeutic contributions, gestalt therapy is about gaining freedom from the tyranny of constraining or painful beliefs and repetitive activities. A person who believes that they "should" be angry with someone may really be trying again and again to get that person to listen to them, "sucking juice out of a dry orange" as one of our group members put it. When the person realizes that instead they are sad because of the lack of a relationship with the someone, they may finally accept the truth of this and stop their futile onslaught. "Unfinished business" is a key concept and this is linked to buried feelings that nonetheless interfere with present-day functioning. In Therapeutic Enactments, individuals are helped to finally express and finish business that may have clogged up their emotional systems for decades.

Body psychotherapy is also involved in Therapeutic Enactment. Our emotional system is located in our body and can become immobilized as a result of trauma. A traumatizing event attacks the body first. Yet all too often the reactions and workings of the body are left out of the therapeutic endeavour. Trained in the 1960s and 70s in individual therapy we had no previous experience of using body therapy. However, we were fortunate to encounter practitioners who had expertise in that area. Slowly we have incorporated an emphasis on body awareness and body responsiveness as part of our action-based practice. Many of the major trauma recovery methods now emphasize the body as an essential part of treatment. The mind-body connection may be broken as trauma and anxiety crush the delicate calibration that allows the mind and body to be in balance, thus decreasing the individual's quality of life. Many people who have been traumatized are numb from holding suppressed emotions of fear, rage, and grief in the body and they suffer from related psychosomatic symptoms such as panic attacks. They can also suffer chronic pain from rigid muscle tension. Many use dissociation as a coping defence and this makes it difficult to work with them therapeutically as in a very real way they are not present. During Therapeutic Enactment therapists have to be on the watch for dissociation and must constantly bring the person's awareness back to their immediate experience. We have had many people in our groups complain that their bodies are out of their control with addictions or eating disorders that help them get away from underlying painful feelings. We emphasize that the Therapeutic Enactment process is not just a mental exercise but includes a large body awareness component. It is important for therapists to use appropriate language that is different from counselling language when working with participants on body connections. This requires proper training and experience in what is essentially an experiential method. Readers interested in further study should refer to Knaster (1996), Levine (1997), Rosen (2003), and Rothschild (2000).

Therapeutic Enactment, therefore, firmly based in established theoretical and methodological antecedents, is a safe and relatively brief comprehensive method of moving through the ongoing distress related to a traumatic event or events in people's lives.

Creating space for the Divine is also important, as some clients wish to include this component in their enactment. Many people who were misunderstood, neglected, or abused feel that their wound is so severe that their souls are damaged. In these cases enacting their scenarios involves including the ultimate witness—God, the Higher Power, the Creator, the Divine Spirit— because they believe their experience cannot be understood, resolved, atoned, or forgiven without moving "beyond the earth" to the divine. It is important for them that a transcendent and compassionate being that understands and sees all things witnesses their experience and that they can, in turn, bear witness to the spark of the divine within themselves. They gain the reassurance that they were not alone after all and are then able to make a meaningful narrative out of their experience along the lines of: "No living person was available or capable but the Power that infuses all Life was there, saw me, and that is why I am living to this day. Otherwise, I'd be dead." This spiritual awareness permeates the group because repair work requires that individuals see that we are all connected to a timeless and compassionate way of being beyond the distortions of culture and upbringing. When the person doing Therapeutic Enactment steps forward into the group circle to do their work, group members often shudder or weep in awe of something bigger, something so deep and real it is sacred.

Five Phases of the Therapeutic Enactment Intervention

The Therapeutic Enactment model has five phases: (1) assessment and preparation; (2) group building; (3) enactment; (4) sharing, reconnection, and closure; and (5) integration and transfer. These phases are shown in the following figure.

The **assessment and preparation phase** involves a pre-group meeting with the individual who wants to do an enactment in order to assess their needs and develop a detailed plan for the enactment event. Within the **group-building phase**, the group begins with the creation of an atmosphere of safety, affection, and cohesion among group members. The therapists work to build feelings of inclusion, belonging, relaxation, spontaneity, and support for one another, which are essential ingredients that encourage member risk taking and participation within the enactment. The **enactment phase** is the point at which clients enact their chosen scenario. These scenes represent a past, present, or anticipated future situation or event. In this phase, the therapist directing the group helps the client create the scene by involving other group members in the enactment. Group members assume various roles as directed by the therapist or act as witnesses to the enactment. Moving through the enactment facilitates catharsis and reprocessing for the client, which promotes repair of psychological injury. In the next phase of the model—**sharing, reconnecting, and closure**—the therapist invites the client and other group members to

Figure. Five Phases of Therapeutic Enactment

Assess Client Needs/Readiness

1. Assessment & Preparation

Interview

Plan Enactment

Safety/Inclusion

Personal Control

Selecting
Participants   Setting Up
                  Scene   Trust/Intimacy
Initiate
Enactment   Cohesion

2. Group Building

Risk Taking

3. Enactment

Expressive Experiencing

Completion

De-roleing Participants

Reintegrating Client into Group

4. Sharing, Reconnection, Closure

Client Self Reflection   Witnesses Share

Identifying Resources

Closure

5. Integration & Transfer

Reconnection with Community

Follow Up

express their personal reactions to the enactment experience. This sharing of reactions helps consolidate the client's experience and further connects members through increased inclusion in the group process. The group has become truly what Winnicott (1965) called "a facilitating environment". We have noticed over years of group practice how quickly people respond to the palpable yet mysterious sense of the group as a living being. Members want to continue to experience the sense of being seen and heard in a lively group of interested people. They desire to carry this experience back into their families, friends, and work groups.

Integration and transfer is the final phase of the enactment process. In this phase, two separate components are at work. The first level of integration occurs when the client reflects on the enactment experience and the thoughts and reflections of other group members. The second level of integration takes place when the client is encouraged to practise transferring or applying the newly acquired learning and insight into everyday life. In this way, the client is able to use the new meanings and felt sense of change, gained from the enactment, as a way of practising new ways of being in the world. It is also at this point that we identify resources for the client such as follow-up counselling for those who need it. We also include a group follow-up to the workshop because participants are eager to get together and monitor progress. This satisfies a commonly expressed yearning for connection instead of isolation.

Recent research (Brooks, 1998) indicates that changes in awareness, insight, and behaviour occur more quickly and tend to be more transformational personally in this integrated group approach than in conventional, one-dimensional, individual verbal therapy alone.

Major Roles

Four major roles in Therapeutic Enactments are: (1) the therapist, (2) the lead (client), (3) the witnesses (group participants), and (4) the assisting practitioners (senior group members).

The therapist has four primary functions: (1) establishing with the client ahead of time the specific scenario that will be enacted with a clear vision of how the enactment will proceed, (2) creating a strong and solid group climate through application of effective leadership skills and group member facilitation, (3) directing the enactment from beginning to end, including the integration of the whole group once the enactment is complete, and (4) follow-up with the client and ensuring they have a connection for continued work with a counsellor if indicated. We decided quite quickly after beginning our work together to drop the psychodrama term "director" in favour of the term "therapist" because ours is primarily a "therapeutic" method. We always use two therapists, one who primarily directs the individual through the scene depicted in the circle, and a second who pays attention to group process, flow and continuity, universal themes, and closing actions.

The client or lead is the individual upon whom the enactment focuses. We call them the "lead" because it is this person who tells the therapist what the enactment scene will be and who will choose the people to enact the various roles. In consultation with the therapists, the lead is responsible for developing a specific plan or scene depicting the trauma. This plan outlines in detail aspects of the enactment, including key elements of what various role-players will do or say and how far the scene needs to go for completion. Further, the lead controls the pace and the ultimate decisions through the process.

Witnesses or group participants are present in the group and are a crucial aspect of the success of a Therapeutic Enactment. In addition to being available to take on specific roles in an individual client's enactment, the witnesses hold, with the support, guidance, and loving presence of the therapists, the role of watching, listening, and understanding what takes place. During the enactment process, the therapist occasionally focuses attention on the witnesses in order to remind leads that their actions are having an impact on those observing. Usually, the lead hardly notices anyone outside their immediate focus because they are so totally engaged in process and enactment. After doing their enactments, however, many leads have told us how the very fact that they knew the witnesses were there enabled them to carry on (Baum, 1994). The witnesses' view becomes essential during the debriefing phase, because the lead needs to hear their perspective on what was seen and heard, as well as the impact that the enactment had on them as individuals and members of the community. From preliminary research (Buell, 1995), witnesses report feeling privileged and honoured to be present for the lead's deeply personal and difficult experience. In many cases, witnesses report that the event linked with their own life story and, through their identification with the lead, they often experience a transformational learning experience in this role.

The effect of witnessing trauma has received new emphasis in recent times particularly for atrocities both local and international. Keats (2003) makes the point that the role of the witness is a necessary public affirmation of the individual's suffering in promoting redemption.

Assisting practitioners and senior group members are involved in larger group enactments. Assisting practitioners are asked to participate because of their expertise with the enactment process. They sit among the witnesses in order to monitor and maintain safety in the group by alleviating member stress reactions and occasionally alerting the therapists to safety needs in the group. They provide support for witnesses, especially if the witness appears to be emotionally triggered or decides to leave the room. Sometimes these practitioners may be referred to as "soul-catchers" or "space keepers", as a way of indicating they are attentive to the psychological, environmental, and spiritual dimensions of the work in progress. Because of their experience and expertise, assisting practitioners are also able to take on challenging or dark roles that the client may hesitate to want other group members to assume.

Clients Who Benefit Most

Our clients carry much grief with them. How does this manifest itself and what is the reparation process for these individuals in the Therapeutic Enactment process? The kind of person who might benefit from Therapeutic Enactment is seeking to regain the parts of the self that were taken or lost as a result of the trauma in their lives. Individuals report that they have lost their "enthusiasm" or "joy", they "never have any fun anymore", they "can't get close to people" or they "have no energy and feel exhausted almost all the time". Under the guidance of trained therapists these people may carefully and safely revisit and reprocess a distressing scenario that they identify as continuing to cause them suffering.

Many individuals who suffered abuse or neglect when they were very young have subsequent difficulty coping with the normal stresses and strains of close relationships. They may tend to withdraw when they should communicate. They may blow up over small things after weeks of suppressing their feelings. They are unable to tolerate their own feelings so when they have a feeling, particularly a negative feeling, often they cannot distinguish or name what that feeling is. They flip into overload too fast. They are easily overwhelmed and then resort to emotional numbing. Their tension-reduction behaviours tend to fall into the "acting out" category: addictions, compulsions, or sexual affairs. Since these individuals are plugged into families and professions, this is not just an individual problem but has wider social implications.

Many people have hardened themselves against the pain of their own wounded hearts. They literally try not to feel. Sometimes this strategy works for them for a long time. Often, it even helps them achieve success quickly on their career path. Many of them go into the "helping professions" and are very successful practitioners. However, eventually they come to us because they have admitted to themselves that their inner lives are barren and close relationships are either missing or superficial. Strangely, these reactions may not unduly affect the individual in the workplace. However, at home, they are going through the motions. They realize that they must do something reparative or they will wither and die.

Individuals who have arrived at this serious revelation are ready for an enactment, especially when they have a specific scenario in mind. Enactments are contra indicated when people have vague "feelings" but no specific distress and no memorable events. Also, if the traumatic event is very recent and raw we will be cautious about proceeding to plan an enactment, usually advising a wait period. We want memory to be consolidated and we want the individual to come back to some central position in their own lives.

In fact, we have certain characteristics in mind for potential leads. Not all clients are ready to be leads because the wound is either too raw or deeply embedded in rationalization or dissociation. Therapeutic Enactment is most appropriate when the individual experiences a sense of connection within a personal or work setting, while at the same time feeling that their interpersonal engagement in this setting does not meet their needs. Enactments are not appropriate with rudderless individuals who are experiencing generalized anxiety that adversely affects their overall functioning. If their lives feel out-of-control then the group experience can be aversive to these individuals. Therapeutic Enactments are not appropriate for people with certain psychiatric disorders as they tend to have little insight into their illness and therefore are not suitable to engage in such an integrated and complex process. Adequately functioning people who have good ego strength as well as personal courage make optimum clients for enactments.

Choosing a Target Event

Individuals identify a critical life event to enact (the "target" as in Shapiro, 2001). There is a difference between a one-target trauma in an "intact" individual and multiple targets related to attachment breaks. Normally the target is one that cannot be fully accessed through a verbal therapy approach; rather it requires a dramatization of the event in which all parts (feelings, actions, thoughts, spirituality) of the person are involved. Similarly, many enactment clients wish to begin their work at the beginning, with their parents. Next to a death, unfinished business with the parents is the most common enactment. During this kind of enactment adults may grieve for the very first time the fact that the parents they had were not the parents they wanted. This allows them to finally separate from fantasies about their parental figures that they have used to buttress a false sense of certainty and control or nourish their own sense of victimization. In many cases, in spite of worldly success, these fantasies have prevented them from growing up emotionally and achieving reciprocal intimate relationships.

It is important in enactments that therapists take this aspect of growing up extremely seriously otherwise shame and dishonour will darken the group's spirit. Many people will say things like: "Oh, I don't want to make a big fuss (about my parents) because I didn't have it as bad as so-and-so." This type of "comparison shopping" of suffering has to be confronted or the groups become competitive and unsafe. We confront the problem of "the struggle against suffering" (Sullivan, 1989). The person has disdained and even disowned their own inner life because no one else has ever seen it or seemed interested in it. Participants in the groups must be willing to descend in a very real way into the dark regressive wanderings of the human soul. As Sullivan puts it, individuals painfully and with difficulty must shift their attitude toward their infantile aspects from "rejection and disgust to acceptance and respect" (p. 64).

In the enactment groups, people struggle to be real. This means facing sorrow, hopelessness, and despair. The question might be asked: "Are some events better for Therapeutic Enactment than others?" To answer this quesion, we can refer to Eye Movement Desensitization and Reprocessing (EMDR) therapists who, when working through distressing experiences, use the sequence—First, Worst, Most Recent—to elicit the traumatizing "targets" they want to work on (*EMDR Basic Training Manual*, 2003). Earlier, potent, and lingering events are better than more recent and less deeply felt events since the latter will continue to cause disorientation. Distance is better than persistent upheaval when choosing an event. Parent and death scenarios are better for restorative purposes than a recent argument with one's boss. Effective scenarios are those that have a clarity of focus as opposed to vague feelings of unease. A felt sense of urgency on the part of the client to get started with the enactment is an essential motivating factor. The trauma has changed the person's sense of who they are and how they are in the world. Scenarios that reflect this altered sense of self and contain a resolve to change negative beliefs into positive self talk are the most potent.

The Group as a Safe Container

Therapeutic Enactments take place in groups that can include anywhere from eight to twenty-five participants, with an ideal group size of twenty members. Two to four enactments are typically conducted over a full day. To gain maximum group benefit and cumulative learning effects, enactments are best done in a sequential rhythm of three to four enactments over a two- to three-day workshop. The authors have conducted Therapeutic Enactments in both residential and conference settings. An individual enactment that includes debriefing with the group may take anywhere from two to four hours.

It is possible to create enactments in pre-existing groups, teams, and families without going through the extended follow-up procedures that we use in the workshops. Planning becomes crucial. Questions to be explored in advance include: What is the purpose of the intervention? What is the family or team goal? Is safety possible in the setting?

Therapeutic Enactments used in this way can include the use of group-based "sculptures", a group exercise in which a client chooses people to silently stage a scene from their past. The method is applicable to reparative mediations or conflict resolutions, such as when two work teams have had to merge but are unable to resolve territorial differences.

It is important when establishing safety within the group to let people know that there will be follow-up after their enactment and after the workshop ends. Our group approach is not a "quick fix". Time is necessary to consolidate the personal learning that results when participants confront their suffering. Most often, Therapeutic Enactment in the group is used as an adjunct to individual therapy. It does seem to either jump-start a stalled change process or open up and begin integration and closure of a file—an issue or "target"—that has choked the emotional life of the individual, group, or team, usually for some considerable period of time. Our overall goal is to create groups where participants may be nurtured and renewed.

The central component of healing is the group. Therefore, whether forming a new group or going in to work with an already established group, group building and group process form the major part of the beginning of the intervention. The group therapists along with the group members facilitate the healing of individual suffering through a public enactment of the individual's story. Emotional expressiveness is facilitated when the process in the group is given over to the existential truth of Virgil's *lacrimae rerum*, the tears that are in things. The affirmation of this potent existential truth encourages people and feeds their spirits. This is the reconnection that traumatized people have been missing.

Symbolizing the Imaginary World Inside

Another important part of the work done in the group is making meaningful narratives out of individual stories and finding the meaning of the group itself. An important task of Therapeutic Enactment is to assist the lead to gradually symbolize the imaginary world, as this gives meaning to the narrative they are creating to explain and dignify their lives. While this is going on, the group is creating a multi-level group identity that is vivid and engaging. These multi-levels are differentiated by Lacan ([1966] 1977) into "real", "symbolic", and "imaginary" realities. Mannoni (1970) describes the "real world" as concrete, literal reality; the "symbolic world" as archetypal, containing cultural and universal myths, the law, language, the spiritual, and dreams; and the "imaginary world" as psychological, containing projections, fantasies, and transferences. The imaginary world is about feeling and reacting, whereas the symbolic world is about meaning. For example, we have real, imaginary, and symbolic parents. The "imaginary" parents may stand in front of the real parents and be experienced as true or false, giving or withholding, loving or hateful, deaf, blind, or dumb. These "parents" are our ego identifications and projections. The poet Robert Bly (1981) expresses this beautifully: "It was a simple wedding ... and the invisible bride stepped forward, before his own bride. He married the invisible bride, not his own."

In psychological terms, the symbolic and the imaginary realms can be as riveting as the real. We have directed enactments with people whose "symbolic" parents came across as dream-like witches, tyrants, kings and queens, beggars and ogres, slaves and slave drivers. One lead had a recurring dream throughout her childhood in which her mother burst into her bedroom wearing a black witch's hat. She never told anyone about this nightmare but it polluted her childhood and made her afraid to go to sleep at night. As Pinkola Estes (1992) suggests, some leads see their parents as ducks and themselves as swans, beautiful but a completely different bird and therefore always ganged up on and eventually thrown out.

We see confusion between these realms periodically in Therapeutic Enactment groups. In one particular group, the lead enacted a scenario in which he was attacked by peers on his way home from high school and badly beaten. One witness, distressed by the scene, complained during the debrief at the end of the enactment that she felt she was one of the people who had stood by and allowed him to be beaten up. She felt that by witnessing the enactment she had stood by again and she should have intervened and stopped the enactment. The witness was confusing the imaginary and symbolic realms with the "real". It is very important not to do this, as Therapeutic Enactment is not about reproducing literal memories and making them into a story but about unlocking painful feelings and making meaning of our life experiences so that we do not live as if we are completely at the mercy of other people and events.

During the Therapeutic Enactment itself and in the group process, we are moving in and out of all three real, symbolic, and imaginary realms. We take them seriously when we see them come up, highlight their meaning, and incorporate them into the process. In one Therapeutic Enactment, a lead who had positioned his father at the outer edge of the circle during his enactment realized for the first time that, while his father (who had emigrated from another country) had arrived physically, his heart and soul had remained in his country of origin. The lead stated that he had always "known" this about his father but had not been able to understand how this symbolic truth had affected both of them. This kind of insightful breakthrough is good practice for participants who may have been holding one or more of these realms at bay in their ordinary lives outside the group. We have been in groups where, watching an enactment about abuse, members have spontaneously begun to pray because they very strongly feel themselves to be in the presence of great evil. Their experience affirms that other non-rational elements are present.

Enactments, therefore, are complex therapeutic interventions. What is it that they are designed to accomplish? In common with all therapeutic approaches, Therapeutic Enactment has to have clearly specified aims. The goals of Therapeutic Enactment include the following:

- letting go of key images and emotions through emotional expressiveness or catharsis;
- reclaiming a sense of self;
- restoring the ability to choose how and when to respond to both inner and outer demands and challenges;
- interacting positively with others;
- regaining a positive sense of personal power and experiencing new kinds of interactions in previously unmanageable situations; and
- moving away from the isolation of shame and reconnecting with others.

Essentially, our approach is restorative and enlivening. Most striking is the client's movement from a previously diminished sense of self to a heightened experience of personal control and integrity, a reclaiming of the self. They may enact the moment in their life when they experienced significant loss of trust or control. Therapeutic Enactment engages or allows for the creation of a reparative process, which transforms feelings of self-shame into feelings of acceptance and self-caring.

Summary

These are the tears of things.
And the stuff of our mortality cuts us to the heart.
—Virgil, *The Aeneid*

Traumatizing events leave clients with a range of possible reactions:

- shame
- secrecy
- vigilance
- numbing
- fragmentation
- isolation

- holding in
- silence
- forgetfulness
- flight
- denial
- terror and rage

In contrast Therapeutic Enactment is identified with:

- safety
- acceptance
- speaking the unspeakable
- truth
- grieving
- connection

- integration
- correction
- reconciliation
- reparation
- love and concern
- community

As teachers and researchers we were acutely aware that psychodrama could produce significant results. In our approach to Therapeutic Enactment we have preserved the parts of psychodrama pertaining to depicting and acting out the trauma. However, we have come to balance the value of spontaneity in the process of repair with the development of safety. In addition, we have commandeered theoretical underpinnings from other therapy approaches. As a basic outline of the Therapeutic Enactment model, this chapter sets out our rationale and briefly describes the framework of Therapeutic Enactment so the reader can grasp the process more easily.

The people who are drawn to Therapeutic Enactments feel emotionally cut off from self and are spiritually adrift. What are they looking for as a result of doing their enactment?

- They want to be free of the distress attached to past trauma. This distress is invariably associated with early experiences of dishonour and despair.
- They want to come back in touch with their own emotional and spiritual lives.
- They want to integrate the complexities and disparate parts of themselves into a new wholeness.
- They want to revive nurturing and satisfying interpersonal relationships.
- They want their work to have meaning for them.
- They want to be able to relax, play, be spontaneous, and experience joy.
- They want their truth to be known.

The best way to comprehend the process of Therapeutic Enactment is to follow the stories of past participants we have called Michael, Darren, and Marion. Each of their stories encapsulates a specific therapeutic problem. For Michael, the issue was unresolved grief due to a death; for Darren, shame; and for Marion, dissociation and post-traumatic stress disorder (PTSD). Their experiences demonstrate what our approach to therapy is all about and we invite you now to follow them throughout this narrative so that you may come to know Therapeutic Enactment through their eyes. We begin with Michael.

The next chapter tells Michael's story and describes our methodology and the changes we made as we went through Michael's story. His story serves as a tangible case history to illustrate landmarks of the process for clients and therapists, particularly with regard to how we work with deathbed enactments. We tell Michael's story in great detail, slowing down a critical event, scene, or affect, like watching a movie in slow motion, so that his story can be seen clearly, poignantly, and deeply.

Michael's Enactment: The Process in Action

CHAPTER 2

Since I still don't know enough about pain
This terrible darkness makes me small.
It's you, though.
Press down hard on me, break in
that I may know the weight of your hand,
and you, the fullness of my cry.

—Rilke, *Vielleicht, das ich dur schwere Berge gehe*

Michael's story is typical of many scenarios we have enacted. His work was primarily about incomplete grieving, disconnection with his father, and loss of identity as a man with subsequent difficulties in intimacy. Michael's enactment was one of the earliest we directed together, and it stands as a turning point for our work. A number of unexpected issues arose that led us forward in developing Therapeutic Enactment in all its cognitive, emotional, behavioural, and spiritual dimensions. Michael's story is a good introduction to our model because the debilitating long-term effects of blocked grief are such a common theme in enactments.

Assessing Michael's Needs

Michael was having difficulties in his relationships at home and at work. His father had died and Michael felt a great deal of anger and grief about his father and he felt cut off from his family. In our initial meeting with Michael, the two therapists did an individual assessment and family history during which he told us about the psychological issues and stresses that brought him to want to try Therapeutic Enactment. Our initial meeting with Michael lasted about an hour as preliminary assessments do for all clients. We later followed up by telephone and then met again briefly at the beginning of the Therapeutic Enactment workshop or planned group session.

Michael was a thin, quiet, rather guarded young gay man in his early thirties with curly hair and a youthful appearance. Michael smiled often but seemed not quite sure of himself, fidgeting from time to time. A teacher who had returned to university for graduate upgrading, he did not seem to have a warm personality and we found him elusive emotionally. He had an expression of sadness on his face that bordered on fear. Michael told us that he had difficulty expressing his feelings and that he had had several individual counselling sessions but had not found them helpful.

Michael came to us because, currently, he was in a long-term relationship with a male partner that was not going well because of Michael's ambivalence. This was during the early 1990s, when the AIDS scare was at its height. Everybody knew about the disease, and Michael and his partner were caught up in the scare. Michael's partner wanted him to commit to a monogamous relationship but Michael knew that he was holding back. He could not understand what it was that was holding him apart from this man to whom he was genuinely attached. He said that he wanted to break through his resistance and truly commit to this relationship. Essentially, Michael wanted yet feared intimacy, distrusted others, and wanted to be in control. He thought that he was not good enough to be loved, yet he also held a prince-in-the-tower dream that an all-seeing, all-accepting lover would rescue him from his emotional prison. This is also known as magical thinking.

Michael's feelings about his family placed him in the insecure-resistant or ambivalent attachment grey area described in Wesselmann (1998). In general, these people view others as untrustworthy and the self as unlovable. They are hyper vigilant in relationships and desire closeness, yet fear it and put up walls or push people away. They suffer from anxiety and repress anger and grief with consequent rigidity in the body. They may resist comforting and soothing. They hold strong negative beliefs about themselves such as "Others are more worthwhile than I am." "No matter who I am or what I say, I will always be rejected." "My feelings and needs are not OK." "Others will not meet my needs." Sometimes their beliefs include "It's hopeless" or "Nothing will ever change."

The discipline of self-psychology (Bragan, 1996) informs us that in the deep structures of the self there has to be an understanding or mirroring, what has been called "the gleam in the parent's eye", in the primary relationship with caretakers; otherwise, what is missing in the primary relationship is also missing in present relationships. Also, children need to "idealize" the parent before differentiating from them. This need is so strong that many grown-ups cannot let go of their idealized parent even when the real parent was abusive or harmful. When this process of attunement goes wrong it goes badly wrong and can affect relationships as life-long struggles around meaningfulness and self-efficacy. This understanding of how the client perception of the idealized parent is frozen in time is crucial for the understanding of reparation through Therapeutic Enactment. In Michael's case, what he needed to get from his father was a sense of being heard and seen for who he really was, not the dream son that the father may have preferred.

As we continued our assessment, a story came out about Michael and his father. Michael had grown up in a family of women: his mother, grandmother, and sisters. His father had been deaf all his life. Michael had a very strong sense that he could never get an audience with his father, who was both literally deaf and symbolically was unable to see or hear his son. The deafness of Michael's father had a strong negative effect on the family. The father, the so-called dominant male, was cut off from speaking with his only son through his deafness, which further alienated Michael as a male among a group of females. Michael was estranged from his father and moved to the opposite end of the country. In reality, though, Michael felt that his father had left him because he couldn't accept his son's sexual orientation.

What was touching was that Michael still spoke lovingly of his father despite the rejection. Michael told us that while he had experienced no sense of emotional connection with his father, he felt that somehow he had to make it up to his father for his deafness. Many neglected children take on themselves the responsibility for alleviating their parents' distress. This overdeveloped sense of personal responsibility is linked to the lasting effects of trauma (Shapiro, 2001). Since Michael's was an impossible task, the result was that Michael felt he was a failure and worthless. Michael plainly had a lot of feelings about his father that were unresolved.

His father had died recently and Michael was unable to be with him before his death. He did not go back for the funeral so, in his mind, his father was still alive and out of reach. Michael planned to enact going back and saying what needed to be said between a son and his dying father. There was a yearning to be in his father's presence when he died, not separate and far away. He needed to hear his father say that he would have liked Michael to be there when he died, why he wanted that, and that he was forgiven for not being there. He also wanted to prepare himself for going home the upcoming Christmas to be with his family and to have them meet his partner for the first time.

Michael asked the usual questions common in therapy: "Why go back? Why bother?" The answer is to retrieve one's sense of freedom to move between the past and the present, the self and the other, without feeling engulfed and aggrieved. During the preparation stage, we often ask leads to think about what they want to get back from the past and what they would like to give up. Many people have become so accustomed to getting on with their lives that they completely underestimate the amount of actual pain they are suffering as a result of early wounds. Many have had to "reduce themselves in order to survive" (Femi and Rothberg, 1997, p. 23). In our workshops we try to create a setting in which there is no rewounding and where participants can grieve past heart wounds safely, without shame. We're counteracting the common message: "Keep it in. Don't feel. If you feel and express, you will be killed."

One of our assumptions as therapists is that early development is pivotal in the formation of how we deal with our emotions and relationships as adults. It was through that lens that we were assessing Michael, his distress, and the work he needed to do. We believed that the difficulties Michael was having were linked to his unresolved conflict with his father and other members of his family of origin. Michael had spoken earlier in the planning about his constant sense in all his relationships, of working alone, of using others as mere props, and of him or them not quite being there, of being unreachable. As a teacher his classroom was a managed environment in which he held himself aloof from both students and faculty. He did not want to repeat this in the group. He had come to the point in his life when his loneliness was more painful than his dread about changing his ways of relating.

In terms of timing, Michael had, during the previous year, received a graduate degree and a promotion and he had moved in with his lover in a committed relationship. Often, we find that people come to do Therapeutic Enactments after they have achieved what they have sought for a long time. They may feel stronger after their achievements and therefore ready to face what they have been avoiding. Or they may feel that in spite of their achievements something important is missing.

Michael wanted to commit to his partner and was bemused because he could not do it. However, how could he commit to someone who is saying "Be mine" when he belonged to and was waiting for his real love object, his missing parent, to return to him? Michael's enactment, then, was paradoxically both atonement with his father and separation from his father.

Preparing for the Enactment

As we prepared for the enactment we were able to assess and understand how being unable to visit his father's deathbed played a critical role in Michael's life and affected the present. Consequently, after hearing the history and a statement of the present distress, we helped him create an enactment. The purpose for Michael was to change his view of where he stood with his father—and by extension in his other significant relationships. This part is like the rehearsal before the event, because, at this time, we agree about details such as what the room will look like, what furniture, dishes, or other props will be needed, or who else will be there. We might ask: "Where is your father's or mother's favourite spot in the house? Where would you usually find them?" "What do you remember about their armchair, table, kitchen, garden, and favourite belongings?" "What did they usually wear around the house?" "What names did they use for each other?" These questions allow the lead to access memories that are linked to body awareness, and other senses such as smell may come into play. People like Michael are likely to dissociate from their body sensations and this affects their memory of events. So these questions access the deeper body memory and helped him reconnect to the past.

The process of externalizing the unconscious into a concrete scene begins to bring the drama of the therapeutic work to life. After all, the crux of drama, according to Aristotle, is to imitate human action. The unique and wonderful part of psychodrama, according to Brooks (1998), is that you get to construct your own play. It was deeply satisfying for Michael to take the central part in a ceremony that recreated the drama of his life story. As he went over the who, what, where, when, and how, the therapists discussed details of the actual incident being enacted and what the key people in that incident might say or do. For example, we asked Michael: "Will the deathbed scene require a coffin, a hospital bed, or your father's bed at home?" Some therapists like to have many physical props available and the group enjoys helping to create rooms and landscapes. We are also listening to the subtext, if you will, attending to the non-verbal cues of the person and sensing what might be a major goal or outcome of the enactment. For example, a key feature for Michael was that the person playing the role of his father use sign language. In physically setting up the scene with his father, Michael had to instruct us how he communicated with his deaf father. Although in the actual deathbed scene later on he talked to his dad as if he could hear, seeing the sign language early on increased his trust in the enactment process and connected him to buried feelings about his father.

The time just before the enactment is set up is the ultimate "buying in" or "buying out" time when we ask the lead: "Do you really want to do this?" Often people remark on how sobering it feels to go through this final preparation before jumping into the circle of fire. We hear reports of heightened arousal, which may be experienced as either anxiety or excitement, or both. Keeping safety in mind, at this point, the therapists remind the individual that we will be consulting and supporting them throughout the process.

Group Building: Creating a Trustworthy Context

The next step for Michael was to join a weekend workshop about a month after our initial assessment meeting. At Michael's enactment we developed group cohesion in the early stage of the workshop by having members participate in group-building activities. One particularly effective group-building activity we used was to learn one another's names by selecting an adjective that begins with the first letter of their name. During group building we also provided an overview of the enactment process, reviewed the goals of the group, and established agreements for safety.

Michael felt his trust level was high enough for him to begin. However, we knew that his ability to go back and release his grief would depend on his safety within the group. Therefore, because Michael was nervous about groups, we encouraged him to think about enacting his scene early on in the workshop. Otherwise his anxiety would increase and prevent his full attention and interfere with his ability to choose his role players. We agreed to time Michael's enactment for the second morning of the workshop. Keeping group process in mind, we were aware that the order of the Therapeutic Enactments may be crucial since it is important not to jeopardize safety by having beginning enactments that take the group too deep too fast. During the first day of the workshop Michael had time to sit in the circle and look for people he wanted to play the roles. He approached them just before breakfast the next morning and got their agreement. If he had wanted to, he could have approached them the night before and asked for a meeting to clarify the roles. Some people need more time to prepare for the role they will play.

In the early days of developing our method we allowed leads to choose the people they wanted to play key roles during the opening of their enactment. Other leads, if they already knew some of the group members who would be attending, decided on their role players before the workshop began. Often these choices were unerringly right. Many, many leads have been amazed to pick someone who appears to know exactly how the key people in their lives were feeling, thinking, and acting. As our experience with the method has developed, however, we prefer that the lead choose their role players, not impulsively, but with careful planning so that we can help the role players prepare. This increases everyone's comfort (and safety) and their commitment to the process.

During Michael's enactment we suggested that he say to the group something like: "I usually feel very uncomfortable in groups. I feel like people are judging me. Then I shut down. I want to tell you this so that I can try and be here in a different way this time." Michael felt vulnerable and exposed and was uncomfortable with emotional intensity. He said that his biggest fear was that the group might not be able to create a safe container for him and therefore he would freeze and be unable to complete his enactment. The therapists reminded him that he would not be out there alone in the circle and we would not let him down.

Beginning the Enactment: Walking, Telling His Story, and Inviting Others In

Michael began his enactment with his confession of fear in the group. He then invited the quiet, rather shy man he had chosen to play his father to join him and the therapist as they walked around an imaginary inner circle within the group. This walk signified Michael's move from being a group member to becoming the lead. The act of walking tends to mobilize feelings, experiences, and memories. Michael was invited to tell his story, introducing the key players as he walked, and began to construct the drama. The very act of doing this, with all the dramatic details such as story, characters, setting, and props, as well as emotional and intellectual intensity (his as well as the witnesses') enlivened and pleased him. He was the one making all the choices and as his choices were affirmed publicly his experience was extremely encouraging.

Disclosing the story as the lead walks around the circle can arouse shame. The lead is vulnerable, hence the therapists remind the group about safety. We might say something to the effect that shame is a common ingredient in relationships, especially when we are in the public eye. Healthy shame reminds us of our limitations while "toxic shame" (Bradshaw, 1988) isolates us. If we receive admiration and appreciation after disclosing to others what we are most ashamed of, and discover that we are not cast out, then toxic shame may be transformed. This is why we believe that, for many clients, repair actually begins as the person is mobilized into action in front of the group. For example, many people feel weak and helpless as a result of having been bullied or abused. As adults, they try not to remember those feelings and cover up the memory, even though it haunts them in unguarded moments because the body does not forget. Describing their story and expressing their feelings in front of a group is often daunting but can be restorative for many people. In Michael's case, we encouraged the group to understand that shame has a place in this enactment and our job was to make a very safe container for Michael so he could do important work.

During Michael's enactment, as the man playing his father began to take on characteristics familiar to Michael, even saying things his father might have said, we noticed a shift in Michael's body. The man playing his father was using sign language and frowning at Michael. He slapped Michael on the shoulder as he walked by him. The therapist noticed that Michael began to freeze (he was unable to move forward). This body reaction signalled the emergence of something critical to the event and also the presence of shame. It also indicated that Michael had already begun to move into actually reliving the times when his father shamed him by striking him in public. He could no longer block his body reaction, memory, feelings, and sensations. He began communicating in a different way (through freezing) rather than by simply using his voice. Such a moment is common at the beginning of enactments.

Any signs of change in Michael's body language, tone of voice, or motion are markers to the therapist about where to move next or about what might need to be changed. For example, when Michael stopped suddenly or walked very fast, the therapist might ask questions such as "What are you aware of right now?" or "Where in your body do you feel the reaction?" This helps to "unlock" the lead and give verbal expression to what they are experiencing. It helps focus their attention on what is actually happening for them in the moment, beyond what they expected in the planning stage when sometimes leads get ahead of themselves, controlling their feelings and engaging in distracting activities just as they do in the rest of their lives. By continually bringing awareness back to what the lead is feeling and experiencing in the present, the therapists facilitate a deeper level of congruence within the lead, a desired outcome of the enactment. Michael was noticing as opposed to fixing. His experience reinforced what several researchers have suggested, which is that "the body knows" or that we have "cellular memory" (Van der Kolk, 1994; Pert, 1999). In this case, when the therapist asked: "What is happening to you right now?", Michael told us he was enraged at his father because his father treated him with contempt. Then he began to weep and this brought back other feelings and experiences about his father. He remembered a time when his father had put his arm around him after his dog died.

When Michael had the courage to let down his defences and begin to weep, allowing himself to publicly mourn what was missing in his relationship with his father, he allowed the rest of the group to feel their participation in "the human condition". This helped to reinforce group commitment and solidarity, because to witness true human vulnerability, bravery, and openness is inspiring. Shame and grief when they arise in groups can create what Livingston (1991) calls "the mystic nurturing power of a vulnerable moment" (p. 91).

An additional factor in Michael's case was the fact that he was gay. Lesbian, bisexual, transgendered, and gay people often feel marginalized, patronized, and even abused in therapy groups. The way Michael was treated with respect and appreciation was not only reparative for him but helped to heal the split in the group created by participants' previous experiences with the way society treats gay people.

Moving in Action with the Father

As Michael's Therapeutic Enactment developed he brought his mother, grandmother, and sisters into the circle and introduced them to the group. He spoke to each of them, expressing his feelings about his father's death. Then he positioned his father at home in his bed as he lay dying. We had thus created the pivotal scene for Michael at the bedside of his dying father surrounded by all the women in the family, with Michael holding his father's hand and speaking directly to him. As Michael moved into position by his father's side, he began to experience diverse unexpressed emotions and unmet needs. The therapists were there to help him put words to them, drawing from the gestalt technique of Incomplete Sentences. In this technique, the therapist places himself directly behind Michael, coaching him to say to his father things he wasn't able to say when his father was still alive. Michael's dialogue went something like this:

Therapist:	What I need most from you, Dad, is for you to tell me …
Michael:	[*completing the sentence*] … that you are pleased I am your son.
Therapist:	Without this I have …
Michael:	… I don't have confidence in myself as a man.
Therapist:	What I fear most is that …
Michael:	… if you reject me, I will feel worthless.
Therapist:	What is most difficult for me to say right now is that …
Michael:	… I am sorry that I got angry and left home when you told me you were ashamed of me being gay.
Therapist:	What I want most from you now is …
Michael:	… to hear you say that you are glad I came.
Therapist:	If I could hear you say that …
Michael:	… then I would know that you really love me. I could relax and tell you all the things I want to tell you about my life. And I could listen to you and get to know who you really are.

As therapists, we want to keep the leads connected to us but not interfere with their processing. We don't want to get in their way but the language is so essential that we want to work on helping the lead say the right things to amplify the emotional expression that accompanies the lead's words. When they are able to accurately describe their feelings it releases the body tension involved in blocked feelings. It is not just saying the right words but articulating the accompanying feeling and intensity that goes with them. This means therapists may have to have the lead repeat the statements with different emphasis until it feels right to the lead, especially in expressions of anger or hurt. In this way memory and emotional expression are tied together to achieve the therapeutic goals of release and catharsis, thus installing emotionally based insight. We can see how cognition and emotion mediate one another. So, for example, we might help Michael complete sentences such as:

Therapist:	I am so angry with you because …
Michael:	… you put your beliefs about homosexuality before your love for your only son.
Therapist:	Dad, I felt hurt because …
Michael:	… you rejected me.
Therapist:	What you took away from me was …
Michael:	… the love that I needed then because I felt very alone.
Therapist:	What you did was wrong because …
Michael:	… you made me feel worthless.

Fritz Perls (1969), the father of gestalt therapy, distinguished between needs and wants. Needs are such truly primary things such as food, shelter, love, and understanding. Wants are preferences and likes that need to be acknowledged and expressed even if they are not always gratified. Needs are more important than wants because, while we can't always get what we want, if we don't get what we need, we will die. Michael needed to experience the mirroring and affirmation of his father's love. At the same time, he needed to discharge the accumulated grief of years of not receiving it. As he began to uncover his needs and what was missing from his relationship with his father, he felt safe enough in the group to express the anger, frustration, and hurt that had not been safe for him to express or experience in relationship with his father. Often, people discover the distinction between needs and wants as they go through Therapeutic Enactment. What was notable with Michael was that he finally recognized that the essential thing missing in the primary relationship with his father—commitment and devotion—was also missing in the current relationship with his partner.

Emotional Release or Catharsis

What Michael was able to express now, in the moment, were some of his unmet needs in relationship to his father, thereby releasing the grief that he had carried both in his heart and in his body. He was able to feel the loss of a relationship with his father. We could also see the importance of ensuring that people like Michael have the safety and space to do their grief work. Most people we know do not like to cry at all, never mind weep in public. Yet people want to unload their pain if this can be done in an honourable way. Blocked grief negatively affects our mind-body system and makes it rigid because of the muscular tension it takes to suppress feelings—and big feelings require big tension. There is no room for creativity or even spontaneity because we are always guarding ourselves against feeling. Until this moment in the enactment, Michael prevented himself from grieving for his father because of the lack of clarity and closure in their relationship. During enactment Michael said what he needed to say and he heard what he needed to hear. This permitted him to reclaim a belief that he was worthwhile, the absence of which had contributed to a lack of energy and hope.

As in any other therapeutic process, empathy is essential to understanding and change. Empathy is the capacity to participate in the feelings and thoughts of the other. Empathy brings people closer together. We no longer feel isolated in our hurt feelings. We are able to restore "the interpersonal bridge" (Kaufman, 1985) by putting ourselves in the other's shoes thereby experiencing some of their feelings. This connection is the good outcome of the empathy highlighted in, for example, a role reversal in an enactment. Role reversal gives people permission to accept parts of themselves that previously had been disowned. Role reversal enables an external frame of reference, moving us out of the narcissistic self. Acting as the other person in role reversal and empathetically walking in the other person's shoes, we tell ourselves we are good people after all.

One of the pivotal moments during Michael's enactment was when the therapist heard Michael say that he wanted to know more about his father. He had Michael do a role reversal in which he literally rose from his knees at his father's bedside and replaced his father on the bed. Playing the role of the father, Michael responded to all his anger, hurt, and rejection over feeling unloved. Although this father in real life had never actually expressed love for the son he rejected, in the role reversal Michael was able to hear and believe in his father's love. This is what we call a "healing moment" and it was an epiphany for Michael, the beginning of his reparation. He was able to claim the unexpressed fatherly love of himself when he took on the role of his father. This is not to say that Michael was fantasizing and making his father into something that he wasn't. Rather, Michael was able to separate himself from his projection of his father as unloving so that he could experience himself as lovable.

Once Michael expressed this truth that he was lovable, it awakened in him what Melanie Klein called "concern" (as quoted in Hinshelwood, 1991), what Christians call "forgiveness", what Jewish adherents call "mercy", and what Buddhists call "compassion". Concern within an object relations context moves the person away from blaming toward reparation. Michael was able to appreciate his father's predicament and release his love for his father. When

Michael, playing his father in the role reversal, was able to say: "The reason I couldn't love you was because …", then Michael began to understand his father as a man. In addition, he was able to say out loud: "I am not unlovable after all because there was a reason he couldn't love me and that was about who he was and not about me." What Michael was coming into touch with was a sense of his own goodness deep inside and a belief that he was worthwhile despite his experiences with his father. Michael changed his negative cognition "I am unlovable" to a positive one "I am lovable." Therapeutically speaking, "I am lovable" is better than "I am loved" since, unfortunately, many people cannot always trust the motives of those who say they love them.

In Michael's enactment, the role reversal was a very powerful moment because at that moment the enactment began to change from catharsis to repair, a noticeable surprise to the therapists who had been observing Michael's process. We were amazed to see that something good had survived this disastrous relationship. Resolution or reconciliation had begun, making clear the next stage of the integration process. As we watched Michael speak directly to his father, we felt tremendously moved. It was an "aha" moment in that we saw in the power of this process that, when grief is released, compassion surely follows. In that moment, Michael was genuinely there with his father, making the connection with his imagination of him.

We could clearly see the importance of allowing a person to give over into grief. Unless a person, as Klein observed, accepts the reality that a disaster has happened to them, it is not possible for them to move forward. Michael used up so much energy to block his grief that there was none left to invest in external reality, leaving him with consequent superficiality and disappointment in relationships, self sabotage, and omnipresent feelings of emptiness. In the enactment, Michael was able to grieve and to achieve closure, if not in the real world, then at least in the symbolic or psychological reality of therapy. This permitted him to reclaim the parts of himself the absence of which previously had contributed to a negative self-concept and lack of self-esteem. He was able to reclaim his pride, energy, and hope for the future.

An important distinction to make about empathy in role reversal is that it is different from the counselling empathy we are trained to understand and use with clients when we identify and reflect back feelings. Rather, empathy in role reversal involves switching to "seeing out the window of the other person" (Yalom, 1985). We take the perspective and the experience of the other, enabling us to accept the other, as well as release our need for revenge or retribution. Most of us remain frozen in an attitude toward the other person, and this allows us to believe that the other person hates, disrespects, or has nothing but contempt for us. In other words, we deeply suspect their motives and assume the worst. Michael was convinced that his father wanted nothing to do with him because he had turned out to be such a disappointment. Empathic immersion in the other's situation opens up the heart and provides awareness of other possible motivations and intents. Our vitality is restored.

Integration and Transfer

As often happens, enacting one critical scene brings up other issues that need working through. Michael spontaneously conceived a second scene so that he could turn from the deathbed and speak to the women in his family about what they had witnessed. He set the role players where people usually sat: his grandmother in her armchair, mother in the kitchen, and sisters in front of the television. Michael had believed that it was very important for his grandmother, mother, and sisters to witness the scene at his father's bedside. This second scene was about Michael taking his place as a man in his family full of women, but he was only able to involve the women after his father affirmed and validated him as a worthy person. While Michael talked to his mother about what kind of a man his father had been, he found himself speaking of his father's true passion, which was puttering about the house, mending, building, and fixing things. Michael suddenly remembered that his father had a toolbox that he took great care of. Michael remembered himself as a child admiring it and wanting one just like it. He asked his mother to give his father's toolbox to him. The therapists were able to create a moving ceremony in which the entire group stood and witnessed Michael's mother, flanked by the other women, presenting his father's toolbox to him.

Receiving the toolbox turned out to be an essential reparative component for Michael. He had always considered his father to be a handyman and himself to have "butterfingers". Yet since he and his partner had set up house together, Michael had discovered that he loved to do home improvements. Moreover he was good at them. This came as a surprise to him. His father's toolbox began to take on an added symbolic significance as a previously unrealized connection to his dad. In the enactment, when his mother presented him with his father's toolbox, Michael was very moved and wept. The presentation of his father's toolbox signified Michael's recognition that a changed relationship with his mother was necessary and vital as his attachment to her had been out of balance in reaction to his lack of attachment to his father.

Dreams and Closure

At this point the Therapeutic Enactment was finished, and Michael was invited to rejoin the group. Meanwhile the therapists de-roled the participants who had been selected to take part in his enactment: the role players were invited into the centre of the circle so that they could step out of their roles, speak their real names, and become themselves again. After a short break, the group came back together and the enactment was reviewed, with emphasis placed on hearing from the role players. Michael first listened to each of the key role players talk about what the experience had been like for them and how it had impacted them personally. As the group debriefed, the therapists from time to time helped speakers clarify or convey their reactions. Some people may need help in recognizing what they are feeling since there is a common tendency to dissociate when faced with another's suffering. Witnesses were asked to keep comments brief, not to give instructions or counsel the lead. They were invited to speak of the impact the work had on them. After the witnesses shared their reactions to what they had seen and heard, Michael closed by "having the last word", describing what he was now aware of and asking clarifying questions. During this integrative phase, some teaching may take place, inferences may be drawn, links may be pointed out, and the group may celebrate their appreciation and relief at a job well done.

At the end of the enactment, in the debrief circle, Michael remembered a dream. Dreams are prevalent and important in enactments. We often ask people to remember their dreams and often we integrate dreams into enactments. In fact, we have done entire enactments around a dream, using props to set up the dream scenario and having the person then walk through the scene just as in the dream. Dreams provide an additional channel that can provide access to blocked grief and can signal that repair has happened or what repair still needs to be done. Michael said he rarely remembered dreams, yet the evening before his enactment, he had what we would call a preparatory dream. In fact, that dream began the process of his enactment.

In the dream, two women were fighting. Then the younger of the women made a presentation in Michael's honour in a place far away from where Michael was living but close to where he was born. Michael felt that this dream was related to him taking his place in his family of origin and his mother and sisters accepting him as the man in the family. In addition, we looked at the dream from the perspective of our work with integrating the masculine and feminine aspects of each individual psyche. We see these not as male and female but as symbolic patterns of being that are present in both genders at all times. We saw the dream as a signal from Michael's depths that the feminine part of his nature, his buried emotions, is honourable and serves as a connection between the inner and the outer for him, and between the past, present, and future. Identity precedes intimacy and thus Michael could stop striving for a missing identity and relax into his relationship. Also the place of honour in the dream signified the long spiritual journey that Michael had to make to find his rightful place.

Michael was able to separate out being gay and being a man, both possible and both valued, by being honoured in the dream. We think this was linked to the funeral of Michael's father and was prescient in terms of the presentation of the toolbox. The dream indicates that Michael was beginning to prize himself as he began to be prized by others despite the fact that, for most of his adult life, Michael felt that his family had not accepted him. Also, because his father was deaf, Michael was prevented from finding his way to his father's emotional interior and thus from developing his own emotional expressiveness. Through the enactment, Michael completed his task to find and claim his place in his real family and also in the symbolic family in his psyche.

Noting the Power of Symbolism
As Michael struggled to take his place as a man in a family full of women, we began to think about the symbolism of family roles and their long-

lasting impact on future relationships. We have discovered as a result of the hundreds of Therapeutic Enactments we have facilitated that the theme of role differentiation, particularly separation from the parents and acting as a grown-up, comes up in the enactments as a problematic endeavour. We have noticed how role confusion, role diffusion, role competition, contamination of roles, and lack of clarity of roles in families, groups, and societies all contribute to unsafe and damaging environments. Repair involves understanding what happened and putting the roles straight again by truthfully communicating in the group the amount of injury inflicted.

In Michael's family, the women overcompensated for the father's deafness by interpreting for him, making excuses for him, and thereby protecting him. All of this led to a role imbalance in the family that made it unsafe. Michael and his sisters had learned that their own needs would not be met. They coped through appeasement and propitiation, always striving to please others to the extent of losing themselves in relationships. This prevented intimacy and engendered resentment. Hence, none of them had been able to achieve ongoing satisfying adult relationships. This is an example of how a senior member in a family who has a lack of clarity about his or her own feelings, roles, and responsibilities can contaminate the learning process of the young. The youngsters, when they grow up, are never clear about where they stop and where the other begins. Michael's father did not act as a nurturing father. He acted as an emotionally inaccessible, irritable male in a house full of females.

An important task of Therapeutic Enactment is to assist the lead to gradually symbolize the imaginary world. On a day-to-day basis we tend to either ignore the symbolic or we put our symbolic template over the real events in our lives and try to crush them into a good fit. Our symbolic meaning of events gets disparaged and discounted. Yet the symbolic meaning is as "real" an event in the psyche as the physical event and is an essential component of balance and depth. Both deserve to be acknowledged. This became clear in Michael's enactment, culminating in the symbolism of his father's toolbox, which symbolized his father's gift or legacy. Michael was affirmed as his only son, who would carry on his tradition with respect. The toolbox also was symbolic of Michael entering into his manhood. Michael lived in an imaginary realm, too, where his father and, by extension, all adult males were untrustworthy and withholding. He had to learn to separate his real feelings about his father from his imagined projections.

Psychologically, Michael's feelings of being misunderstood and rejected by his father were equivalent in the symbolic realm of Michael wrestling with the themes of Prodigal Son and Atonement with the Father (Campbell, [1949] 1968). Symbolically, and in practical terms, atonement with the father means coming to an acceptance of one's identity (as the child of one's father) and integrity in the face of authority and reality itself. Michael's archetypal theme is only one of many common themes in Therapeutic Enactments that are important for both men and women.

Although his enactment was completed and Michael indicated that he felt a great deal of relief, as well as a sense of wholeness and a desire for intimacy and commitment, it was important for us as therapists to follow up with him. Follow-up is essential and the therapists committed to contacting Michael a few days after the enactment to speak with him to continue integrating more of the experientially based learning that may have occurred. Checking in twenty-four hours after the enactment, we found Michael was feeling a little "down", daunted by what he saw as the tasks ahead of him. This is a normal reaction and leads can be warned in advance that it may occur. Later, at the six-week debrief meeting with the whole group, Michael reported that his enactment had not only helped him achieve his original goal in his relationship with his partner, but he also said that he was acting more directly and with more confidence in many of his work and social relationships. He reported having a lot of energy for the first time in awhile.

Ten years later, when we met up with Michael by chance at a presentation we were giving, he reported that he was still with his partner and happily using his father's toolbox.

Summary

> *What is sorrow for? It is a storehouse of barley, wheat, corn and tears.*
> *One steps to the door on a round stone.*
> *The storehouse feeds all the birds of sorrow.*
> *And I say to myself: Will you have sorrow at last?*
> —Robert Bly

By retelling Michael's enactment we have tried to show how the therapists guide the client through each of the phases of Therapeutic Enactment. This narrative-in-action approach helps individuals know the self more fully, begin being, doing, and relating differently, and ultimately reach a better resolution and understanding of how their history and uniqueness enriches their daily lives. The next chapter explains more about what the client experiences, during what we call the "core processes" in Therapeutic Enactment.

The Core Processes of Individuals in Therapeutic Enactment

CHAPTER 3

The cure for pain is in the pain.

—Jalal al-Din Rumi, "There's Nothing Ahead"

In a dark time, the eye begins to see.

—Theodorr Roethke, "In a Dark Time"

In reading Michael's story we saw how therapists work with the client in enactment therapy. This approach to therapy involves certain "core processes", some of which focus on the individual and others which focus on the group. The major processes for the individual are assessment, planning, resources, enacting, and then debriefing. More specifically they can be described as follows:

(1) **Assessment and preparation**
   - finding and defining the core scene for enactment
   - establishing nuclear scripts and organizing principles
   - developing and installing resources: bringing strength and finding the child within
(2) **Enacting the narrative by making concrete parts of the self**
   - remembering through action and emotional experiencing
   - doubling
   - expanding the understanding of the self through empathy in role reversal
(3) **Debrief**
   - de-roleing and bringing people back into the group

Finding and Defining the Core Scene for the Enactment

Unlike psychodrama, in Therapeutic Enactment we emphasize the necessity of doing preparatory work with individuals about their planned enactments. The pre-enactment assessment is crucial. We have learned the efficacy of preparation in terms of streamlining, depth, and outcome. Individuals can be supported and prepared for their work in a number of ways. For example, EMDR sessions may be helpful in conjunction with an enactment.

Using EMDR to Help Prepare for Enactments

Eye Movement Desensitization and Reprocessing sessions can help individuals choose a specific trauma target that becomes the enactment scene and prepares them emotionally. Developed by Shapiro (2001) EMDR is a non-drug, non-hypnosis psychotherapy procedure. The therapist guides the client in concentrating on a troubling memory or emotion while moving their eyes rapidly back and forth following the therapist's fingers or using some other dual attention stimulation such as tapping on the back of the client's hands. Rapid eye movement (which occurs naturally during dreaming) or focusing attention on tapping or auditory stimulation seems to speed the client through the healing process. During EMDR clients can face distressing memories in a safe setting so that they do not feel overwhelmed by the emotions that are released through the process.

EMDR is helpful in preparing the trauma scene and preventing helplessness and retraumatization. In addition, we have incorporated resource development and installation (Korn & Leeds, 2002) as a key element in our assessment and enacting phases. More recently, we have begun to use a variation of the basic EMDR protocol to uncover negative beliefs and install positive cognitions. We ask the person to tell us about the distressing event. We ask them about their feelings and where they feel the sensations in their body. Then we ask them what negative belief they have about themselves when they remember it. Finally, we ask them what belief about themselves they would like to have. We incorporate this information into the enactment by having individuals look at the scenario they have created and tell us what comes to mind about themselves as a person as they look at it. Occasionally, leads have chosen two players to represent the negative and the positive cognitions. At closure, they have sent the negative role ("I am not lovable") out of the room and embraced the positive ("I am a good person").

During assessment a lead may be clear that they are distressed but unclear about what the critical scene is. We help leads to recognize and name their despair but we don't want them to be overwhelmed by it. As one of our leads said to us: "It's amazing how you can live with things that are so burning and yet not speak of them." In order to be able to surrender to a public expression of intense emotion a person needs to feel protected. If they have not had early experiences of being protected, they tend to believe that they need to protect themselves. The major benefit of the early assessment is to make the lead feel safe working with the therapists, who provide encouragement and support. Also, while we want leads to be able to open up and express themselves in the enactment, we are looking out for the possibilities of premature abreaction (intense and involuntary expression of emotion), flooding of the defensive system, dissociation, potential depression, or self-harm. We are also looking for present and future resources.

Adlerian Early Recollection

When working to find the core scene to be enacted, we used to employ a variation of the Adlerian Early Recollection technique. The client identifies a concrete event (an internalized representation of the self in a situation) that represents the issue, struggle, and their pain. We ask the client to hold, in their mind's eye, a visual image of the event that is charged with strong emotion and connected to the traumatizing event. Often, this is viewed as a snapshot that represents one important aspect of the short movie of the event. For example, a client might say: "I felt very upset when my supervisor complained about my work. I felt frightened and helpless. The image is of my naked self, very small, hiding behind my office door." Then we ask the client to imagine letting themselves float back to an earlier time when they had a similar strong feeling. They identify the strong feeling through body awareness. We might ask them: "Where are you feeling it in your body?" Sometimes we might ask them to place their hand on the relevant place where the feeling resides.

This is similar to the notion in Watkins (1997) of the affect bridge. Sometimes the client will have an "aha" moment when they will not only recognize an earlier event but also some form of insight that arose from it. For example, they might remember being sent to their room as a small child to wait until their dad came home so they could be beaten. Often the clients show understanding that their affect (emotion) is out of proportion to their present circumstances. The link with the earlier scenario is strong. The client might feel knots in his stomach or feel that his chest is tight. Another client might feel that her legs can't support her and she begins to sag toward the floor.

Another example is a snapshot of the client as a small child cowering in the corner as his mother points her finger and criticizes and shames him. He says that he feels very alone and sad. He believes that nobody loves him. If we ask him, he might say that he feels tightness in his throat and upper chest. In his present life he often feels the same sense of discomfort when he is invited to discuss his work because he believes he will be criticized. Regardless of the event enacted, a strong body component normally operates during assessment as the client anticipates the event to be enacted.

Drawing the Scene

To draw out the particular scene to be enacted, we ask the following questions:

- What trauma would you like relief from? or What was the traumatic event?
- Describe the event. Where did it happen? Who was there? What was said? What was done?

- What scene, event, spoken words, reaction, or aftermath sticks in your mind?
- What was the worst part of it for you?
- What sentence or word sticks in your mind to describe the belief you have about yourself after this event?
- Where do you feel this in your body?
- What would you rather have happened? What belief would you prefer to have about yourself now?

We find that these questions help the person to focus. We write everything down and later, just before the enactment, we double-check for any changes or further information. The reason we are after a particular scene, as opposed to generic feelings about life, is that a scene can be conceptualized and enacted in the group (the scene at a dying father's bedside or a ceremonial giving over of the toolbox). Sometimes the scenes are actual scenes that the person has experienced as wounding, such as a mother dragging her two-year-old child down the stairs by the hair or a father yelling and belittling his six-year-old son in front of the neighbours. Other scenes have not actually occurred, but are set up as part of the reparation process (a woman speaking to God about her parents' suffering during the Holocaust).

One of the things that Michael's enactment taught us was how elusive it can be to locate what we call the critical scene, the concrete event that is the source of a person's underlying nuclear script. In another Therapeutic Enactment we worked with a woman whose single mother had been a 1960s hippie, moving house, district, or country every year or second year during the lead's childhood and adolescence. This lead had a deeply felt sense of resentment toward her mother. She saw her father infrequently even though he had been settled in one place throughout that time. She said that she could not pin down one scene that encapsulated her sense of dislocation. This lead had a certain ethereal quality and was interested in philosophical discussion. In her present life she was moving from relationship to relationship, always choosing partners who did "not want to commit". As the assessment progressed, she told us of one day, while living in a rural commune, she came home from school early and was alone in the house. A man who she thought was involved with her mother came by. She remembered feeling very lonely and scared, wondering where her mother was and feeling that she did not want to be alone with this man in her house. This was the scene that was chosen for the enactment.

Almost everyone comes to the enactment process struggling with vital parts of their selves that have been split off because their parents or teachers could not or would not tolerate them. For some it was their rebellious spirit. For others, it was their curious searching mind. These parts need to be reclaimed. During the assessment, leads speak of what is missing for them in their present lives, often very movingly describing inner alienation and loneliness. Many people are cut off from their bodies and do not realize how much emotion they are holding back. Going missing from the body is an unconscious adaptive response to trauma. When we settle on a specific scene we know that, as we approach retrieving these parts, the emotions connected to them will emerge and be expressed in the body when the lead gets into the circle and the enactment begins. This means that therapists pay as much attention to what is going on in the lead's body as to what they are saying and help the lead focus there.

Establishing Nuclear Scripts and Organizing Principles

Most individuals who come to do a Therapeutic Enactment have experienced primary environmental deficiency and impingement that began in childhood (failures of "affect attunement" as in Stern 1985). Interactions with the primary caregivers were experienced as emotionally depriving rather than fulfilling. They may have been forced to feel—or not feel—emotion. Affect attunement is more than empathy in that the caregiver is responsive to the child's emotions, recognizing and matching them with appropriate feelings of their own in a way that is both soothing and strengthening to the child. Absence of affect attunement "can be disruptive and damaging to the self" (Bragan 1996, p. 20). The child grows up plagued by negative beliefs about the self. We recognize that problems with attachment began with a primary wounding, break, or insult to the person, preventing the development of healthy relationships. Infants are not yet separate selves and are helpless. If the care given is defective, the infant can internalize a sense of themselves as defective. This feeling of worthlessness can permeate the whole self and become a core self script, such as "I am defective." Brooks (1998) describes how many people who come to participate in enactment groups arrive not expecting to deal with the issues of early object relations material (their parents), but inevitably do because they realize that they are still coping with the fallout. That is why, in choosing an enactment scene, we like to go back to as developmentally early a place as the client can tolerate. Early wounds resulting in the development of negative self scripts require the balm of empathic resonance from the therapist and the group for healing.

We want to assist in uncovering core beliefs that result in self-defeating "nuclear scripts" (Tomkins, 1962) that ultimately limit people's lives. The nuclear or core script is the principle under which the whole self and personality organizes itself and how the self relates to the world. Individuals unconsciously anticipate and create new experiences to substantiate beliefs about how the world works, such as "There is no safety in the world for me" or "I am unlovable."

We have to identify the concrete event that is part of a person's underlying core script. The core scripts, as described by Young (1999), that we identify the most in our work include:

Core Scripts	Possible Core Beliefs
• abandonment and death	"I have no right to exist"
• mistrust and abuse	"I am dirty"
• defectiveness	"I'm useless"

- shame   "I have to stay hidden"
- social isolation   "I'm infectious"
- incompetence and failure   "I'm a loser"
- dishonour   "I am weak"

Often constellation scripts surround the core script, complicating the process of getting to the main organizing principle. For example, one woman with whom we did an assessment felt completely devalued by her parents and complained about not being able to get close to people. Like Michael, she said she wanted intimacy but could never have it. She also said she felt she had to do everything for everybody else and be really competent at it so that people would love and value her. In her case the levels of the constellation scripts, in descending order, look like this:

Constellation Scripts
- "I cannot get close to people (I don't or can't trust others)"
- "I have to do everything myself (in order to get love)"
- "I cannot trust anyone (to give me what I need)"
- "I am not safe" (helplessness)

Core Script
- "I am alone (I'll die)"

On the surface, it may seem like this woman's core script was "I can never get intimacy" or "I'm the one who has to do everything" but, in fact, the real core script was "I am alone in the world and (therefore) I may as well be dead." This was a woman who had ghost-like parents. Her drive to do for everyone was a neurotic compulsion to connect despite her deep-seated belief that she would always be alone no matter what she did. This individual, coming from a ghost family, was terrified that in agreeing to do an enactment she would find herself in a ghost group with more lies and dissociation. She was afraid that she would hold back for self-protection and not get what she wanted from the experience. Holding back like this compounds the problem and can be a self-fulfilling prophecy that Young (1999) calls "schema maintenance or schema avoidance". Group therapists have to be aware of this possibility both during the assessment and as the enactment begins.

Another common core script has to do with abuse and damage in childhood. When a parent beats a young child it is likely that the child will internalize the idea that they are loathed and deserve to be beaten. Their nuclear script at various levels might be:

- "Nobody loves me because I'm so evil."
- "It's not safe to be who I am." [a constellation script]
- "I have no right to exist, I may as well be dead." [core script]

Some survivors of childhood abuse act as if they have never been born and so they are ghosts themselves. One lead's words were: "There's nothing real in this family. It's a dead zone." Another said (about close family members): "Because I do not know you my body is dead. My feelings are frozen. There's nothing there."

Core scripts are similar to what is called, in the EMDR approach to trauma repair, "the negative cognition". A negative cognition is more than just a belief. Shapiro (2001) states: "the cognition represents the client's current interpretation of the self, not merely a description" (p. 58). Shapiro points out that most negative beliefs seem to fall into three categories:

Core Scripts	**Possible Core Beliefs**
• responsibility	"I did or am wrong"
• lack of safety	"I'm in danger"
• lack of control	"I am helpless"

We have found that these themes are common in relation to self-tormenting core scripts revealed in our enactment work. Overly responsible people will say things like: "It was all my fault." "I am a coward." "I didn't do enough (to prevent the trauma)." Others, who never feel really safe anywhere, will say things like: "I am going to be hurt or rejected." "I am going to die." Some say: "I may as well be dead" or even "I am dead." Ongoing feelings of helplessness are a significant sign of trauma, observed in people who say: "I am inadequate", "I am at the mercy of others", or "My situation is hopeless because I cannot change it."

Death is a core script for many, linked to a constant self-tormenting bottom line of guilt and existential terror ("I am so guilty I deserve to be annihilated"). One lead commented: "My parents did not love me so there must be something terribly wrong with me." Klein (1975), when discussing reparation, emphasized that the individual feels terribly responsible for and guilty about the traumatizing loss. This is true even if they were the target of abusive, neglectful, or narcissistic parenting (Pressman & Pressman, 1997). This terror is not a functional state of being. Moreover, people who are terrorized have great difficulty perceiving that they are no longer in danger. They are constantly vigilant and startle easy. Shapiro (2001, p. 260) describes this state: "As long as clients remain at this undifferentiated state, they cannot escape the perceived danger; it is fully internalized … (with concomitant fear and self-condemnation)". Enactment clients feel anxious and harried. Moreover, they think this is a deserved state of being because of past transgressions. One of their aims is to relax and change negative beliefs such as "I deserve to suffer" into the positive, such as "I have suffered enough. I deserve to be happy" or "I'm safe now."

Developing and Installing Resources: Bringing Strength and Finding the Child Within

Before proceeding through the enactment scenario we recommend that the therapist take particular care to bring into the circle resources the lead has chosen. Resources may include people, places, objects, animals, or music. This process of bringing in resources is essential for witnesses as well as leads and is linked to issues of safety and trust. Leads have to be able to exercise self-control, self-regulation, and self-soothing behaviours. Resources may be one or more of the lead's own repertoire of self-regulating behaviours such as an easily accessible visualization of a "safe place". As part of our written memo for participants before they come to a workshop, we now include a section on bringing resources.

We begin to discuss resources with the lead during the assessment phase. We tell potential leads that, when they step into the group, we advise bringing as many resources as they want to support them during their work. People are asked to think about personally meaningful positives associated with well-being. These can take the form of images of good, self-soothing experiences such as kayaking on a calm ocean, personal traits such as courage or compassion, memories of nurturing, and joyful occasions with loved ones or lifesaving activities such as reading, riding horses, swimming, music, or artwork.

As soon as the lead steps into the circle, even before telling the story, the therapist encourages him or her to bring in their resources. Leads have passed photographs around the circle, displayed precious objects including family Bibles and albums, described "safe places" either real or imagined, and introduced important people from their past or present. One lead showed a wooden box full of childhood treasures. Another lead produced baby clothes and infant shoes. One individual had earth and stones from their country of origin. Leads comment on how bringing in their resources seems like a mini-enactment to them. Of course, resources are a major safety measure and have a salutorious effect not just for the individual but for the group.

As some leads cannot come up with resources from their unsafe childhoods, it would be a mistake to ask for one. People who are unable to come up with "safe places" from horrific childhoods are assisted to think of a time when they felt strong, safe, or cared for and choose an image, name, or feeling that captures that sense of themselves.

Resources increase the lead's safety in the group. They add authenticity and spiritual depth because the resources are symbols, often of a sacred nature. The First Nations concept "gathering medicine" describes this process very well. An example of this might be bringing in sweetgrass for smudging the circle. In addition, resources serve as cues later on when they are taken back into the "real" world. They remind us of a time when we felt loved. They are associated with a positive goal state or future self so that the person carries or transfers the learning to the "real world". When the workshop takes place in a beautiful setting, people often take away "resources" in the form of stones from the beach or leaves from the forest.

Frequently, in choosing resources, after the lead has selected the key members of the scene, the therapist asks the client: "Is there anyone else who should be here from your family, or maybe your partner, who should witness what you are about to say?" Sometimes leads want their parental ancestors and often their cultural or racial group to be witnesses to their heir's suffering and reparation. Continuity from generation to generation is particularly sought as it confirms identity.

For some time now, we have been following protocols in Shapiro (2001, pp. 434–40) and Korn and Leeds (2002) for installing resources with bilateral stimulation. Also, we often use self-soothing techniques such as the Butterfly Hug (developed by Jarero et al., 1999) during intense group process. The Butterfly Hug is accomplished by having a person wrap their arms around themselves, so that each hand touches the opposite upper arm or shoulder. Then they are instructed to pat their shoulders rhythmically. The person imagines good things such as "My heart is a treasure" while administering this self-stimulation. People can use the Butterfly Hug to feel safe and get to sleep at night.

Why is the need for resource installation so strong in enactment work? The sense of having been deprived of something essential often persists into adulthood as relationships are unable to compensate for the early lack. Despite their ability to behave as high-functioning professionals "out-in-the-world", people who have experienced trauma feel empty inside. They feel tormented by negative beliefs about themselves and unable to change them. In terms of overcoming helplessness and thus restoring agency—a sense of being in charge of one's own actions—they have to experience themselves in a different way in the enactment. The therapeutic process entails helping them move from feelings of being trapped inside their own suffering to being able to relate to others and make choices. This helps the individual feel calm and centred, an experience they can take away as a resource to use for good coping and to help in the development and maintenance of appropriate boundaries. This positive experience helps to increase "affect tolerance" (Linehan, 1993), which is one's ability to choose how to respond to incoming messages as opposed to feeling constantly acted upon. Leaving people with this experience and with other practical resources to take back home is a key component of the enactment process.

EMDR therapists install resources by bilateral stimulation (Shapiro, 2001). They measure the strength of the positive cognition by how true it feels to the client. We ask leads to scan the enactment scene and hold their positive cognition in their mind, for example: "I am lovable." Sometimes we ask participants to state a positive cognition they hold about themselves at the end of the group, for example: "I am a worthwhile person." For our purposes, installing resources means bringing them to consciousness, feeling them in the body, and speaking them out in public. Many people comment in follow-up meetings that when they feel anxious at work or home they imagine themselves in the group and feel supported and loved.

The lead may decide to bring a real person to the enactment such as a therapist, friend, or partner. Or they may choose to bring a photograph or object belonging to a person important to them. They may decide to bring objects from their own past or present. One of our deaf clients chose as his major resource his own indomitable spirit, role-played by the group member who played his double. He clutched on to this man throughout the enactment and later said he couldn't have done it without him. This is one indication of how important touch is for growth and connection. Touch plays a big part in enactments and in the group as a whole. Being able to hold on to one another is a major resource, although the therapist has to demonstrate boundaries in this regard as witnesses may need guidance so as not to overdo or violate privacy. However, many people who have been traumatized literally feel "out of touch". Coming back into touch and restoring the ability to feel is part of the reparation that occurs through enactments.

Another lead brought in a veritable bookcase of her important books and deposited them in the circle. She said that, when she was growing up in her injurious family, reading these books had saved her life. Many leads ask role players to depict loved relatives or friends, resources that will sit on the edge of the circle. Some leads have brought music to play. Resources help to promote the continuity of the lead's life. They are a counter message to isolation and disconnection. When working with First Nations groups, the Creator is usually present in the group as a resource. Many First Nations people like to begin and end their work with prayers of gratitude and appreciation to the Creator.

Many leads take a physical resource away with them, either an object of their own or given to them by a witness, for example, ruby slippers, a twirling skirt, or a cowboy hat that came in as a prop and left as a good object. Some people take photographs, create art objects like masks or collages, or beautifully decorate journals with pieces taken from the workshop environment. These objects have become associated in the lead's mind with the strength and support of the group.

The Child Self as Resource

The child double is a particularly important resource installation in the enactment process. We may ask the lead to choose a child double as well as an adult double, particularly in situations where the scene is set in childhood. This is an example of the split between the competent adult self and the little child that still carries the hurt. The child double may serve as a resource or, during role reversal, provide important input for the lead. By tending to our own little child we are internalizing nurturing for the self. We have noticed leads get stuck and then recover tenderness and vitality as a result of viewing their enactment through the eyes of their child double.

Increasingly we have found that enactments dealing with what happened to people in childhood require that we have the lead bring into the group the "small self" or "child self"—the self that existed pre injury. Not only does selecting a good, pure, and alive self act as resource installation to keep with them when they return to the traumatic event, the therapists often bring in the "small self" at key points to show the lead what happened and what was taken. The therapist's goal is to help the lead rediscover this "lost self" and integrate this part into the existing self. Meeting and working with the "small self" reminds them of hope and that repair is possible, regardless of what was taken in the trauma of their lives. For example, we have begun enactments by going back to see the small self fishing or gardening happily with a grandparent. Once we enacted a particularly harrowing experience with a lead who had been forced by his stepfather to live outside in a shed from about age one until he started school at age five. The Therapeutic Enactment ended when the role players the lead had chosen as his siblings came and got the small self from the shed, carried him into the house, and placed him in his own little bed. They covered him with blankets, got him a drink, and read stories to him.

The Witnesses as Resource

The group itself in the form of the witnesses is also a resource and plays an essential function in mirroring and reinforcing the new, positive self-script for the lead. During enactment, leads are so in the moment that they are unaware that a new self script is being installed. They seem to have no awareness of anything other than immediate feelings and reactions. It is only later, in the integration phase, that leads become cognizant of the change. Both master's and doctoral level theses research on the relevance of the presence of witnesses indicates that leads are acutely sensitive to the presence of witnesses and others who are supporting them. These findings reinforce what Watzlawick et al. (1967) have shown: that to understand ourselves we have to be understood by others. This confirms the essential value of the group setting for change to occur. When witnesses share their deep understanding of the lead's process, they validate the person: "I really felt connected to you when I saw your pain and you had a right to feel dishonoured." Then leads may come to understand that they haven't been dishonoured forever. Witnesses are able to speak forthrightly to leads because, in most instances, the leads' enactments have touched deep parts of themselves.

There's a truth and a congruence to this reciprocity that draws forth tenderness. Not only is the content of what people say important, the very process of having people speak in a heartfelt and supportive manner in public, allowing strong feelings, often holding one another, mirroring acceptance and affirmation, confirms the lead as a valuable member of the group. It's a ceremony of communion. The witnesses have the experience of participating in something intensely meaningful that is greater than any one of them. This in turn results in revisions to the lead's previous negative beliefs about himself and his situation. Although everyone feels like an outsider some of the time, traumatized people feel that "outsidership" is an ingrained part of their personality. If the group can create a warm, accepting space for everyone, no matter how wounded or socially marginalized, then reparation in some form is possible for all participants.

Part of therapeutic change is to experience validation from the group for what Kohut (1971) called "omnipotence" and "exhibitionism". Many people who have been brutally treated and had their noses rubbed in their helplessness exhibit what we call the self-righteousness of trauma. Their core belief is that they have been treated unfairly and the world owes them something. They think: "Somebody owes me and you are standing in front of me so it may as well be you!" They feel entitled to make continual and excessive demands for special treatment and generally this behaviour evokes contempt and distancing in others. Through experiencing the support and mirroring of the group they feel free to drop this narcissism when they see they can get their needs met without alienating people. They experience themselves as agents in the group and this includes an affirmation of the solitude and privacy of the self that is deeply satisfying. The therapists and the group are not experienced as engulfing, impinging, or withholding. The group instead installs an "internal representation" (Stern, 1985) that is taken away as a resource.

Enacting the Narrative: Remembering through Action and Emotional Expression

The leads now moves into action. They begin to experience for the first time a concrete representation of who they are or what has happened to them. Unconscious emotional frames of references (introjected schemas) that guide how they relate to others in the world may be revealed.

After the resources have been identified, the therapist invites the lead to stand and they both begin walking around the inside of the group as the lead begins their story. As the walking and co-constructing begins, leads may or may not know where they are going, but having the therapist stay with them promotes their sense of safety and they can move beyond thinking to feeling, sensing, and remembering. This awareness allows them to experience their bodies more fully. For instance, the therapist never says: "This is what you must do" but rather asks throughout the co-construction such questions as: "Do you want to proceed here with this?" "How would this be?" "How would your father or mother walk?" and "Who else should be witnessing this?" The lead feels supported, not controlled, and from time to time takes charge. Leads may say: "No, that's not right" or "I can't go there." Sometimes they will remain silent in response to a suggestion and then the therapist moves on. This collaborative process enhances trust and can stimulate insight. For example, one lead who felt marooned on a desert island with his two non-English speaking parents suddenly remembered a visit from an aunt who lives in the old country. He had been young at the time but he remembered how much he had enjoyed her and realized that she had somehow made a bridge for him between himself and his parents. He brought her into the circle as a resource, someone who loved him unconditionally and whose company he enjoyed.

This kind of realization occurs often during the enactments as the measured and focused moving through the scenario evokes concentration. Sometimes, leads can piece together or become aware of important aspects that they had lost in the chaos of the event. One lead, who as an adult had almost been murdered, had a body memory in the middle of the enactment of the murder scene: that the perpetrator had taken him by surprise and stabbed him the minute he answered the door, not after a struggle down on the floor as he had believed previously. This was a new and important realization as he had tormented himself for years with questions about how it was possible that he had been so weak as to have been overpowered in the struggle. Thus his sense of agency and trust in himself was restored.

As leads begin to move into action they begin to feel mixed emotions: shame and relief, fear and excitement, dread and anticipation, all at the same time. Often dramatic voice changes or changes in posture or movement appear to accompany these internal shifts. The therapist may stop the walking to amplify these shifts. We also find it important to look for spontaneous reactions or playful qualities in the person as they tell their story. Sometimes the therapist will stop, turn to the lead, and say something like: "Oh, you're laughing!" or "What a loud voice you have!" Other times leads may choke up, gesture, or feel a sense of initial panic as the story arouses shame, rage, or grief. Sometimes when a person begins to choke up they will stop momentarily. The therapist, who is always paying attention to these verbal and non-verbal clues, will ask the person: "Something just happened didn't it?", "What are you aware of?", or "Where do you feel it?" The therapist is directing the lead's attention back to the body. Or the therapist may gently guide the lead to finish incomplete sentences such as "I can't speak because …" or "I don't want to go there …" or "I don't want to say that …" or "I don't want to do that because …" ("I'm afraid that if I … or this will happen if …"). The therapist may ask the lead to begin: "What is holding me back is …" Or the lead may say: "I have to go now but before I do …"

Sometimes the therapist will quietly stand close to the lead and wait, perhaps with a hand on their shoulder, before proceeding to evoke verbalizations. The lead will probably only hear a few words from the therapist but will feel movement and touch so that, instead of feeling choked and wanting to hide, they know that someone is present, gently guiding them, and facilitating both the experience and expression of the blocked emotion. The therapist's physical touch, respect, and reassuring voice are essential. Leads feel supported by the reassuring sound of the therapist's voice, of not being hurried or felt to be a burden, of being able to slow down and reflect, and by non-verbals such as a light touch or walking shoulder to shoulder in close proximity. The early death of a loved one or a violent assault can be a life sentence for the survivor. Since one of the results of traumatization tends to be isolation, the company of the therapist conveys a strong message to the lead that they are not alone. One lead said that she mainly remembers that the therapist's voice was like a lifeline. Other leads may find, as they move into action, that they cling to the therapist as a necessary support as they move through their feelings of grief. It is important for the therapist's voice to remain calm and even. Any sign of the therapist jumping on the bandwagon of the lead's emotions by requiring them to exaggerate their feelings, or even over empathizing by invasive interpretations, can lead to lack of safety in both lead and group. The non-verbal component of communicating is very important to leads who are in action, experiencing the enactment.

As the lead and the therapist continue with the story, the therapist encourages the lead to bring people into the circle to play the roles of the family members. Once the role players are in place, the lead can start to set up the scene. One of the biggest fears of the lead is that they will stall and won't be able to go through with the enactment. People are afraid of making a fool of themselves and, again, it's about trust. Leads often voice their anxiety that they will "stay in their heads". Once moving to action, however, the individual experiences being "back in time", and the past becomes the present: they have returned to the event and are in the moment, and the event tends to move ahead with its own momentum. They have a sense of moving through the trauma, not becoming trapped in it or identifying themselves as one who is traumatized. The therapist has to exercise judgment between keeping the process moving and not moving too fast thus missing catharsis. The therapist wants to draw the lead's attention to feelings but not to the extent of their becoming stuck in them.

One way to think about Therapeutic Enactment is to imagine that distressing information has become frozen as a package in the brain and body. The person is unfreezing the package in the enactment while regaining feelings of personal control and movement forward. Presenting the material back to the individual as a coherent whole that can be safely explored is crucial and is therapeutic in itself. Chaos is reduced to manageable bits through the therapist's assistance and thus a safe container is formed. The primary objective is to make sure the client does not feel immobilized, overwhelmed by anxiety and strong emotion, or retraumatized.

Doubling

Safety and movement are reinforced through the use of "doubles", people who are selected to take on the role of the lead, as a sort of "stand in", as with Michael's enactment. Doubles provide a safe distance for the lead person doing the enactment. A common technique in psychodrama, doubling is used in Therapeutic Enactment because of the value it provides in helping the client with insight and empathy. The lead usually selects the double during the preparation stage and this person may stay close to them throughout, helping the lead clarify and express a deeper level of emotion and understanding of what occurred. There were several examples of doubling in Michael's story, both by the person he selected to be "him" and by others who came forward to help say the words that needed to be said by him when he was with his dying father.

The double is a good resource to have in the enactment setting. We often use the double to literally "back the lead up" as they walk around the circle telling the story, and from time to time the double is asked to stand in for the lead to permit them to observe what the scenario looks like in totality. The double is able to suggest and express inner experiences and statements that may also be helpful. On occasion the lead will watch while the double runs through a pivotal scene. Therapists may "freeze" the image so that the lead sees and feels the impact of it. Then the double can quietly step aside and the lead can take their place in the scene.

Child Doubles

Leads may choose child doubles as well as adult doubles and we are promoting this increasingly. Leads can always set aside the double or the good-enough self (from the "good-enough mother" in Winnicott (1965)) when they feel ready to say and do the action themselves. The double or good-enough self serves as a "transitional object" in Winnicott's terms, symbolically standing in for sources of security in the real world. Leads often cuddle with their child double or sit quietly, holding them tenderly. Child doubles can be used in several different ways. For example, the lead may protect the child and affirm a renewed sense of agency. Or the lead may nurture and soothe the child thus reawakening the lead's self-soothing abilities. The child double can be placed in a safe place—on the edge of the circle perhaps or with playmates—and the lead can go over and be with this representation of his childlike curiosity and liveliness at will.

Reparative material includes exposing abuse and humiliation, confronting the abuser preferably as a community thus excising the isolation, and redoing the scenario in the preferred way. For those who were robbed of childhood, an enactment that provides a revisited experience can facilitate moving the person away from the earlier role confusion that unfortunately may have resulted, paradoxically, in a child psyche in an adult's body. Many leads, when they see their child double having to act as an adult, and say or do inappropriate things with adults in the family, are really struck with the impact of it, often for the first time. They may have to express clearly what this took away from them, lose the faint hope that they could ever have different childhoods, and feel the resulting grief and anger. One woman became stuck in the middle of her enactment. She was unable to feel and thus her vocalizations did not ring true. Her child double made herself very small and approached the father, who yelled at her and tried to wrench her arm. The lead was galvanized! She dashed into the circle, grabbed her father, and ripped him away from the child double. She screamed at him and ordered him out of the room. Then she went down on the floor, held the child double in her arms, and wept for a long time.

Reality must always prevail. We know that we are not in the business of training people to find and keep illusions. However, reality can marry with ongoing sources of satisfaction and security for the individual. Consequently, the way in which the individual experiences and expresses the world can be spontaneous and creative. Reality is not just external and concrete but has an internal coherence and vitality that is a remedy for despair. We are dealing with "unfixable suffering" in these scenarios. What was taken cannot be replaced. Repair is not about replacing but about having the resources to carry on living. As one lead put it to the group: "When I'm alive I want to live. And when it's time to die, I'll die."

The presence of a child double alerts the group to focus on safety. Many leads were traumatized as children but they are grown-up now and tend to minimize the effects of trauma on their small child inside. When they see someone acting as a small child being abused they can be retraumatized. To complicate the situation further, the participant playing the small child can suffer retraumatization. Therapists have to very carefully manage the bringing in of the little child double. Senior group members acting as safety monitors are put on alert to watch for signs of abreaction or dissociation in other witnesses or the "child". Warning the group in advance and finding a senior group member to back up the child is essential. As well, the "child" has to be thoroughly debriefed after the enactment.

The use of doubles confirms that some pieces of work are simply too overwhelming at first for the lead to stay present. One lead wanted to enact a scene in a restaurant when she was eleven and her dying father had vomited blood on the table and floor. Everyone in the restaurant had been frozen. The family, in our lead's words, "cowered in shame, slunk outside, and drove away". She chose to watch her double enact the scene but it was still too potent for her to step in. The double was able to express her shame, outrage, and grief in a very believable way while the lead held on to her from behind. She chose to enact another scene without her double where everyone behaved differently and helped the family. We had to enact this last scene several times until she was able to physically accept that we are all capable of coming through for one another. She commented later that, as she was driving home from the enactment, she felt a vivid physical sensation of sitting in her double's lap. This is another example of taking an imaginary resource away from the workshop.

Expanding the Understanding of Self through Empathy in Role Reversal

Empathy is key in all therapeutic endeavours and empathic resonance is an important factor in Therapeutic Enactment groups. Our advice is that, when you don't know what to do, fall back on empathy! However, one of the traps of empathy in the enactment is that the therapist may overdo it and inadvertently force the lead to feel what the therapist believes they are feeling or should feel. The purpose of the therapist is to offer themselves to someone else to use for his or her purpose. Alice Miller (1981, p. 32) calls it "the idea that good objects allow themselves to be made use of". The goal is to comfort and protect not confront leads with their shortcomings or break down their resistance. Kohut (1971) was especially clear on the alienation and isolation that individuals with open childhood wounds suffer. His emphasis on "empathic immersion", that is, allowing therapeutic dependency without early interpretation, changing, fixing, or premature insistence on "right" behaviours, means an acceptance by the therapists and the group that the lead is in charge of the story but they are not alone in trying to make sense out of it. Therapeutic Enactment provides for the possibilities of the repair of attachment and intimacy disasters as the group provides a safe place, a refuge, for the person to expose the wound and prepare it for healing. The therapist and by extension the group provide a sense of "calm holding".

One of the ways to arouse and practise empathy in enactments is through role reversal, as with Michael's Therapeutic Enactment. The therapist judges when the lead, stuck in one way of seeing a significant interaction, is ready to take a different view. If a lead says that they do not understand why a significant other could not love them or is confused about why that person did or did not do some important action, then a role reversal may be indicated. Role reversal simply means at certain times that the client changes places with one of the key "others" to gain perspective outside of themselves. This is not so much that leads get to imagine what the other person was thinking or feeling, but it gives leads permission to accept parts of themselves they previously had disowned. Role reversal enables an external frame of reference that moves the person out of the narcissistic self. For example, a depressed lead believed that her mother and father had never loved her, that she was a burden to them, and that they regretted the responsibility of having her as a child (this was a female physician who was the head of her department in a hospital). In role reversal, she realized that her parents were trying to protect her from the suffering they had endured as refugees during the Second World War. They were filled with sorrow but it was not sorrow about her specifically.

The empathy in role reversal is not necessarily about affirming the other person's feelings. It is about understanding perspective so that we can detach from feelings that do not belong to us. In this case, the lead had confused her parents' sadness with her sadness. She understood that to give up her sadness did not mean she was dishonouring them. Role reversals can sometimes work like magic because a person, miserably stuck in their sense of things being one way, suddenly does a 180 degree turn and realizes a different perspective. Accompanied by release of feelings, this can be quite beneficial.

We have noticed many other similar reparative shifts during role reversals with dead or somehow flawed significant others. Once we suggested a role reversal in an enactment in which a brother was talking furiously to a much-loved, dead, older brother who had committed suicide. Both brothers had been physically abused by their father but the older had taken the brunt of it. The lead was angry at his brother's "selfishness" and "cowardice". In the role reversal, however, speaking as his brother, he was astonished to hear himself say that while he was sorry for the pain he had caused he wanted his brother to do him the honour of affirming his decision-making even if he disagreed with the decision; also he wanted his brother to let him go and yet remember him to his children when he had them (they were both young men). By taking the intense pain of their distressing upbringing upon himself, this lead was redeeming his brother to live a better life. This reframed the suicide in meaningful terms for the living brother and aroused his grief, thus allowing him the freedom to move out of his rage and guilt. In fact, at this point, the lead at last bowed his head under paroxysms of grieving, the denial of which had made us very worried about him. Dying with his brother had seemed preferable to him than living with the feelings that the death had aroused.

Typically leads don't have a sense of where the enactment will ultimately lead them. They are highly charged and consumed with feeling. Having said that, after a role reversal, leads often change the direction of their enactment based on a critical moment of new awareness, consulting with the therapist on the spot and experiencing the return of flexibility. A new analog for the self, a new self-script, can emerge and is installed as a result. Brooks (1998) points out that the enacted scene with its positive after-effects becomes fused and inseparable from the initial, "real" scene, as when the lead re-did the tragic scene in the restaurant. One lead whose mother died tragically in a mental hospital enacted a role reversal during which the lead felt loved by her mother. After the role reversal she went around the set-up exuberantly dragging out all the hospital furniture and replacing it with an imaginary garden full of flowers and growing plants.

Many leads comment on their physical memories after their enactments. One man who had never known his biological parents and had been adopted and then abused had said: "I yearn to be held by my mother." This yearning had been validated during his enactment as he was held and his sense of himself as a person who is always yearning for something was affirmed as important and real. He said to his mother: "Thank God you have come. I have missed you so much. Thank you for giving me life." Even years later this man was able to contact the physical sense of being held by his mother. He said: "I felt it in my bones." Another lead commented: "I'm gonna hold on forever to that ten minutes when I felt fathered." His "father" had carried him on his back around the circle and introduced him with pride to the group.

De-roleing

An essential process for the safety of the group is to have role players physically move through a de-roleing process. We de-role the participants before the group debriefing begins. If de-roling is not attended to, participants may experience troubling and distressing residual effects from the negative roles they assumed in the enactment and/or the lead may experience feelings of guilt or self-recrimination for having asked others to take dark roles. Since many enactments are intense and painful the group has to come back into balance, otherwise there is the prospect of vicarious traumatization. Participants de-role by coming into the centre of the circle where they are asked to imagine the role as a cloak, covering them from head to toe, that they then let fall to the ground.

They say: "I am no longer … [role], I am … [own name]." Then, once the role players have taken their places back in the circle, we make the transition to the debrief by participating in a ceremony that cleanses the space and releases grief. We may use a prayer, blessing, or silent coming together. Sometimes we send participants outside in dyads or triads for ten minutes of breathing or holding. Sometimes we say something like: "Is there anything that anyone needs to say into the circle at this point? Just say it. We may not be able to do anything other than hear you right now. In speaking our pain we can feel it more fully and let it move through us. Better outside than inside!" That way everyone is as available as possible for the debrief, is centred, and not carrying unshed tears or the heavy burden of other blocked emotions.

Debrief

The last phase of the enactment is for the lead to return to the group; witnesses and selected members who took roles are invited to share their reactions to what they have just observed and experienced. This phase is more than the lead hearing from others. It involves giving the speaker a chance to express both their feelings and ideas within the group. For many of the participants, they report having been transformed to some extent by either witnessing or being selected to take on one of the key roles. The therapeutic process is deepened for both the lead and others during this phase. As the members speak to the lead they affirm what the lead has done for them and in this way the group connections are also reinforced. Increased cohesiveness and safety is the result, making way for the next enactment to follow. The lead may feel encouraged to take the new awareness and be conscious of how this can be brought to their life outside the group.

The impact on the lead is evident soon after the enactment is complete. During the debrief what is often observed are noticeable physical shifts in the person who has experienced catharsis, just as we noted at the beginning of the enactment. For instance, the body is relaxed, the whole face is different, the voice may have moved into the chest or deepened; it has more power. It's almost as if we can see the eyes more clearly now. The lead also notices a shift. The old self-script doesn't hold the power it once had. It becomes history and doesn't tip them into extreme emotion or the blocking or numbing of it any longer. This is similar to what is reported after EMDR. Clients say that they remember the traumatizing event but it has lost its power to captivate or distress them.

Despite the sense of connection that usually follows an enactment, therapists need to be reminded to continue to maintain the safety of the group. If the group is big, more than fifteen participants, for example, we have found it better to divide into small groups of five or six for the debrief with a senior member in each sub-group. In this way, people can relax, get more air-time, and feel safer to let down their emotional guard. When the smaller groups return, a member can report the highlights of the contributions. Then people who want to speak into the big group can add in.

What leads usually experience during the debrief is not just reconnection but a new connection that feels deeper than they've ever had. They feel calm and supported and are often commended by the group. They feel a sense of accomplishment, a sense that "I did it!" However, others in the group will have felt the impact on their own feelings and core scripts. They have to come back into balance and feel both contained and respected. They also have to prepare themselves to witness the next enactment. It is essential to make sure that participants are not worn out, misunderstanding or distorting what's being said and done. Some group members, including the lead, may want close physical contact and comfort with a key person or persons from the group as they listen to feedback from the group. Sometimes we cover them with a blanket and get them water to drink. At this point the lead is in an altered state (and maybe others in the group as well). The therapist limits or blocks inappropriate or too lengthy feedback from other members, especially when directed at the lead, who may be so emotionally spent, or so empty, they can't actually take in or give out cognitive feedback from others. Since leads often tell us how much insight they get from the debrief, especially from those in key roles, we sometimes videotape enactments with permission of the group, so that leads can absorb more later. Other leads have contacted group members at a later date as a way to further integrate and understand their experience. Often gratitude, appreciation, and generosity is expressed at this point, and by no means just from the leads. There is a sense of group solidarity: "We came through this together!"

This liveliness indicates that a common yearning or pining for connection and community has been met during the enactments and their aftermath. A sense of shared identity and purpose has formed. Participants feel that they are inside a palpable group spirit. This motivates many to stay in touch. Or some people will start putting energy into forming their experience of community into a transformation of their "real world". They proceed differently in their circles of family or loved ones as well as in their work settings. In these ways, the group becomes a laboratory where the lead can practise new behaviours, make mistakes, and observe results. In one Therapeutic Enactment the lead was about to visit his elder brother in another country where he now lived. The lead had felt abandoned by his brother when he left home early to get away from conflicts with their father. The lead idealized his brother and saw him rarely. He realized as he planned what he would say to him that he felt a lot of anger toward his adored brother that he felt it would be wrong to express. Consequently his relationship with his brother felt superficial and false. In Therapeutic Enactment he got a chance to rehearse a scene in which he was having dinner with his brother during the visit. He got to tell his brother the truth of his sense of devastation and loss, firmly asking his brother to hear him out. He thus reclaimed a sense of personal agency as well as a return to an honest relationship with him. During this particular rehearsal, the therapists and the group gave the lead specific suggestions to help refine and enhance his plan for the meeting. The planning became a kind of "mini-enactment" that was timely and useful. Such mini-enactments keep up the commitment and involvement of the group.

The lead, in reconnecting with the group, is able to begin to integrate what they have experienced into the newer schemas of the self. Each lead goes through a cognitive and emotional reprocessing during which support and connection are crucial. The therapist will call the lead within forty-eight hours of the enactment. Sometimes key role players will call too. The therapist may need to normalize a movement from euphoria to depression related to loss and change. Leads may experience themselves as very vulnerable and shame may make an appearance ("I exposed myself"). The group provides venues for this through various stages: (1) the debriefs after each enactment, (2) the process that the group goes through in the closing hours of each workshop, (3) the follow-up debriefings (we used to have just one follow-up six weeks after the workshop; now we often have two: one at two weeks for leads and the other at six weeks for the whole group), (4) the spontaneous individual follow-ups with the therapists and with fellow-group members, (5) sometimes leads become senior group members and rejoin another workshop, and (6) occasionally groups do not want to stop and they continue to meet periodically to follow-up and to pursue new work with one another.

We encourage leads at each of these stages to consider the ways in which they may be different and to begin putting these differences into practice. We begin with visual imagery, perhaps asking people to imagine out loud what it will be like when next they meet their parents, colleagues, or partners. What will they do, what will they say, what are their goals? What is their contingency plan for safety? We go through the negative and positive cognitions. What do they feel in their bodies as they imagine this process? We may do a short practice role play. The individual lead may make a plan. Discussions with the group may give people new ideas of what they might do differently, especially since some members of the group will have been through this stage already.

At the six-week follow-up meeting, leads often remark on new awareness they have continued to process out of their enactment. If the size of the group warrants it, at this follow-up debrief we may divide the group into smaller groups to give people adequate airtime to check in and process their experiences. This enlivens participants and they get more time to discuss what has happened to them in their re-entry to the world. We come back into the big circle after about forty-five minutes and listen to the group reports. People have an opportunity to add pieces into the group as a whole. We finish with a short leaving ceremony.

The groups become what Bandura (1986) called "self-generated social environments" in which participants can practise self-efficacy and enhance their self-esteem through the ability to work with multiple resources, experimentation, and reinforcement in a safe setting. Bandura states: "The belief in one's capabilities to organize and execute the sources of action required to manage prospective situation, results from one's experiences of mastery, vicarious experience, verbal persuasion, and physiological states." Enhancing skills and reinforcing new awareness through social learning and modelling prepares people to re-enter the world with a greater potential for resiliency and effectiveness in managing their lives. This is the phase of integration of personal learning. The participants, through powerful, cathartic experiences and authentic engagement with others, form strong emotional bonds that sustain and fortify their ability to fulfill their intentions. For example, a lead may promise to fulfill certain actions and have this vow witnessed. These bonds are not about conscious, interpersonal feelings of attachment or love although they may feel like that. Rather they are about the bond of life itself. The intense emotional environment "stamps in" the individual ability to carry over the learning when they return to their "real" life, as they must do.

Brooks (1998, p. 303) describes the implementation of therapeutic change as "recontextualization, integration, practice, commitment to action, and generalization". This means that the importance of the therapeutic group in providing a new context for the individual's experience cannot be overemphasized since, in the individual's experience, their previous group whether family or work setting was a context for trauma. In those earlier groups, to feel seen was to feel shame because individuals felt painfully diminished by the experience. The enactment groups, in contrast, provide a public context in which the individual can feel affirmed, encouraged, soothed, and honoured. Leads can both differentiate and integrate their experience, and thus enhance their willingness to follow through when they return home. However, before they move out of the group, leads have had to assert their presence in the group in a fundamental way. They must reveal themselves, warts and all, and use courage to test the tenet "I am loved because I am" (Fromm 1956, p. 33). This cannot be strived for and exposing oneself is a risk. When love comes, it comes as a blessing.

Behavioural rehearsals, coupled with a new inner schema of self such as "I am a competent person" and "I can risk doing things differently" even saying "No, thank you!" as opposed to the old schema of "I am trapped" increase the chances of following through with new goals.

Eventually what has been learned is integrated into the lead's psyche. At the same time leads develop strategies and approaches to act differently, be more aware of the body, build self-esteem, and embrace a belief that change is possible and sustainable. Individuals may change their scripts to "I am alive." One individual commented that her script had changed to "I am recalled to life."

Individuals now prepare themselves to return from the highly charged communion of the group to their personal and work worlds. Two things typically occur following repair work. First, members experience a sense of mastery and begin to build confidence in this. The world and the people in it look different now and are less contradictory and difficult to deal with. Second, by acting and believing differently in the world, people are socially reinforced, which encourages greater risk-taking and thus enhances feelings of ability and competence. It cannot be overstated, however, the sense of loss present in the bare fact that everyone has to leave the group and go home.

Summary

We sit around in a circle and suppose
While the secret sits in the middle and knows.
—Robert Frost

Essentially, the healing properties in enactment groups remain mysterious. Spiritual processes are pivotal to the individual lead's learning experience. An abstract sense of timelessness and transcendent meaning permeates the groups. Each therapist conducting Therapeutic Enactment will come up with their own set of comfortable activities to deal with these hidden properties. We do not want the reader to run enactment groups exactly the way we run them but in their own way, informed by our experience. This chapter has attempted to address the primary processes related to change and the restoration of "self within the group". Participants in Therapeutic Enactment are struck always by the power of the group in affecting change in people's lives. Building the group is a delicate and difficult endeavour requiring considerable knowledge and expertise about how groups in general work and about the roles and obligations of therapists. We think group processes are so important that we have devoted the entire following chapter to them. We believe that our approach to creating safe and sacred groups is new and yet can be taught. The next chapter will take you through the processes involved.

Developing the Group

CHAPTER 4

You're crying. You say you've burned yourself.
But can you think of anyone who's not hazy with smoke?

—Jalal al-Din Rumi, "Fragment 551"

There they go. I must haste and follow them
for I am their leader.

—First Nations leader,
a participant in an enactment group

Since Therapeutic Enactment occurs within a group context, the therapist must know about how groups develop and possess a variety of skills to form a safe group. In this chapter we set out the core processes participants in the group experience at various stages of group development. In the next chapter we provide some tools for the therapist to use in leading and maintaining a safe group.

Of primary importance is the therapist's skill at creating and maintaining an effective working climate in the group. It is the therapist's ethical responsibility to ensure safety and care because the risk of hurt for individuals in groups is great. Many casualties were left after the Encounter Group Movement in the 1960s and early 1970s. As a result, we keep safety uppermost in our minds in order to contain the intense and often threatening emotions that arise when people work with their own painful material.

All groups go through developmental stages: a beginning, middle, and end. These stages are seen in some form whether the group lasts for one session, a weekend, twelve sessions, or as an ongoing group. Each developmental stage has its own focus, task, and activities. The stages of development are reviewed below, from the initial stages when we establish safety and develop the group as a container for the enactment, to the middle stage of working with the shadow and unexpressed emotions, to the termination stage of closing and preparing to leave.

Initial Stage: Safety

The main focus at the initial stage is to form a working climate and establish the role and function of the therapist or therapists leading the group. In the early part of the group there is a "milling about" (Rogers, 1961, 1985) as people try to find their place, and this invariably brings in the shame and grief associated with dependency, concerns of acceptance, or possible rejection. Group members are confused, frustrated, searching for structure, clarity, and the "real" leader. Schutz (1958) suggests that group members first have a need to feel included, to belong, and to become a part of the group. This need is expressed in questions such as "Is there room in this group for me?", "Will I be accepted?", "What will other group members expect from me?", and "How will I relate with the therapist?" This need to belong does not mean that members have to like or be liked by everyone in the group. They may even feel uncomfortable in the group initially. At this point group members also typically ask themselves: "How much of an investment do I want to make and what kind of a commitment do they want from me?"

In addition to striving to belong, members have a need for some personal control (Schutz, 1958) in respect to what they do or what happens to them. Anxieties related to fear of being manipulated or disrespected by members or the therapists are evident. Individuals try to find out how much control they have over what will happen to them as group members, asking themselves: "Can I be free to be myself in this group or will I be forced to feel and do things I don't really choose to?" They try to figure out how much they can influence or control the group and how much the group can control them. Typical process issues arising at this stage are associated with leadership, competition, and comfort with the degree of perceived group structure. In Therapeutic Enactment groups members need to see that the therapists are clearly in charge in order to feel safe. In groups where this is not the case and where the therapist as leader is "not the leader", Bion (1961) warns of the danger that the craziest person in the group will assume the role of leader. Being in charge means setting up the parameters by which the group can function and work, at the same time paying careful attention to perceived and stated needs from the members.

Clarity about starting and closing times for the group is one way therapists provide structure for the group. Being vague or unclear in leadership roles engenders anxiety, defensiveness, and acting out. We try to avoid having latecomers or early departures as it breaks the continuity of the group process and is very disruptive to learning. Outlining expected outcomes, goals, and guidelines for the group process to be followed contributes to the development of stability and predictability for the members.

With increased feelings of belonging and a sense of personal control in place, levels of safety or trust begin to increase. Affection for the group develops, characterized by the expression of positive feelings, sharing, emotional support, respect, and enhanced member-to-member attachment in non-exploitive ways.

With increased trust comes greater risk taking and self-disclosure. Increased self-disclosure in a safe context enhances trust. Intimacy in the group is only possible when high levels of trust and self-disclosure are present. Without these they feel at the mercy of the other in the relationship and cannot relax enough to allow openness and vulnerability. The tone for the development of trust and self-disclosure are created by the therapists when they state clearly what is expected, the feelings that may be aroused, the method of addressing one another in the group, and the means by which speaking the truth to one another can be supported without inflicting hurt. Supporting without hurting has to be experienced and tested in the group before members are confident it works. The therapists prepare themselves to be confronted and tested early on as to whether or not they have both the willingness and the ability to be open and non-defensive. These skills must be modelled by the therapists first before members can act in a similar way. Safety resides in an open and respectful process, not in stifling strong emotion or suppressing disagreements.

How do you build safety, especially in preparation for enactments that can activate a range of member reactions due to the volatility of traumatizing events? How do we approach this matter without violating defences? A person's defences are often their saviour. To try to knock them down can either harden them or push the individual over the edge. For many people, it is not just the traumatizing event that is an issue but the way those around responded to the injury. The way group members respond to them can arouse strong reactions, particularly shame, helplessness, and even despair. For example, one woman, who was seven months pregnant when she was assaulted in the street, said that although this was a deeply distressing incident what she remembered most was the way the ambulance driver and policeman said to her: "What were you doing walking out alone at night?", implying that it was her fault she was assaulted. Just at the moment when she was most in need of care and protection, those responsible for her care acted inappropriately and exacerbated the traumatic injury. She felt she had been treated with contempt. This, likely, is a sign that the caregivers too may have had difficulty tolerating the feelings aroused by the traumatic event. In any case, people bring into the group unfinished business from previous experiences with groups and helpers. They can react to group business with disproportionate emotion by projecting onto others. In reflecting on the pregnant woman's experience we are reminded of how essential it is to pay attention to how people communicate with one another in the group. Remember often it's not what's said but how it's said. This is especially so in contexts where inner defensiveness is already high, so typical of people coming to do trauma-related work.

The group "eyes" or "witnesses" contain and publicly support the individual's actions. We remember the words of Martin Buber (1965) that childhood's spell has been laid on us resulting in our withholding ourselves because of an impenetrable inability to communicate ourselves. Each of us is encased in an armour whose task is to ward off signs. These "signs" are the eyes of the other.

When these eyes meet ours, we have a superstitious fear that we have been penetrated and this we try to avoid. When we come into a group, we both long for and try to avoid the eyes of the other. The group, therefore, contains all the hidden and overt elements necessary for its members to achieve completion and wholeness. Participants have to believe that they do not have to guard their backs but can be honest and open. With feelings of safety they can risk to speak their truth and experience. They need no longer suffer in silence.

When the therapist provides leadership in the initial stage, a context for emotional repair is created that is central to our method of trauma repair. We therefore teach and model effective ways of communicating early in the group to help avoid unnecessary threats to safety. This doesn't mean we only want "positive" or "nice" comments; instead we want clear and open statements.

Initial Stage: The Group Container as Foundation for the Enactment

With a solidly contained group in place the enactment now becomes the focus. You have seen how the lead in the enactment relies on the group formation and process to enable moving through the enactment. The container is a good metaphor for a Therapeutic Enactment as the group has to be able to "hold" the individual and their enactment. If the lead does not feel safe, especially since the most awful disclosures of personal degradation, torture, and torment are possible and common in enactments, then reparation will be impossible. The full nature of the event must be told. The lead needs to feel free to speak and act without fear of offending, embarrassing, or creating fear in the witnesses. In addition, the lead needs to know that witnesses will remain present and will not abandon them.

One Therapeutic Enactment is an example of a situation that developed spontaneously after the group had formed a solid container. A lead planned an enactment that included a scene in which he was to go around the group and state that he was loving and lovable. As he was walking with the therapist, telling his story, he reported that while he knew people loved him, he just didn't believe that they respected him and this compounded his feelings of worthlessness. It quickly became apparent that he wanted to tell the group that he had attempted suicide. (He had never told any of his friends or colleagues this secret although he had made a point of telling the therapists in the assessment phase.) Now he alluded to his loneliness and the ways in which he held himself apart from people, including keeping from them essential information about his despair. He said that he would like to change but was afraid. The therapist asked him if there was anything specific he wanted to tell the group. He said there was and he needed a lot of help to do this. The therapist asked the group to stand, draw closer together, and say or do whatever they thought they could to make it possible for the lead to make such a big self-disclosure. While terrifying at first because he had been concealing his "weakness", it proved remarkably reparative for him to blurt out his story in a group of fellow professionals.

As another Therapeutic Enactment began, a lead expressed his confusion about why he was complaining about his parents since, as he pointed out, they had never done anything bad to him. He told the group that he felt like an impostor and believed that someone with more important issues should be doing their enactment instead of him. However, as he told the story of his loneliness and his parents' unwillingness to have any kind of close emotional contact with him or even show any interest in his accomplishments, he realized that, to all intents and purposes, except for the stability of food, clothing, and shelter, he grew up as an orphan. Later still, he became aware that he envied his wife and her family their close relationship and this had become a problem in his relationship with her. It is important for the therapists at the outset of situations like this to make sure that the lead understands that they are not judging him, comparing his suffering to anyone else's, and that they are taking his unique context very seriously. Otherwise the lead may be shamed.

Another example that illustrates the power of the group is a lead who was a rather well-known local professional and suffered from depression. The most shaming thing for him to do was to stand up before a group of people and try to communicate this. Simply going around the circle speaking out and having the group mirror understanding and affirmation was reparative for the lead. This was a mini-enactment in itself. It was as if he almost didn't have to go through the rest of the enactment. Another lead was the widow of a man well-known for his altruism. She felt sick with shame when she told the group that he had routinely beaten her and her two sons. We find that with behaviours that carry a lot of attached shame, for example, suicide or bullying and physical assault—anything associated with weakness or not measuring up—the lead finds speaking the truth in the group remarkably freeing.

Before the enactment can begin, the therapists must be satisfied that they have prepared a group climate experienced by the members as cohesive and accepting. The group is often referred to as "sacred space". It is safe and non-judgmental as well as fulfilling because it evokes a spirit that transcends the individual ego. Preparing the group in this way is the first step in the therapeutic process. The lead's process and the success of their experience depends on the promise of safety, trust, and control. Deciding to enact a critical and emotionally charged scene from your life is a courageous act that requires taking huge emotional risks in front of others. A group member who decides to do an enactment needs to feel they belong to the group, that the group won't shame them, and that they will not be forced into doing or feeling just to perform and get it over with. This means that group members do not criticize the lead or argue with the content of the enactment.

Once the group is safe, members begin to move through expressing and enacting their story and they begin to take personal responsibility in their own change process. The lead must accept the reality of their life and what happened to them (it was awful and can never be undone), while at the same time empathizing and making space for other people (not only did they have it bad too but we can support each other). The lead, at this point, is ready to give up their dependency on abusers, neglecters, shamers, parents, bosses, and so on because they have moved into a potent sense of agency, which, oddly enough, is fuelled by grief or rage. Expression of anger can be a releaser as the anger helps people move from depression to action. However, for those who are accustomed to pretending to hold up the entire world ("Look how strong I am") it is better for them to collapse into grief momentarily. Remember that releasing grief unlocks spontaneity and creativity and these are the primary factors that drive or fuel the enactment.

Moving through individual enactments promotes openness, transparent process, and high equal involvement, moving the group to higher levels of cohesiveness and safety. This serves to mitigate predatory or narcissistic acting out. We observe that cohesiveness continues to increase over the life of the group and further deepens with the completion of each enactment.

The Middle Stage: Working with the Shadow or the Unexpressed

In the initial stage of group life, the therapist and the participants are predisposed to like each other and feelings of persecution and guile are set aside. Sometimes a sense of "false communion" prevails as everyone "makes nice" and negativity is suppressed. Enchantment is a necessary first stage in attachment and commitment to the group. However, enchantment may be difficult to give up, especially when the therapist knows that subsequent developments will include darker elements such as conflict and complaints. The therapist may try to hold on to enchantment by momentarily becoming the slowest member, holding up the group by focusing only on content and trying to ignore complaints and power struggles. Yet these later processes are an essential part of testing the therapist and expressing autonomy. In the initial stage, when the container is forming and these darker elements (the shadow) begin to appear, the therapists must be aware that they are a test of safety. The therapist usually finds the darker elements unpleasant, but their appearance and acceptance is essential to the group's progress.

In Therapeutic Enactment groups, safety is linked to evoking and embracing the shadow. Stein (1984) describes it as: "The shadow refers to all those rejected and repressed aspects of the personality; it contains infantile, inferior and morally reprehensible tendencies, but it is also the carrier of many rejected natural, life-promoting impulses" (p. 59). The shadow includes the feelings of shame, grief, rage, loneliness, envy, scapegoating, helplessness, masochism, and terror that are aroused when we confront the suffering of self and others in public. Individuals usually suppress these feelings, judging their environment as inhospitable to such strong, socially primitive, aggressive, and uncooperative aspects. Groups that are unable to contain the shadow are unsafe and members withdraw their commitment and energy from them. Gladding (1999) is alluding to this when he warns of one of the limitations of the method of psychodrama: "if the group is not carefully constructed, the emotional part of the theory and the here and now emphasis will override the integrative aspect of this approach" (p. 443).

The concept of working with the shadow is very helpful as it reminds us that the "unexpressed" will be acted out in ways that threaten the container cohesiveness and impede the individual therapeutic work of the lead. Participants bring memories into the groups of the many variations of family and work groups that they find injurious. The group mind, as Bion (1961) called it, can be tormented by these transferences and the container will be unsafe. In groups, members enact the transference from their family of origin. Participants who have had problematic relations with their parents have lost their dream of the good-enough family. They may be looking to the group to replace this loss. Or they are filled with anticipatory anxiety or resentment, fully expecting the group to repeat the original group nightmare. If grieving is an identifiable group process early on, members can begin to recognize these transferences and let them go. In any case, members are seeking to find their way through the miasma that early experiences from their families of origin cast over the group. Part of the excitement and efficacy of group work is to embrace this challenge, opening up the possibilities of repair.

Members of the group must feel that they can work with the shadow in the group without suffering emotional injury or secondary trauma. Safety must not be confused with an absence of strong feeling. The therapists as group leaders carry an awesome responsibility for providing and maintaining a safe place when incidents involving the shadow happen. Naturally, we will make mistakes. Both therapists and group members must take responsibility for bringing these critical incidents and breaks in the container to the attention of the group as a whole. Therapists respond by validating the experience of the member who brings it up, not deflecting or avoiding it. Otherwise, maintaining safety in the group is impossible.

The Middle Stage: Regressive Energies

The container has to hold what Bion (1961) calls "discontent"; what Melanie Klein (1975) calls "primitive part-object relationships"; and what we call the "shadow" (unexpressed, socially unacceptable negative feelings). In one group, a man raged so powerfully at his father that it took five of the men, with their whole strength, to hold him back as he gave the rage his full force. This left him feeling cleansed, if a little sheepish. The group's containment aroused feelings of concern in the lead instead of possible shame and resistance. However, many in the group were afraid and one or two were terrified by the unleashed intensity and potential violence. This had to be addressed before the group could proceed to the debrief. The lead's rage at his father, and then the group having to contain that rage and their need to dispel it through the debriefing, was a major safety issue.

Some people go into Therapeutic Enactment wanting to symbolically kill their abusers. Yet quickly, as the enactment unfolds, the lead may move into an entirely different understanding and emotional acceptance of their own situation. This frees them from being bound up with the oppressor. They can let them go. The feelings that follow are often an excruciating combination of gratitude, grief, concern, and mercy on self and on others. One lead who wanted to kill his father was afraid that in confronting him he would become just like his father, so enraged that he would be evil as well. After he allowed himself to express his rage he was overcome by grief at the loss of love between himself and his father, as well as by grief at the unfulfilled love in his father's life that would never be restored because he was now dead. This process can only happen if the group makes room for the shadow. If members want to prevent or protect out of their own anxiety they will shut down the lead and abort the reparative process.

We had an individual in the group who was extremely oppositional, passive-aggressive, and hard to approach. He was a man who James Hollis (1994) would describe as living "under Saturn's shadow". In order to survive at work, to maintain dominance and protection, he had given up his soul. This was a man who had been treated sadistically by both parents. He had made his way in the world by being exceptionally competent while giving the impression that he could not care less. He controlled others by maintaining distance, inflicting small but constant jabs like knife wounds, and, while appearing to comply, made sure that no changes could occur in his relationships. Eventually one of the therapists said to him: "You seem really determined to annoy everyone and yet you are not enjoying it. What is it you would really like to do?" He replied that he really wanted the group to do what he wanted. He agreed to make a sculpture in which he would position the group members where he thought they should go. He ended up positioning them in the corners of the room, away from him. He looked at the sculpture and burst into tears, saying that he felt alone and isolated. He asked the members to come closer and at last he positioned them in a circle with him inside, each of them touching him.

After the break, he expressed "shame and anger at being manipulated into joining the group". However, when he expressed this loudly and heard the members' non-hostile responses, he was able to accept that he was an important and valued part of the group. He had "acted out" in the group and then he had "acted in". For him, reparation had to occur after he realized that the group saw him clearly (as difficult and provocative), yet wanted him to belong without requiring that he pay some huge price to belong. For some people, speaking the unspeakable in the group is itself reparative. This individual had indeed, for many years, been at the mercy of his family, who did not have his best interests at heart. He was filled with shame and rage at the memories of his neediness and his helplessness. He was determined never to admit to need and to make everyone suffer who had to be in a relationship with him.

Our experience confirms that if shadow or unexpressed content is encouraged, groups will be potent, disturbing, and anxiety provoking. If we as therapists become anxious, then the group begins to feel anxious and unsafe.

Our strategy is to consult each another openly about our anxieties in front of the group. Fearful leaders make for fearful and constrained groups, so we always try to work with a therapist who is a little less afraid than we are.

In groups of twenty or more, self-disclosure of shadow material is not an easy process to begin and foster. People worry about being scapegoated. Yet this is a necessary step in preparing the group for Therapeutic Enactment. A huge disclosure can bring the shadow into the group in the forms of shame, grief, fear, and envy—the Four Horsemen of Group Process. When these intense feelings come into the group, it means that something desirable and beneficial is going on and the therapists can relax. We may feel annoyed, irritable, bored, or indifferent, but this means that a group is actually happening. We can feel betrayed, emotionally drained, exhausted, or want to run away. This is normal balancing going on. We can feel greedy, deprived, resentful, and guilty. We can feel left out, shut down, raw, and bleeding. We can feel giddy, loving, and grateful and never want to leave. We can feel feelings we have never felt before. We can be awed. Some of us can even be rendered speechless. But when we look around the group and see shadow feelings in action, we realize that the group is really working in a robust way and is ready to hold the intensity of the enactment and its aftermath. We permit the shadow, allow the group reactions to the shadow, and, at the same time, reinforce feelings of support and safety. The net result is diminishment of early feelings associated with shame. It is a type of desensitization in the best sense of the word—people still feel their feelings without a need to cover up or diminish—and there is no retraumatization.

Shadow material is germane to therapy groups. However, enactment groups are rarely vulnerable to major shadow elements such as scapegoating, envy, power struggles, or other narcissistic attacks because the intense, negative emotions are right out there in the circle for all to see. It is only when there is a failure to confront shame and when the shadow is split off in groups that scapegoating can arise. Instead of the group openly confronting unattractive or scary feelings, they are projected unconsciously onto one individual. In some groups, including families or even entire professions like counselling, members are supposed to be "nice", reasonable, understanding, forgiving, empathic, and non-hostile. What an intolerable burden to carry. We sometimes say in our groups that when someone says they feel "fine", it means they feel fucked up, insecure, neurotic, and empty. Being "nice" begins with feeling numb. In some groups, members are supposed to listen to the others in the group and not act out. Often, they will feel like doing the opposite. Instead of receiving and holding, they will want to reject. There has to be room in the group for the expression of these shadow energies that otherwise could be at war with each other, producing scapegoats and destroying the group.

Therapy groups may be vulnerable to envy because dependency—its brutalization, exploitation, and betrayal—is a large part of the therapeutic experience. In the group, the very existence of the therapists may arouse the spectres of dependency and distrust left over from the parents if we do not deal with it directly. Envy is more common in human relations than we would like. Parents can envy their children simply because they are children. The dying can be envied simply because they are dying; similarly, the bereaved and the traumatized. But envy destroys reality itself, spoiling the good simply because it is good. Group members who struggle with envy can become implacable enemies of reality as it is experienced in the group process. For example, they may envy the therapists or any signs of healing, specialness, or communion in the group. Feelings that look like indifference, coldness, or withdrawal actually may be guards against envy. Other indications of the possible presence of envy are the "impostor syndrome", comparing self unfavourably to others, political or social hypersensitivity, authority problems, untidiness, inability to finish things, lack of spontaneity, or difficulty with commitment and intimacy. We discuss envy forthrightly early on and are successful in warding off its destructive potential.

To reiterate, the groups will only be therapeutically safe if the members believe that they are able to deal with shame, envy, scapegoating, and the other shadow energies. For example, in one Therapeutic Enactment we had a medical professional in our group who was taking antidepressants. This was an enormous shame to him because he felt like a fraud advising his patients how to deal with their depressions. He thought he was a failure and a sham. With great difficulty and trembling, he slowly got it out to the group that he was taking treatment for depression. In response several members of the group threw their own antidepressant pills into the circle. His face was a study. Finally he just burst out laughing.

The Middle Stage: Grieving in the Group

Probably the major reason that enactment groups are not prone to destruction by shadow elements is that public grieving is accorded a central place. Shared grief redeems the group from shame and helplessness. Suffering and grief evoke community life and call forth the deepest emotional resources of the participants and the group. They affirm the identity of the group and the members' commitment to it. People who grieve in the group, not just the leads but the witnesses also, must feel that their grief does not set them apart or make them pitiful and that their dignity is inviolate. For the first time people experience a balance between the loneliness of suffering and connection with others in the same situation. This is "reciprocity" and is a necessary component of therapeutic groups. The *Oxford English Dictionary* defines "reciprocity" as: "Expressing mutual action or relationship, giving and taking, existing on both sides, felt or shared by both parties; To return, requite, the action of making a return, a function or expression related to another that their function is unity."

In Therapeutic Enactment groups everyone is involved in the process and has a task to perform. The leads, therapists, role players, witnesses, and experienced group members all make their essential contributions. This evokes a meeting of equals. In therapy groups, the therapists have to find a way to affirm the autonomy of group members—restore reciprocity—in what is an unequal power relationship. If group members are "inside" the process doing all the work—thinking, feeling, and acting—and the therapists are "outside" doing all the guiding and controlling without being emotionally drawn in, then the relationship between therapist and group members will be out of balance and healing will be difficult. This is especially important for group members who are in the helping professions. If they get stuck in the helping role then their relationships will be one-sided, making them sterile and frustrating. Reciprocity is needed in Therapeutic Enactment groups to create a space of high involvement for everyone.

Reciprocity is not about cause and effect, action and reaction, but about balance and connection. People after a lifetime of blaming others or a self-as-victim identification can return to a sense of themselves as a sovereign individual. Questions asked at the beginning of the group—"What did you give up?" (in your early development) and "What do you want to get back that you lost?"—draw attention to the longing to have returned that which was lost. Replies often include "my honour", "my self-respect", and "my self."

Schieffelin (1976) describes a tribal society that has rituals to restore balance, discharge grief, and redeem "outsiders" (those who have been wounded) to bring them back into the group. The point of the rituals is to ensure that people can experience their grief without being immobilized by despair. Schieffelin's description is reminiscent of the process in Therapeutic Enactment groups. When one has been injured, one loses one's place in society in a symbolic but nonetheless deeply felt manner. This sense of dislocation has to be repaired. Schieffelin's society does this by means of ceremonies called Gisaro. "Gisaro is a drama of opposition initiated by the dancers but played out by everyone (in the group). Within a structure of reciprocity, the action of the performers and the feelings of the audience are brought into a relation with each other that allows intelligibility (meaning) and resolution" (p. 197).

The grieving ceremonies in Gisaro reveal and affirm the principle that, when something is lost, something else must be restored. Lost honour must be restored otherwise there will be a split in the community. In this way, reciprocity ensures that the relationship remains just and never breaks down into violence. Gisaro ceremonies typically were not about restoring the actual loss but about returning the relationship and the community to wholeness. This is a useful analogy for enactments as they are performing very similar functions for the leads and the group and, by extension, the larger community to which all belong.

Grieve But Do Not Grieve Alone

Unless the group is able to find a way to express the intense feelings of grief and rage that come up during the enactment, they will be unable to move into concern for self and others. In fact, they may engage in destructive, acting-out, or scapegoating behaviours. After a particularly intense enactment, we have noticed that the group is unable to focus, members quarrel about small things (such as lighting or room temperature), or people run in and out or go missing. This leaves members of the group feeling chaotic, insecure, and disturbed. Balance has to be restored before the group can move on to the next task. At such times, we understand the link between reparation and grieving. In addition, we understand how essential it is to be together through empathic and physical resonance so that we return to ourselves and to our shared humanity.

In one Therapeutic Enactment, the lead, when very young, had been subjected to different kinds of abuse by several members of her extended family because her alcoholic teenage mother was unable to protect her. When the group came together again after her enactment, there was a palpable energy in the circle that was close to despair. How were we to come back together after such a thing? The group had to find a way to discharge feelings of terror, grief, and rage, otherwise this energy would likely be acted out destructively. In such circumstances, grieving circles and ceremonies of purification work to discharge the negative feelings held within, to normalize the experience, and to facilitate the member's reconnection to the group. In this case, we went outside through the wood that surrounded the property and down to the ocean. It seemed important to be in nature and feel the earth under our feet—a form of grounding. This community walkabout was restorative in that it brought everyone back to the present moment away from the surreal trauma of the lead's enactment. This allowed everyone to return for the debrief and many heartfelt things were said and done in that particular debrief. The participants were able to be fully present and not numbed or vicariously traumatized by what they had seen and heard.

Carrying out a specific enactment often helps to trigger and or release feelings in this way for all group members. It has a cathartic effect if effectively managed. In fact, the enactments perform a similar function to the therapeutic "cleansing" described by Van der Hart (1997). Grieving is not an intellectual process but an expressive, experiencing event. If the group can grieve together then there is no isolation, and the natural aloneness that we feel even in the most intimate of contacts is no longer to be feared and avoided. A balance is achieved between the sovereignty of the individual and the contact in the group.

Facilitating and Responding to the Expression of Grief

Therapeutic Enactment groups inevitably hold loss and grief. When we sit in a group, we experience loss, whether it be loss of face, faith, illusion(s), dreams, secrets, control, camouflage, or the giving up of tried and true habits of relating to self and others. Even a change for the better is a loss as we may have to give up the past. We probably will have to give up any faint hope we might have for a better past or a different life. There are many more losses that people experience as they participate in the groups. These object losses bring grief into the group.

Grief is present from the very beginning of the groups. Schermer and Pines (1996, p. 99) comment: "For authenticity to occur, there must exist a high level of interpersonal trust in which group members can risk being vulnerable. In groups based on issues of death, dying, and bereavement, the authenticity concern is highlighted by the extraordinarily profound and difficult consciousness of mortality. The same need for authenticity is a foundation of all therapy groups."

Public grieving restores a sense of agency. By telling the truth in public, within the group, the person no longer experiences themselves as a pawn of fate, of powerful non-personal forces. They get back a sense of movement, autonomy, and personal control through action and grieving. When these intense, often disturbing feelings, are no longer suppressed or rejected, but welcomed and taken seriously, then the group can be experienced as real. The enactments can proceed because the shadow energies are both conscious and contained. In groups that are balanced in this way, the amount of reparative work that can be done throughout the group is truly remarkable. The members of the group feel their connection to each other in immediate and powerful ways. The group has become safe enough so that members can practise trusting one another and being close without having to be unceasingly vigilant about attacks or betrayals.

Enactments that confront fundamental loss and at the same time arouse the spectre of cultural taboos are extremely challenging for the group as a whole. The helplessness of grief if not contained can turn to lashing out. The group must be able to contain these strong emotions as well as aggressive impulses (Bion 1961). Consequently, at the same time as tending to individual reparation, therapists must pay attention and ward off damage to the group itself. This is a complex process demanding advanced group skills and experience from leaders plus a willingness to put judgments aside and follow the lead of the group. Therapeutic Enactments are only as successful as a group enables them to be, and, therefore leaders have to be able to move back and forth, tending to both the individual lead and the group members in general.

Helping the Group to Express the Shadow

All the "-isms" out there in the world can make for difficult group process, including racism, narcissism, sexism, ageism, and so on. Other splits related to differences may involve gays and non-gays, or divisive religious or political beliefs. These divisions are part of the normal wear and tear of groups. A part of the "shadow" that can arise in Therapeutic Enactment groups has to do with gender polarization. Our therapy groups are unusual in that we tend to have an equal distribution of men and women in attendance. This makes for an excellent group environment to tackle inter-gender wounds. We have had enactments where women raged at men or were assaulted by men and this called forth the need to heal the group before the debrief. Groups, when members become anxious or angry, can easily break down into an "us versus them" reality and begin scapegoating. The topic of gender is potent because even to criticize the opposite gender in public usually is frowned upon. After an enactment in which a large male had raged at two small females who played his mother and ex-wife, the women in the group, before moving into the debrief, had to break off into a small group to compose themselves. The men felt that they had been "banished" and they expressed some hurt and angry feelings. The women agreed in general that they had witnessed an attack on women. However, when everyone got back together for the debrief, the climate of the group was one of support and concern. The women were able to express their feelings of fear. The men were able to describe how they felt scapegoated just because they were "males".

This was further illustrated in the enactment of an isolated, distrustful male who wanted to have closer working relationships with his work team. He had difficulty connecting with women both at work and in his private life. A self-contained intellectual, he began by "warning" the group: "I get emotional and then I get off balance because I don't know how to protect myself." He felt that he had no control over his feelings. He was either inappropriately angry or in "shutdown mode". In his enactment he decided to practise confronting a very strong male in his workplace. His father had died when he was a boy and he grew up feeling that he did not know how to relate to dominant males. He had mixed feelings of resentment and love about his father, feeling that his father was "perfect" and that he could not live up to him. This left the lead feeling resentful and guilty. While he was walking around the circle, telling his story, he was struck by an early recollection of his father pulling him up from under the water and saving him from drowning. He wept as he remembered his love for his father and how much he missed him. This man was experiencing what Hollis (1994, p. 83) calls "father hunger". He had no positive older male influences in his life and no male friends.

His grief about this brought up his sense of loneliness. In addition, a related and difficult topic was raised through his enactment, that of gender stereotyping and his polarized views of male and female characteristics. These had caused difficulties in his ongoing relationships. This man expressed certain negative feelings about the women in his life. He blamed them for his troubles in relating to men. He fell prey to isolation and futility and tended to blame and offend the women with whom he worked. He felt literally cut off and was not always sensitive to the feelings of others. For individual reparation to occur, the lead had to be able to express difficult topics without being attacked and destroyed. For group reparation to occur, the members had to bring the underlying issue of gender stereotyping to awareness and handle it as a group issue. In this case, the lead did arouse female consternation but it was openly expressed. He was able to "hear" it without collapsing or becoming aggressive. During the debrief, members were able to speak openly about fears and losses in their relations with the opposite gender and this was experienced as both unifying and freeing. A process like this, which leads to increased connection with others, may be similar to what Yalom (1998) calls "developing socializing techniques" and what Adler (1939) calls *gemeinschaftsgefuhl*, translated as "community feeling" or "social interest".

In another example, a male lead's father had been shot in a hunting accident. He had never known his father and was brought up by his mother and grandmother. They constantly reviled his father, implying that the lead was "just like" his father. This left the lead with deep ambivalence about women and an inability to sustain relationships. He felt deeply angry with everyone. He constantly veered between the two polarizations of domineering demands, coupled with neediness and possessiveness on the one hand with oppressive silences on the other hand.

During the enactment he literally dragged his (symbolic) father around to various "stations of the cross". For example, at one station, he had his grandmother nag him about his grades and compare him with his "useless" father. He wanted to show his father what he went through "without your guidance and support", saying to his father out loud: "If you had been here, I wouldn't have had to endure this." Poignantly, this enactment ended (at the suggestion of the member playing the father role) with the action previously described—the father actually carrying his son on his back around the stations. As a result, the lead was able to give himself over to his grief completely. Later he said that he realized he had idealized his father and allowed himself to form "fantasy bonds" in other relationships that, of course, could never measure up. He said: "I have allowed my self-involvement to separate me from real relationships."

Releasing Fantasy Bonds

The traumatized may choose "fantasy bonds" (Firestone, 1985) that are illusions of connection instead of human attachments. Loss is a condition of attachment. As soon as we love someone, we open ourselves to the possibility of losing him or her. For the traumatized who are unable to tolerate any more losses, giving up attachments may be seen as a pre-emptive strike to give them autonomy and control. Unlike real relationships, fantasy bonds can be controlled. However, they feel lifeless. This lead had to drop the fantasy bond with his idealized father. He began by expressing his grief and rage at his father's "abandonment". He was then able to work through (successfully) some delicate gender blaming with his group peers.

These enactments shed light on the process whereby the group unconsciously tries to raise and heal gender problems that bedevil individuals outside the group in personal relationships and work. We live in a world where there are few rituals to assist us in developing and integrating a real sense of lively feminine and masculine ordering principles or archetypes. In our groups, we notice that men choose other men to develop rituals that initiate themselves into the company of men. Women similarly choose women for rituals that affirm their membership of the group of women. A large part of the reparative strength of these enactments lies in the group's willingness to divide into gender role sub-groups without destroying integrity and trust. We have had groups of men join together for this purpose either to help prepare a lead for his enactment or to welcome him back into the company of men. Groups of women have initiated a lead into a mother role or blessed her in the name of the feminine. Often after ceremonies like these, the entire group comes back together. Just as rituals are instruments of cultural engagement, so, in Therapeutic Enactment groups, rituals are used to create a culture that promotes equality of dignity between men and women and encourages communion.

Termination Stage: Closing and Preparing to Leave

The termination stage (involving closure) is the time in the life of the group when members' feelings about leaving and disconnecting from the bonded group occur (emotional closure). It is at this point that members begin to prepare for leaving as well as consolidating and beginning to integrate what was experienced and learned in the group (integrating personal learning). Closure is the most delicate and complex aspect of therapeutic relationships. It is all too easy for the therapist to encourage dependency and help the client to cling to relationships that are not intended as substitutes for real life. The therapists need to be careful to allow enough time near the end of the workshop for proper leave-taking. Occasionally there is a risk of the group either terminating before the appointed hour just to get it over with or trying to hang on and postpone closure. This often is the point when feelings of abandonment and loss are retriggered. Therapists must address the needs of group members so that the re-entry back to the "other world" is as smooth and productive as possible.

An important part of the therapeutic process involves idealization of the therapist, therapy, and group. However, if this is coupled with the participant's desire to be protected from the human condition itself, then having to leave the group will pose a problem. There is an ethos that arises in the group: "This is wonderful. Let's stay here." The refusal to leave is a defence against the responsibility of making good on the pledge or promise to act differently, since this will lead to transformation and is deeply unsettling. A large part of our leadership role is to facilitate the transition at the end of the group: "What we are doing here is real. However, we have to leave this place and return to our real lives." In our groups, we try to face this dilemma calmly.

Participants need to come together, grieve, recharge their batteries, and leave willingly. The group process is such an integral part of Therapeutic Enactment that the feelings aroused in the group by the enactment itself or the group as a whole must be affirmed. Ethics are involved in closure, however, just as in the "real" world. We must all be allowed to have what Livingston (1991) calls "vulnerable moments" as the pain of leaving can bring up other losses. "All relationships take place in a temporal context in which loss is as much a factor as attachment" (Schermer & Pines, 1994).

During the termination stage, Therapeutic Enactment groups assist the individual to focus on the relationships in their "real" lives, carrying the learning, insights, and intentions forward, so that they do not exchange the immobilization of traumatization for that of dependence on the group. People who have suffered injury in their early attachments may have difficulty leaving the group with grace. Yet, all relationships must entertain the notion—in fact, the reality—of separation, loss, and grief. In the groups, members learn to allow this truth to revitalize their relationships rather than kill them emotionally. When the participants return to the world, they want to go with energy and anticipation. A planned and focused closure that permits people to acknowledge the attachment, honour it, and grieve it enables them to complete the closure, resulting in an energized sense of self.

Summary

We're all falling. This hand here is falling.
And look at the other one ... It's in them all.
—Rilke, "Autumn"

In this chapter we have provided the theory or model of group development: the expected dynamics and processes involved. By now the reader understands that therapists must be highly skilled group experts. Supervised practice in planning, leading, and evaluating group process is essential in order to achieve the outcome goals of effective Therapeutic Enactments. Specific "tools" or approaches to build the group follow in the next chapter. For those wanting more extensive theory on group development and group process, please see Amundson et al. (1989), Bion (1961), Gladding (2003), and Yalom (1985).

Tools for Developing the Group

CHAPTER 5

*Love is not changed by death and nothing is lost and all
in the end is harvest.*

—Edith Sitwell

*It is an old ironic habit of human beings to run faster
when we have lost our way.*

—Rollo May

The therapist serving as group leader can prepare and accelerate group development by introducing activities that provide members with essential knowledge, skills, and emotional confidence to help them participate more fully.

We often don't have as much time as we'd like to focus on group process and development because our groups come together for a specific purpose as enactment weekends and not as ongoing therapy or counselling groups. Therefore the suggestions provided in this chapter will be of considerable assistance to the therapist working on a short timeline. In addition to showing you how to quickly initiate and plan interventions in the group, we provide some specific ways to respond to events that spontaneously arise in the group. Knowing how to respond to the unexpected ensures greater feelings of safety and confidence among group members. It also ensures with greater likelihood that group solidarity and cohesion developed early in the process will not be reduced or threatened, hence limiting the overall effectiveness of the enactments and the overall group experience. A number of specific interventions are provided by the therapist in both a pre-planned way as introduced group activities, or in response to what's happening spontaneously in the group at any moment.

Introduced Group Activities: How We Build and Develop the Group

We begin our groups in a planned manner by being both directive and facilitative in the initial group building. We subscribe to the group process mantra that the group must exist and the group must have a leader. We are democratic and participatory at the beginning but we have an agenda that we set and we make it clear at the outset what the expectations and goals are to be. The demeanour and language of the therapists leading the group is crucial at this time as is our demonstrated ability to deal with any ruptures in the safety of the container. Once the leaders have set the group in motion we can assume a more facilitative role, which we term "holding the space" as opposed to the earlier role of "making the container". Therapists encourage participants to speak into the space and this, in turn, increases members' sense of control and commitment.

We make sure from the outset that everyone gets a voice. This is essential for two reasons. First, it stems interference from the destructive, repressed shadow as members exert their influence in the group in open and vocal ways. Second, enactments often contain the theme of "losing your voice" and "reclaiming your voice". These enactments would not be possible in a group where members feel constrained or silenced. Members may begin to use their voice by saying who they are, why they are here, what they hope to get out of the group, and what they are prepared to give. We make it clear that people can say as much or as little as they want (just their name, for example) and that they may later revisit their contributions at will. Everyone is encouraged to work at his or her own pace. We tell the group that, except during enactments, they can bring forth unfinished business at any time.

Members can assess their own "fit" in the group, identify with the goals and intentions of others, and in general move from feeling alone and ashamed to beginning to feel they belong. Much of the anxiety of not knowing if they fit or are included may be projected outward as defensiveness, withholding, or critical attacks on others or on the meeting room or facilities. In the early stages of the groups, members may complain about the food, the lights in the room, the parking, the chairs, or the administration. To quickly reduce the need to act out around issues of criticism or resistance it is extremely important at this point for the therapists to be non-defensive, open, empathic, and matter-of-fact. Responding to these needs early on in this way contributes to building a sense of personal control in the group.

The opening circle of an enactment workshop is crucial to the formation of inclusion. Everyone needs to feel that they have a purpose, not just the people who have prepared to do enactments. The therapists take this opportunity to do a bit of teaching about the background to trauma, the process of reparation, and the role of the witness in trauma repair, and to overview the process of both group and Therapeutic Enactment. A review of the five stages of Therapeutic Enactment at this point is sufficient. Although we provide handouts and summaries of the process, group members have to experience (and not just read about) the group process. The handouts that are made available during the groups describe specific aspects of group process and the five phases of the Therapeutic Enactment method.

A key part of group building is to lead the group in establishing rules and setting group guidelines to guide the process. Immediately following the opening go-around activity, the therapists help set in place the rules about interpersonal communication and respect. We explain that the rules are always open for discussion so that the group may eventually commit to their own norms. For example, one of the suggested rules may be that members do not speak to one another in evaluative or judgmental terms. This momentarily reduces the fear of being attacked, allays anxiety, and allows people to listen carefully and maintain focus. We say "momentarily" because later this rule may be tested and made into a norm but that later process, too, is a part of ensuring group safety. If handled properly, it strengthens the container. It is our view that norms cannot be imposed on the group. This would make them rules. Norms have to arise out of the group process and validating, testing, and reaffirming them is ongoing. The basic difference between rules and norms, and both have their place in groups, is that rules are imposed on the group, while norms arise out of the group. This has to be done in ways that ensure that the container is stable because, of course, there will be dissent, struggles, false agreement, and sabotaging before the group finally creates a space where members feel safe enough to take risks and speak candidly with one another. That means bringing any signs of violence, sarcasm, passive-aggression, or narcissistic attacks to the attention and consideration of the group. Repair of the group is as desired an outcome as repair of the individual.

As we did with Michael's enactment, early on we identify for the group a few experienced ("senior") group members to help us support others who may have strong reactions while witnessing enactments. Once or twice, a group member has had an abreaction—an intense emotional reaction that overcomes the ego—during an enactment and one of the identified senior members will move to sit near them, hold them, or even take them outside of the group for a period of time. This is a very delicate intervention, however, and has to be done carefully and then integrated into the group. The senior group members who assist the therapist in this way have to be sensitive about their own needs to "fix", or palliate, or be important; they need to make sure that they are responding to a true need in the other person and not a need in themselves. Senior group members, in addition to having had group experience, are typically counselling professionals. They can identify when another witness needs support. They are given advance warning by the therapists that they will be asked to play this role in the group. An awful lot goes on in the group during any enactment and the therapists, concentrating on the lead and the role players, may not be aware of everything. They rely on experienced members in the group to either draw the therapists' attention to a developing situation or to handle it themselves.

Sometimes in the debriefing, group members will comment on how hard it was to witness the content of the enactment and it is important to answer these comments honestly but firmly: "Yes. It is hard. It's supposed to be hard, because the lead is doing important work." This acknowledgment strengthens the container and validates the members' sense that they are performing a crucial task together. We have discovered that the witnesses, like the leads, also often have to be prepared for a difficult enactment as well as being debriefed. In some cases, the therapists have had to do a quick round of the group as an enactment is beginning so that everyone is clear what is to follow. Sometimes the lead has had to get a verbal commitment from each member that they can handle this or that they will not abandon him or her. Sometimes the lead asks the group to do difficult things such as put on masks or turn their backs. The lead finds something in the group that can be made available to him or her as a resource; for example, their willingness to take directions from him or her without rancour. This increases the lead's sense of self-efficacy, which is the sense of being safe enough to choose a course of action that is right for him or her.

Once we had to revisit this process in the middle of an enactment. The lead momentarily lost his courage and had to recheck with members that the group was able to hold all the distressing emotions and scenes being expressed. This was a way of reconnecting with others and feeling less alone. The preplanning with the therapists, and the in-the-moment guiding, consulting, and checking-in as the enactment proceeds, reinforces to the lead that they can move ahead with security and confidence knowing that everyone knows what to do and that, while the lead is in charge, they are not going to be left alone. In rare cases it may mean that a member may choose to leave the group before an enactment because their own personal experience means that they believe they will be unable to tolerate the content and remain. If this is cleared ahead of time, the lead will not feel threatened and will proceed with the enactment successfully. If it is not planned for but a member spontaneously leaves the group, then the therapists, and later the group as a whole, may have to re-establish safety.

At the end of a Therapeutic Enactment we come together in a big circle and have everyone contribute to the debriefing. If it is a very large group and there are sufficient therapists or assistants, we will divide off randomly for the debrief of the enactment. Time spent in the debrief group—altogether or in egalitarian small groups of four to six people—is extremely intense and often mini-enactments happen spontaneously. For example, in one such mini-group, a member was speaking of her emotions during the part of the enactment when the lead had said to their partner: "You abused my trust and you had no right to do that!" She had endured date rape many years previously but had never admitted to herself or to anyone else that it was a rape. She told her mother what happened and her mother replied: "That's what boys are like. What did you expect?" When she told the story in the mini-group, several of the men said to her: "That was a terrible thing that happened to you. He raped you and nothing was your fault. He betrayed your trust." She reported that she finally allowed herself to feel the enormity of what had happened to her because she felt she was in a safe group of people, particularly males, who would treat her experience seriously.

A sense of anticipation or urgency builds up in the group as in athletes readying themselves and stepping up to the starting block. Ultimately, they will go beyond what they expected and reap more benefits. This is why we believe that leads must perceive that the therapists are the kind of leaders who will bear the weight of the container, leaving them free to take the necessary space and to complete their process without interruption. Leads must see themselves as woven in, included within the body of the group and not alone. This is not about false communion where everyone is on their best behaviour. Higher trust in the process and in the therapists promotes higher risk-taking, and with higher risk-taking comes the freedom to be spontaneous. People believe that they are being seen for who they really are. It is important to remember that the opposite of this is to feel anxious and defensive. This is where good, safe group process becomes essential. When group members are coping with fears and anxieties that threaten to overwhelm them because there is not a strong-enough container, caution, withdrawal, and acting out in negative or self-defeating ways may ensue. At times when this does happen, the therapists must go back to work with the individual and the group in order to help reconnect that person with group members. It requires often doing or saying things as a leader to re-establish the trust necessary to go forward. These events are not planned nor can they always be anticipated, but that's why the therapists need to have the skills to respond when such an event occurs. We see this often when the enactment is trauma focused and this can trigger others in the witnessing role.

Introduced Group Activities: The Magic Shop

The next activity to build the group is focused and serves to motivate group interaction and to help stimulate individuals members toward a Therapeutic Enactment with a possible core script theme. We use the Magic Shop exercise as another way to prepare participants to go deeper into group process. The Magic Shop is useful in the early stages of the group as it tends to help members become involved, self aware, and motivated to participate toward making or desiring change. If this occurs, the therapists will work with the group member to prepare the enactment. Using this activity near the end of the day brings group energy up because it can be fun and is personally very meaningful.

The Magic Shop invites people to re-evaluate their values and life goals in a manner that involves negotiation with one of the therapists, who assumes the role of "shopkeeper". The Magic Shop is easy to set up because we use no props other than a table and chairs, although, depending on the predilections of the leader and group, we can make the Magic Shop as elaborately staged as desired. The therapist not playing the role of the shopkeeper helps people choose what it is they want to buy. They ask the questions: "What do you want to buy?" and "What will you give up for it?" Participants come up one at a time to the "shop". Common purchases are serenity, peace of mind, clear boundaries, caring, courage, assurance, and self-confidence. For example, a woman wanted to buy anger because she believed she could never get appropriately angry; a man wanted to buy courage to help him face a challenge in his life; another man wanted to acquire a family; and another woman wanted the experience of having a baby.

It is when we get into what people are willing to give up that the exercise becomes intense. The bargaining brings up issues of sacrifice, loss, and grief. To physically give something away changes an aspect of the self-script. The person becomes a giver rather than someone who is always being forced to act against their will. Many participants give away secrets that they have carried for some time. The woman who asked for a baby was thirty-nine-years old and felt that it was now or never. However, she had no partner and she and her previous partner had tried unsuccessfully for years and this was a factor in the break-up of their relationship. She asked the shopkeeper if she could buy a baby. He asked her what she was prepared to give up. She wept as she replied that she did not want to raise a child on her own. She said that she would give up being able to choose when and with whom she wanted to have a child. She thought that she was no longer young. She realized that she would have to give up her dream that she would remain young and beautiful, that men would always want her.

The man who wanted clear boundaries realized that he would have to give up his constant need to be wanted and needed by women. The woman who wanted to buy anger realized that she would have to give up her "persona of sweetness and her all-seeing, all-feeling helpfulness". The person who wanted to buy a family discovered that she had very good caring friends who had stood by her. She realized that she was hanging on to a faint hope that her abusive and neglectful family would finally see her true worth and come to her.

Another woman wanted to sell self-protecting denial that helped her avoid certain painful or boring things. The dialogue between her and the therapist went like this:

Therapist:	What do you want more of?
Lead:	Surrender.
Therapist:	What would your life look like if you had that?
Lead:	I'd take more risks.
Therapist:	What if your heart gets broken?
Lead:	My heart's already been broken several times so what's the big deal?

At this, she broke down and wept. She said that she was thinking of the Tin Man in *The Wizard of Oz*. She decided instead to purchase a heart. For that, she'd give up her memories of past breaks and her self-pity.

Another individual wanted to sell tenacity and her ability to make judgments too quickly. Her dialogue with therapist went like this:

Therapist:	What would your life look like if you had fewer judgments?
Lead:	I'd be more in touch with my feelings, especially my likes and dislikes.
Therapist:	How would your life be different?
Lead:	It wouldn't feel so empty. I skim on the surface of the water and have no intimacy.
Therapist:	How would we notice the change?
Lead:	I'd be quieter, more thoughtful. Oh, and I'd be more tender.

For that she would give up her need to be right and her impatience. Another woman came to buy more confidence—both personal and professional—so she can embrace intimacy in relationships, "be less sharp", "stop sabotaging", and "allow people in". For this she would give up control, consistency, and predictability, but again, not all of them. She agreed, cautiously, to twenty-five percent.

Another man wanted to buy approval. He said that he wanted everyone to love him and for this he would sell his soul. The shopkeeper said there was no market for other people's souls and he'd have to give up something else. The participant decided he would give up his ability to pretend that he was feeling okay when he wasn't. He turned to the group and said: "I love you people. And I realize that the group I work with doesn't and they don't appreciate my particular and peculiar contribution. This makes me very sad." He realized he had been avoiding this truth with all his strength since the workshop began.

Another man wanted to sell his own darkness. Again the shopkeeper said there was not much of a market for that kind of thing. The participant replied that he was frightened by his own darkness and wanted a spiritual source and strength inside himself. He said he would be willing to give up his secretiveness, but not all of it. They haggled, settling on thirty percent. "How would this make your life different?" "I wouldn't always be seeking new gratifications all over the place. I would be calm," he replied.

The Magic Shop is a useful exercise to open groups since the activity attracts members' attention and does not feel "too much too fast". It can also be used to close groups, preparing people for the change from intense emotional work "inside" the group to moving outside and preparing to leave.

Sculptures: Getting into the Group

Sculptures are very helpful in enactment work. In the beginning they can initiate lower levels of risk taking. They may also be introduced at any time throughout the life of the group as requested by the lead. Sculptures differ from enactments by being static and motionless in nature. They are non-verbal and primarily visual. They involve the lead asking members in a reflective manner to depict parts of the image he or she wishes to construct in the group. Since sculptures are mostly wordless they are very effective at depicting emotional material in a contained and less intense way. This has the effect of increasing safety and allowing the members to settle into the process of the group in a timely and contained way.

An example of a sculpture would be of a lead asking five people to each take on the posture of a stressor in that person's life. The lead's double would be in the centre of the room and the lead would bring each of the five stressors into the centre and place them in proximity to the double so they could stand back and see what this much stress looks like. Sometimes the lead will change places with the double so they can experience the sculpture from the inside.

Sculptures introduced by the lead have several benefits. One is that some people are more comfortable showing us statically what is going on for them. It's less risky to them; they feel safe. At the same time it empowers the lead to express what they wish at their own speed. The sculpture also helps develop or encourage the group. Because it's visual, people can identify with parts of it. One way we build inclusion at the outset is to select a sculpture activity that brings in a lot of people.

There are different sculpture themes, including personal and family sculptures, work sculptures, dreams, and sculptures depicting a death scene. To give you a better idea of the range, multiple examples are outlined below.

One lead set up a sculpture of the family car with mom, dad, and three kids all either ignoring or annoying one another. Another lead set up a moving sculpture: he set up the room filled with big cushions, footstools, and other pieces of hard and soft furniture so that he could run around the room without his feet ever touching the floor. He said that this was how he felt his life was going right now: jumping from obstacle to obstacle and never feeling grounded or satisfied.

One woman wanted to create a sculpture of her immigrant family of origin. We got a huge ball of red wool and she set her family—mother, grandmother, and ancestors from "the old country"—in front of her. Then she was tied to them in great tangles of red wool. She was almost completely immobilized; in the end she had to break her way out. Another woman wanted a sculpture of her mother forcing her to have her hair cut. She set this up in the hairdresser's salon with other customers watching in horror and her mother forcing the hairdresser to cut off all her long hair. We helped a third lead set up a sculpture of her abusive father taking holiday photos and humiliating wife, son, and daughter in public. The father stood in front while the mother and two children cowered before him as he waved his arms and mouthed insults. We had a small child watch this one as a child double. Passers-by looked on with disdain.

In yet another Therapeutic Enactment the co-director of a residential treatment facility was losing to retirement his female co-director of twenty years. He had to let her go and stand alone. Half the group emotionally left with her. The sculpture showed the split in him and in his group. Another lead, the hereditary leader of a group, was extremely self-effacing, "leading from behind". This caused consternation in his group plus competitive jockeying for position and a survival-of-the-fittest mentality. His sculpture depicted the chaos in the group and his "outsider" position. A third lead, who had been in a mental hospital as a youth, set up a discharge interview. The set-up included a long table with the hospital staff lined up in a phalanx high on a platform, confronting a vulnerable patient on his knees before them. In another sculpture, a treatment team had two directors: one clinical and the second a business director. They had to integrate a new business manager into a team that had never really accepted the split. The sculpture depicted the split and had the team turning their backs on the new manager with the other one frantically gesticulating but not being heard.

Another man asked that the sculpture be formed in the dark, which is an "unusual" request. He had two women kneel and one man lie on the floor. Six outsiders or extended family members stood in a circle pointing and chattering among themselves. The lead was the man or boy lying on the floor and the two women were his mother and his grandmother. His father had disappeared soon after he was born. He said that the sculpture looked like a ballet. He had such a strong image of it on his retina that he wondered if it was a dream. He realized, as he peered at the murky figures in the half-dark, that his whole childhood had been like that; the people seemed motionless, inaccessible, staged, and silent. He said, weeping, that he really had underemphasized how harsh and cold his so-called "normal" childhood had been.

Dreams can be potent sculptures and are a safe way of opening the group. One team member had a dream in which he was travelling through a desert at night. There was a hill in front of him and he climbed it. As he looked down the other side he saw a narrow path that led to a square white building. He tried to get down the hill toward it but birds came and tried to prevent him. Another lead dreamed that she was trying to get into a stable to visit her horse, but a cat had had kittens right in front of the door and she could not get past. When this lead set up the sculpture she saw that the animals were not "chores" but integral parts of her inner life, showing her that the animal images held value to understanding the parts of herself. Prior to this awareness she hadn't seen the connection.

Death sculptures are mostly self-evident. First the person who has died is brought into the group and placed in the way the lead would have imagined them to be. Next the lead chooses the family and community members who should have been there—either at the bedside or grave—and weren't, or were there and shouldn't have been. Each member is carefully placed in relation to others, in terms of intimacy or dominance: some stand, others kneel. This sculpture initiates intense feelings very quickly and is very effective for bringing about closure for those who have been held in suspended grief or loss.

Moving into the Enactment

After a sculpture, we would expect to begin our first enactment, generally within the first two hours of the group beginning. You might think it would be safer to leave it longer and build the group slowly toward the first enactment. However, our experience tells us the opposite. Moving too slowly actually increases anxiety and fantasies. Moving to action early provides a structure, increases safety and spontaneity, and adds to the robustness of the group because a challenge was successfully met. This helps to build trust and cohesiveness as the members see risks being taken and experience success.

An example of an enactment suitable at the beginning of a group involves a woman who wanted to enact meeting her dead father coming home from the Second World War. In reality he had died in the war when she was two but she wanted to experience meeting him as he disembarked from the train. She only had a photograph of him as a young man. Her father's early death violated the natural order of things in which she should have grown up and known him. Her enactment got many people involved immediately and moreover was very poignant. Another beginning enactment involved a war, allowing us to bring most of the group in as soldiers and other participants in the fighting. Thus everyone experienced their ability to move through extremely emotionally intense material in a contained environment. This provided more psychological space for participants, who did not feel constrained or trapped.

A sculpture that involves the majority of the group demonstrates a principle from Wolpe and Lazarus (1966), that one cannot be anxious and absorbed at the same time. The completion of the sculpture helps the lead to talk about themselves more fully, witnesses remark on connections to their life, and the therapists' observations can be offered. These kinds of whole-group sculptures will sometimes move into enactment, when the therapists and the lead agree they'd like this to happen. A good example of sculptures leading to enactments often occurs when dreams are constructed, resulting in an obvious issue that the lead previously did not see and wishes to develop an enactment around that. For many participants, however, the sculpture is all that is needed, as it does externalize for the first time an internal representation with tremendous meaning for the person. A gestalt image is left for them and serves as guide or image in very practical ways following the group.

Rituals and Ceremonies

Rituals and ceremonies are introduced into the group at various points for very specific reasons. One goal is to shift the group away from the interactive and the interpersonal focus. Rituals have four components: (1) community, (2) belief system, (3) narrative, and (4) repetitive behaviours. Therapeutic Enactment groups incorporate all four components of rituals as follows:

(1) Community through the group process, community-forming norms and events, and a continuing exposure to group members over time.

(2) Belief system through the theoretical underpinnings involving psychotherapy, trauma, suffering, and reparation.
(3) Narrative through individual stories, as well as myths, universal themes, and the history of the group that are part of process.
(4) Repetitive behaviours through the structure of the setting-up, enactment, debriefing, and follow-through.

The advantage of rituals—ritualized grieving, for example—is that one does not have to think about what to do. Our view of Therapeutic Enactment in groups is that they are ritualized opportunities for reparation. Gilligan (1997, p. 179) defines rituals as follows:

> Healing rituals provide recovery from trauma and reincorporation of the dissociated person into the social-psychological community. And atonement rituals provide vehicles for apology and redress of damage done. In the present view, a ritual is an intense, experiential archetypal structure that recreates or transforms identity. It is intense, in that participants develop heightened absorption that excludes all other frames of reference. It is experiential in that analytic and other processes of the cognitive self are depotentiated, leaving participants deeply immersed in the primary processes of the somatic self, such as bodily feelings, inner imagery, and automatic (spontaneous) process. It is archetypal in that the thoughts, feelings, and behaviours stand for collective, ancestral meanings . . . And lastly, rituals perform meaning at the deeper levels of identity: they affirm or transform in a deep cultural language a person's place in a community.

For rituals to be successful, preserving the emotional links between people is key. Neumann ([1954] 1970, p. 271) states: "The emotional bond between members of the collective has nothing to do with a conscious-feeling relationship or with love . . . Common descent from the same tribe, the sharing of a common life, and, above all, common experiences create emotional bonds." Connection with others has to be safe. If we lived in a community that understood this, then we would participate in a series of rituals or ceremonies that contained the most extreme and painful of human experiences and gave them meaning. If we lived in a society that took reciprocity seriously, rituals would be available that could bring society back into balance after a critical incident. The task of the ritual would be to contain the emotions, evoke grief, make room for compensation (payment and redemption), and endorse suffering as an alternative to violence. Individuals would find themselves in an environment in which they were affirmed in their desire to clear out, repair, and restore the connections among their heart, soul, and life's purpose.

The groups themselves are ceremonies of reparation, which begins when the person is finally able to piece together the fragments of events, details, and who-said-what-to-whom into a narrative, a whole story that has meaning. However, the enactment is not designed as a faithful replication of the remembered traumatizing scenario. It is a symbolic construction, not a video record. It depicts an essential truth but is not a factual report. In the enactment, a mimetic or creative whole is constructed that evokes depth, meaning, imagination, and engagement. This entails creating the scenes as in a play that has an internal coherence and a beginning, middle, and end. What Therapeutic Enactment offers is a safe place to pull together those pieces into a whole.

Closing Ceremonies

There are as many ceremonies to close a group as there are groups. The ritual ceremony tends to be mostly about acknowledging people, events, experiences, and the group in symbolic or metaphoric ways. Ceremonies are designed to close the group in a way that leaves an image or picture in the mind that the members take away with them. It has a formal quality, reinforcing the dignity of the participants and recognizing the group's accomplishment as a whole.

Here are some examples of the closing ceremonies we have used in Therapeutic Enactment groups:

(1) We have the group make two circles: an inner one containing the leads sitting on chairs and an outer one containing the witnesses standing. We play music and have the people in the outer circle slowly move counter-clockwise around the group placing their hands on the shoulders and heads of the seated group, saying or singing goodbye.

(2) We have members say into the group their answer to this question: What is one thing you are taking with you and one thing you are leaving behind?

(3) We use huge drums that four or six people can drum simultaneously as well as small individual drums.

(4) We sing and dance.

(5) We gather by the lake to throw pieces of our work into it while saying goodbye.

Responding Effectively to Group Events, Dynamics, and Processes

To respond effectively in group situations that require skilful reaction, there are primarily four functions of the therapist as group leader: (1) assessing, (2) directing, (3) facilitating, and (4) influencing. In order to carry out these functions a range of leadership skills are required. These include three skill areas: (1) reaction skills (active listening, clarifying, empathizing, and summarizing); (2) interaction skills (moderating, linking, blocking, supporting, limiting, and consensus taking); and (3) action skills (questioning, advanced empathizing, confronting, exhibiting immediacy, self disclosing, process observing, consensus taking, goal setting). These skills are fully described and defined in Amundson, Borgen, Westwood, and Pollard (1989). With these skills in place, along with a solid knowledge base in group psychology, the therapist is able to meet the critical incidents that inevitably arise in the group. Successful responding and handling group concerns promotes a safe group climate that enables personal exploration and transformation.

Responding and Managing Critical Incidents

One of the crucial areas requiring attention by the therapist is being able to respond to and manage critical incidents. The group has to be strong enough to hold the chaotic emotions associated with the necessary individuating from real parents and parent figures. Therapists have to be prepared for this by being sensitive to critical incidents in group (Donigan & Malnati, 1987) that occur as the group struggles to make this process conscious in order for them to know how to respond to the incident. The therapists make sure to recognize critical incidents in which a group member or members experience emotional reactions that shake up the status quo. The group process does not move on until the effects of these incidents are brought to awareness and are reconciled. When the group is in "false communion" it may look as if the process is proceeding, but no real work can be done under conditions of suppression. If critical incidents are not integrated into the truth telling of the group, any decisions taken will be sabotaged. When the group sees that conflict and anxiety can be constructively managed, there develops a greater feeling of closeness and a sense of group accomplishment, resulting in increased levels of self-discipline.

How do therapists do this? When the therapist models good communication skills group members learn how to hold other members with respect as they struggle with the unexpressed and all of the intense emotion associated with it. By validating a member's feelings of jealousy or anger, the leader affirms that person, helping to reinforce openness and honesty so essential for holding the space during the enactments.

One example of a critical incident was when one group member, talking about another member who was present, revealed private information about that member to the group. The discussion proceeded for a while in a desultory fashion but eventually the therapist brought the group back to the point of the revelation. The betrayed member broke down, as she had been feeling frozen and shamed by her exposure. Others in the group commented on their fear and inability to confront the incident. If the therapist as group leader does not notice the critical incident or is likewise frozen, someone in the group has to break the silence or the group will be immobilized.

Safety to confront the truth gets lost in a group that is unable to handle critical incidents. The critical incident may be one group member rudely challenging the therapist, who ignores it and thus leads the flight away from conflict, consigning the group to a lack of emotional energy. This is both an individual and a group issue. As Bion (1961, p. 65) states: "Group mentality is the unanimous expression of the will of the group." Individuals, including therapists, contribute in ways in which they are often unaware. Allowing fighting, fleeing, or over reliance on the therapists' direction deadens the group. When critical incidents are contained, group members feel that they have control and that they can, in fact, feel safe even when they are working with strong and disturbing feelings.

The therapist is the one responsible for maintaining the group and intervening by using specific responding skills, describing to the group what happened, and focusing how the event or statement may have affected individuals and the overall group process. Following identification of what has happened, the therapist will focus on the individual or individuals involved, ensuring that their feelings and reactions are validated and in some cases inviting those involved to speak directly to one another to repair the relationship between the members. Finally the therapist refocuses the group back to the group task at hand by pointing out that they are healing the critical incident in a transparent manner. In doing this, safety is re-established as members know in the future things won't be allowed to be covert and undermining of the group process.

Summary

> One must still have chaos in one to give birth to a dancing star.
> —Nietzsche, *Thus Spake Zarathustra*

Although building the group is just one of the competencies required for running effective Therapeutic Enactment groups, it is the foundational component in this multimodal approach to change. In this chapter we have described the specific ways the therapist can initiate events in the group and respond effectively to the core issues, dynamics, and processes that occur. We have not been exhaustive, rather we wanted to outline the basic competencies for therapist success in groups designed for enactment work. Now that you have a basic understanding of how groups are formed and how leads function with the group, let's look in the next chapter at an introductory enactment, one dealing with the common theme of shame.

An Introductory Enactment: A Story about Reparation of Shame

CHAPTER 6

*Nothing confirms more clearly the impossibility of amorality
than our capacity to be humiliated. Our rage itself is
a commitment to something, to something preferred.
Indeed, how would a person immune from humiliation
know what a good life was?"*

—Adam Phillips, *The Beast in the Nursery*

*The only way to escape from the abyss is to look at it,
measure it, sound its depths, and go down into it.*

—Cesare Pavese

Some enactments embody common themes and are relatively easy
to set up. They are excellent pieces with which to begin Therapeutic
Enactment groups. When planning workshops, we keep potential
enactments in mind that demonstrate common themes from our shared
human experience. Enactments that evoke emotions that are familiar
to the group ensure safety for all participants and are structurally
uncomplicated to enact, resulting in high group commitment.
Enactments with clear themes of shame and humiliation are two
examples of such common themes, and usually do not require complex
assessment or preparation because they are a universal experience and
understood by most group members.

Shame Enactments as Prototypes

How heartening it would be if shame were the most talked about and
welcomed feeling in therapy groups. Unfortunately this is not the case.
The power of shame is such that it makes people, even therapists, shy
away from its presence. When we talk about shame, we are not only
referring to the original experience of humiliation that the individual
endured as a result of an injurious event or relationship, but also to
the arousal of feelings of shame by any or all members of the group
during the group process. If shame, arising naturally in the group, is
not acknowledged early, then repair cannot happen. The group itself

may simply become another shaming experience. People can be paralyzed when they witness the shaming of another. Shame can so easily be brought up in groups because other groups, the family or classroom, were usually where shame originated.

When an enactment is about shame, the therapists have to be even more aware of the safety of the group as a whole. Shame enactments are prototypes because they are such common experiences. However, leads as well as group members in general are also vulnerable to retraumatization. The group may shut down in the face of exposure to humiliating enactments because this is a raw place for most people. Therapists have to set the scene carefully and attend to the reactions of non-leads. This is where the therapists as group leaders rely on safety monitors and experienced group members who will look out for abreactions in the rest of the group.

A person who has been shamed may imagine the group as an audience witnessing their dishonour and find this overwhelming, toxic, and isolating. People feel exposed and worthless. Their instinct is to hide, lie, and blame others. Shame is about the "whole" person, whereas guilt, in contrast, is solely about the behaviour. We all suffer in the sense that many "ordinary" passages in our lives, for example, committee meetings, public speaking, family dinners, or work presentations, cause us to suffer through the torments of hell.

The Potency of Shame in Groups

Shame can be like a stun gun in the group. The group may appear to be functioning, but the onset of unacknowledged shame inevitably results in discussions becoming superficial. Members are unable to say what they mean and mean what they say because they are afraid that their feelings of shame will be exposed in the group. For example, a member, trying for inclusion or just to reduce their anxiety, may say: "I think we should introduce ourselves; maybe say our names into the circle" and someone replies: "I think that's a really stupid suggestion. Besides you are not the leader here." Not only the member singled out in this manner but many in the rest of the group will experience the shame of exposure and belittlement at this point.

Or shame can slip into the group in subtle ways. The notion of feeling "dropped" by the therapist as group leader opens up a narcissistic wound and is a harbinger of shame. For example, if a member expresses certain emotions such as sadness, fear, or embarrassment and the therapist ignores what they are feeling and continues to proceed with a rigid agenda, the whole group may fall off into shame. It is up to therapists to be aware of this possibility and slow down the process of inclusion and mirroring, especially at the beginning of a group. The member may feel further ashamed if the therapists draw attention to their tears. Even empathic regard can induce shame in the one who feels penetrated by premature understanding. They feel "seen" before they are ready to be seen. Therapists must find a way to bring the group's attention to the presence of shame without singling out individual members. We might say something like: "There have been important feelings expressed in the group. Let us pause here for a moment and recognize how difficult it is in a group to express one's innermost fears or feelings. We appreciate hearing these."

It is extremely important not to underestimate the effort it costs many people when they speak up in the group. If their contribution is criticized or ignored, the whole group may feel the impact. In other cases, members may be shamed because the therapist "forgot" them, for example by ignoring them at a check-in or debrief. Conversely, another member may be shamed because the therapist focuses on them. Since we cannot, as therapists, cover every possible eventuality, we harvest the resources of the group by drawing attention to the omnipresence of shame, asking for attentiveness and kindness. This means paying close attention to body language, silences, and the therapist's own feelings and intuition. One technique is to canvas the group by saying: "Anyone want to open an issue that they think has been missed?" If a member replies, as is usual: "We haven't talked about shame yet" then the therapist might say: "Yes, shame is always a factor in groups because of our past experience. Let's be sensitive to this and watch out for our own feelings and those of others."

For so many people, just to sit down and join the group means that they sit down in shame because they are accustomed to being denigrated and despised. The reason for this is that people still carry the grief of the wounds of childhood disasters with them and they nurture this grief in secret. As a result, a sense of separation from the shaming becomes a part of the self and can foster dissociation. In groups, because everyone at some level wants to be included, this can result in ambivalence at best, passive-aggression at worst. It is better if therapists introduce the topic of shame early on and speak to its universality. Therapists can advise the group that if witnesses are "triggered" (meaning they are experiencing strong feelings linked to their own past traumas) they can bring it up in the group later.

Our notion of therapeutic repair includes reclaiming a sense of who we were as vulnerable children when something important was taken from us or we were forced to say or do things against our will. A large part of the reparation of shame has to do with not feeling helpless anymore. Groups, therefore, provide possibilities both for continuing the nightmare and for reparation. We want group members to feel safe enough to experiment with group and self-boundaries. The groups provide for the possibilities of the repair of attachment and intimacy disasters. The groups have to provide a setting where we can practise choosing how and when to respond to both inner and outer challenges from others in ways that preserve our dignity and autonomy.

The groups are not about confronting people with their shortcomings or about breaking down resistance. That would seem to us to be a recipe for retraumatization and despair. Kohut's (1971) emphasis on empathic immersion, that is, allowing the therapeutic dependency without early interpretation, changing, fixing, or premature insistence on "right" behaviours, means an acceptance by the therapists and the group that the client or lead is already perfect in themselves. The difference between empathy and empathic immersion is that, in empathic immersion, the individual feels the warm glow of unconditional positive regard. The therapist, and by extension, the group, provides a sense of "calm holding". Thus the groups are about creating a space wherein an individual who feels demeaned and dishonoured can feel that their honour is restored. They feel affirmed, admired, and respected.

Many adults carry with them lessons they learned painfully as a result of some terribly humiliating scenario played out with parents, extended family, teachers, or other authority figures. They learned that they were nothing, worthless, beyond redemption, helpless. This learning is likely not to be forgotten. The objectification that comes from being publicly shamed often results in later self-destructive soothing behaviours. We treat ourselves as the bad object we were told we were. Self-soothing behaviours become addictions. We remove ourselves from the possibility of intimacy because of our terror of reinjury and shaming. Our emotional life lies in the dust. As therapists we have helped plan playground interactions, street scenes, and family dinners where people were bullied, harassed, and brutalized. We have reprised graduate degree oral examinations and other rites of passage where people have been left feeling sick and humiliated. We have enacted courtroom and crime scenes, as well as bureaucratic nightmares, where people have felt tormented and helpless. In several cases we have directed scenes in which leads were patients who were given terrible news by physicians more intent on protecting themselves than in helping the patient. In all of these scenarios the person had been left with a deep sense of distress that had affected their ability to let people know them. They had coped but been left with lingering feelings of shame and negative beliefs about their abilities.

Darren's Story

Darren was a good candidate for a beginning enactment because he had a specific scene in mind and the themes were clearly shame and humiliation. Darren, a man in his forties, was finishing a master's degree in psychology as a mature student. He ran his own business and had studied part-time for his degree over a number of years. He was divorced with children. In his family of origin he was the only son and second child. When he was younger he had struggled with substance abuse. He was a slight, fair-haired man with a wry sense of humour. He seemed shy in the group and often appeared sad.

Darren's story was a familiar one. He had been the target of a sadistic teacher in high school. Almost thirty years later he still blushed and trembled when he thought about the incident. At fourteen years of age he was in French class one afternoon when the teacher began picking on him as usual. Darren attempted to block him out and "keep a low profile". Nevertheless the teacher asked him a question in an insulting and shaming way. Darren did not reply. The teacher threw a piece of chalk at him, hitting him with a stinging blow on the neck. Then the teacher came down the aisle, lifted him up by the hair at the nape of his neck, and dragged him to the front of the class. The teacher made him stand there while he yelled at him, calling him names and humiliating him. He threw him out of class, sending him to the principal for punishment. Darren had to return to this teacher's class the following week and every week until the end of the year. He coped by shutting off his emotions and mentally removing himself from the scene, a strategy he had adopted while very young in his family of origin.

Darren's father was a bully, a large, hardscrabble workingman who was remarkably different from his slight, bookish son. He was a dictatorial, physically and verbally abusive man who cowed the women in the family and kept Darren, his only son, in a perpetual state of fear. Consequently Darren thought that men who wanted to "kill him" surrounded him. Darren's older sister was terrified of their father also but somehow managed to keep out of his way more than Darren could. Darren's paternal grandfather was an abusive alcoholic who had tyrannized his family. Darren's mother was a drinker and would never intervene on behalf of her children when their father was on one of his rampages. She too came from alcoholic parents. The family was not educationally motivated and Darren ended up in a technical high school where he took woodworking and welding courses. His first job was as an apprentice carpenter. When we encountered him, he was finishing up his counselling practicum. He paid the rent by accepting contracts to create hand-finished wooden staircases and doors.

With trepidation Darren said that he wanted to enact this awful scene in order to erase it from his mind. He felt tormented every time he thought of it. Also, he believed that the fallout was reflected in not only his relationships with men, particularly older men, but with women. He said that he was always looking to women to "kiss it and make it better". He wanted to change his ways of relating so that his relationships were more adult and equal. He had no primary relationship at that time and his relationship with his ex-wife, the mother of his four children, was described as "dismal". He had also run into some difficulties with female colleagues in his graduate program who told him that he was "dismissive of women".

Darren had no male friends either. He said that he was "lonely" and really only spent social time with his children. He reported that he had not been fortunate enough to have male friends at high school, but had been a solitary boy who spent time in the library. His main interests were his computer and jazz music. During his enactment, Darren's resources were his double and another witness who acted as a second double to offer physical support. When the first double was enacting the scene for him, the second double kept his hands on Darren's back during most of the enactment. He later commented that he could feel how hot Darren was during the classroom scene. His two male doubles became extremely important to him.

Darren's enactment was completed early in our development of Therapeutic Enactment, before we were as scrupulous about bringing in resources as we are now. If we were doing this today, Darren would be asked about his support systems and which people or objects he would choose to have with him while he did his work. He might have brought in some of his woodworking creations or photographs of them. He might have brought in pictures of his children. Filling the circle with resources in this way establishes a bridge between the lead's "real life" and the symbolic enacting of the trauma. These treasured objects help the lead relax knowing that he or she is being truly seen in a historical and rounded fashion.

During Darren's enactment we quickly co-created the scene in the classroom, setting up desks and the teacher's station. Ten "students", including Darren, sat in chairs in rows. The teacher stood at the front. Darren's double sat close to him. Darren decided he wanted to have his father and mother witness his humiliation and he placed them slightly off to the side. These days, we might also ask Darren to choose a child double who would act as a resource throughout.

The teacher began to ask the class questions about French in a loud voice. He began to zero in on Darren, who was sitting near the back. The teacher's tone changed to a hectoring, bullying one. When we are being publicly humiliated, we move into shock, so we expected that Darren would have difficulty actually "hearing" the abuse. The teacher said sentences like: "Well, Mr. Johnston. If we could trouble you to have your undivided attention for a moment …" and "Of course, we know you are too important to be in this class with us mere paysans …" and "Give us the benefit of your superior wisdom …" and " What is the French word for …" (the last sentence was screamed at the top of the teacher's voice). Darren hesitated and the teacher threw a piece of paper at him, hitting him in the face. He then dragged Darren to the front of the class and held him there by his hair while he berated him for being "stupid", "worthless", and "without redeeming feature". "You're a disgusting boy. Everyone in this class thinks you're a loser. You don't deserve to be here." Darren had given most of these sentences to us in the pre-enactment assessment and we were able to cue the role player. As abusive roles can take their toll on the players and witnesses they need clarity and support while they are enacting. As an important safety feature we often encourage witnesses to go and stand behind such a role player, giving emotional support to them during the enactment. However, we are careful about ad libbing as this can break the flow of the interaction between lead and therapist and so the support is more about physical presence and sometimes about touch.

Darren appeared frozen while the role player enacted the French teacher's abuse. The therapists were watching for this and asked him to return to his seat and watch while his double enacted the scene. Suddenly Darren ran up and extricated his double from the teacher's grasp and expressed his rage at seeing his double maltreated. Although frozen when the abuse was happening to him, he was able to charge into action when he saw it happening to another. Now that Darren was freed to act, we decided to reprise the entire scene, redoing it in the way he wished it had happened. This time the members of the class took an active role. They told the teacher that he was out of line and that what he was saying to Darren was wrong and unfair. Some of them expressed themselves in an extremely forceful manner: they rose from their seats and came to the front to take Darren out of the teacher's hands; then they placed him at the front in a chair and had him listen to their feedback on what they had seen and the effects it had on them: "What happened to you was wrong. He had no right to say those things to you. They are not true. Teachers should not take advantage of their powerful positions. He abused his power. He abused and betrayed you and this should never have happened. What he did was very wrong. He disgraced his profession. None of this was your fault." Finally, they turned to Darren and each "student" approached him and asked for his forgiveness for not intervening sooner to protect him.

By this time Darren was deeply moved. To see him relaxed and leaning back into the arms of his two doubles was a wonderful thing. His whole face had opened up and he looked vibrant. At this point he decided to go over and speak to his parents, telling his father that it was because of his "hard-heartedness", "bullying", and "lack of control" that he, Darren (his son), felt weak and worthless. Up to this moment he had believed that he deserved to be abused by his teacher because "that's the way the world works". He said to his father: "What you did was not right. You took advantage of a vulnerable small boy. You gave up the responsibility of your father role. You were selfish and scary. You betrayed your son. This shouldn't have happened to me." At this point Darren wept. He turned to his mother and said: "You always supported him. You chose him over your own children. You're a disgrace as a mother. For your own comfort to avoid rocking the boat, you supported a monster. I'm ashamed of you!"

Then something happened that we had not planned. Darren decided that he wanted his deceased paternal grandparents to hear this. He quickly chose two group members to play them and sat them on chairs side by side in the middle of the circle. He told them that it was because of the way they were that his father was the way he was. He said that their bad behaviour and abusive parenting had had negative effects down through the generations. The worst thing of all, for Darren, was that it was affecting his own children. He said: "In the presence of these witnesses, I swear to my children that I will tell them what happened here today. I will tell them what I said to my parents and grandparents. I will promise them that I will not carry this behaviour on. The buck stops here. I promise that my children can come to me and I will listen to them with respect and support no matter what the content." He then sent his parents and grandparents out of the room. "It's finished," he said.

During the debrief, Darren sat on the couch flanked by his double and the man who had taken an active role as the supportive second double. This man said that as soon as the enactment began he had recognized the similarities with his own story and was able to feed sentences to Darren and the double in the classroom scene. He said that the sentences came to his mouth automatically. Darren was laughing and doing a little bit of horseplay with both of them. He was absolutely full of beans. He commented that having the two men stay so close to him, helping him and "reading me like a book", had somehow fulfilled a longing in him that he did not even know he had. Darren was demonstrating his longing for male companionship, intimacy, and playfulness, what Hollis (1994, p. 123) called to "risk loving men".

Several witnesses were still upset, however. The shaming had triggered their own stories and they were unsettled and anxious. At this point in the group process, it was essential to find a way to bring the group together before proceeding. Usually a physical activity is recommended. The whole group might stand and come together in the centre of the room, perhaps holding on to each other. Or participants given roles might sit in their chairs in a circle and the rest of the witnesses might revolve around them, placing their hands on their shoulders as they pass. What is being re-established is connection and support. In this case, Darren felt released from his lingering shame; it was the rest of the group who had to come together. We did so by inviting those who had been activated to say and express their feelings in the moment.

The group has to be able to create a space in which contact can be maintained despite the presence of distressing emotions. In Darren's enactment, both Darren and the classroom role payers felt outraged. They had to express this rage but in a safe manner, which means no physical attacks and no scapegoating. Feelings of rage, narcissistic posturing, and self-aggrandizement will damage the group if they are allowed to rampage through without containment and protection. To promote the individual over the welfare of the group as a whole means to allow individual aggression, or to do individual therapy, thus forcing the group into observer mode. The group has to be kept in balance.

Darren's enactment about shame was a challenge for the group in that it evoked universal bad memories. However, these enactments are important contributions precisely because the theme is so common and the scenarios themselves are easy to reconstruct. We have many examples of shame-based enactments. One woman, a gifted counsellor, felt ashamed because she could not bring the kind of intimacy she experienced professionally into her relationships with her husband and child. A huge gap in intimacy existed between her and the two she held most dear, which was a repetition of her childhood situation. Her parents had died when she was very young and the loss was still a raw place for her. As an adult she could not stand the idea of losing the ones she loved. Thus she held herself aloof from her partner and son. She was perfectionist, private, and hypersensitive and felt ashamed of her feelings because they failed to measure up to her high expectations.

Another woman felt bound by the people in her life. She experienced her relationships with family, parents, siblings, patients, colleagues, and students as burdensome and felt guilty and ashamed as a result. She set up her enactment so that all these people were clinging to her and piled on top of her while she lay curled in a fetal position on the floor. She had to push them off to stand up. During her enactment she realized that she both wanted and did not want to stand on her own two feet. She wanted to be held up and looked up to. As the eldest in a family of girls where there had been very little money or material security, she was the first family member to attend university. A lot of family sacrifices and ancestral hopes rested on her shoulders. This woman had an epiphany later in the enactment when she finally stood up and looked around at the circle of everyone in her life and the rest of the group. She realized that she was looking at well-loved faces. Furthermore, she realized that her family members were separate people who had their own lives and aspirations different from her. Suddenly she perceived this as freedom rather than oppression. She asked the group to sing a much-loved song that had been part of her wedding celebration. For her the repair was in the felt experience that the people in her life were separate from her, that she could stand alone and yet be connected, and that was a good thing.

Revealing Secrets to Reduce Their Power

Shame thrives on secrecy and isolation. Perhaps a necessary step in the restoration process is to go up against secrets or, as Pinkola Estes (1992) calls them, "secrets as slayers". Family secrets are a part of archetypal myths resulting in both suffering and redemption. The myths of Oedipus who killed his father and married his mother, and of Theseus and the Minotaur are but two of many myths we retell in the groups. Oedipus had his eyes put out but he wandered the land so that everyone could perceive his suffering and know its causes. Because of this, he was redeemed. Uncovering secrets and talking about them is an antidote to the isolation of shame, which persuades that only the hero can be featured, only the one over-functioning on the daily round, and there is no room for anyone else. One of the problems of heroic survival and achievement after a merciless childhood is that the one who endured it comes to believe that only heroic and lonely effort will ensure continuing survival but these survival skills are now self-defeating.

Family secrets are a powerful way of holding off truth and maintaining the status quo. In Therapeutic Enactments we hear, spoken loudly, the hard, unvarnished truth. To say in public, usually for the very first time, that "Mine was not a happy family" or "My parent was an alcoholic, physical abuser, mentally ill, a liar, hateful" or "I was beaten, raped, taunted, bullied, neglected, or unwanted", can be remarkably liberating and life-affirming. As working therapists, we are repeatedly surprised by the variety of the secrets people carry and the subtle and powerful methods they use to carry them. The advantage of the therapeutic group is that if the individual is able to reveal a secret there, once it is out in public, it can never have the power to terrorize the individual again. They feel affirmed by the group. However, this is only possible if the individual does not dissociate. If they turn away or the head goes down or they are unable to make eye contact, then chances are they are dissociating and will not feel the group affirmation and support. It is important for the therapists to check for shame and dissociation once a self-disclosure is made.

Darren's secrets were that his father beat him, that he had no friends, and that he had failed his children. Other types of secrets revealed in enactments include sibling sexual abuse, mental illness of close family members, and the suicide of a grandparent.

Sometimes a tragedy leaves a big dark stain on the family. If nobody is able to acknowledge this mark it becomes a secret. The darkness grows around it and covers all life. And it can harden everyone against one another. As Yeats said in his poem "Easter, 1916": "Too long a sacrifice can make a stone of the heart." This happens particularly in families where there is addiction. However, secrets terrorize everyone and the truth becomes a distant shade. In one enactment, the lead was attempting to break through the oppression of violence, grief, idealization, and immobilization that haunted his wife and her family: his wife was trapped in it and he wanted to help free her. He had to confront the "monster" in her family, her absent, murderous father who, when she was an infant, had killed her mother and gone away to prison. Nobody would speak of him but his ghost was deeply felt. The lead tracked his wife's father down after the enactment and found him to be an objectionable human being but not a monster. The lead was able to grieve for his wife and her family without minimizing their tragedy, trying to fix it for them, or having a secret relationship with their pariah. For this lead, the meaning behind his enactment was his belief that people need to know; that they need to remember what actually happened and get back to reality; that they need to hear the perpetrators admit to reality. Often, this process offsets the need for revenge. Both sides can come back into balance. However, this particular lead saw that this could not happen in his wife's family and he, at last, was able to understand and accept this. He was a counselling professional and had always believed that the family should be doing more about their grief. He was released from his need to play counsellor with them.

Secrets bleed life out of the system. They may provide an illusion of safety, power, and being special, but this proves false in time. Speaking secrets out loud can imbue the self with renewed vitality. Sometimes depression and sorrow follow a confession but this is often a necessary and temporary corollary, what Dabrowski (1964) calls a "positive disintegration", to an emerging self. The kinds of secrets that people keep while in group and which suck energy out of group life can be about the current process such as declining to say honestly: "I felt hurt by you when you said that I was always complaining but never did anything constructive" or "I felt ashamed when you told the group that I called you and invited you for coffee and you did not want to go" or "I am very angry with you because you interrupted me in the middle of a sentence and began talking to someone else in the group" or "I envy you because you always look so perfect and never seem to be vulnerable."

Secrets may relate to hiding from the group information about important things that have happened in the past. For example, one group member did not speak in the group for a long time. It turned out that his younger brother was in prison and one of the two therapists, in a previous position, had been his correctional officer, something he realized during the very first hour of the group. He was immobilized by the shame of the therapist's knowledge of him and his silence, in turn, immobilized the group. Eventually, one group member said to him: "You have been very quiet. I am worried that there is something troubling you and that you are afraid to say it here." This was taken up by another who said: "Yes, I feel the same way. I want you to know that I miss your contribution and if there is any way I can help you I will." Several others who knew him outside the group weighed in with concern. The mirroring, admiration, and affection of the group provided a healing salve for the individual hiding a shameful secret. He was able to disclose the secret with great relief.

When the shame of abuse is hidden, combined with secrets and lies, shaming can be used to torment or scapegoat people. Shaming can become a sadistic means of social control in shame-based individuals, groups, families, societies, and professions through the use of unrelenting destructive criticism, sarcasm, put-downs, constant carping, and negative comments. As an antidote, early in the process, individuals should be encouraged to openly express both shameful feelings and outrage in safety. For example, a therapist, correctly reading body language, might opine to the group that undoubtedly many people present have suffered shaming attacks in other situations and groups. "If anyone is willing to talk about these experiences this will serve to ascertain that this group does not repeat these kinds of mistakes." Self-disclosures like this can assist the group to deepen the contact between members and create a setting that is safe and deep enough for people to do their reparative work.

This is particularly crucial for group participants who come from the counselling and psychotherapy professions, where it is essential that practitioners maintain a necessary demeanour of self-control and do not exploit their relationship with clients. The practitioner has no opportunity within the counsellor-client relationship to safely discharge the shadow. This does not mean that the therapist should make use of the group to self-disclose or do their own therapy. Rather it speaks to the necessity for reciprocal and reparative opportunities to exist elsewhere for counsellors to discharge their own secondary traumatization and do essential self-care.

Healing the Pain of Intergenerational Secrets

If the enacted event was a secret, known only to a very few in the family, then reliving it in the group can be extremely intense. Alcoholic parents are notorious for keeping truths away from their families and for putting themselves ahead of their children. Darren's grandparents had been pillars of rectitude in the community who managed to keep their dysfunctional family under wraps. Darren called his family life a "sham". The grandfather was an alcoholic and the stern, unbending grandmother made excuses for him and lied to her own children.

Many families have skeletons in their closets. We have worked with

Holocaust survivors who never told their children the truth about their past. We have worked with survivors of the notorious residential schools for Aboriginals who never told their families what happened to them. Certain events deemed shameful—cancer, affairs, suicides, abortions, illegitimate children, behaviour in a war, even loss of cash and property—can assume a huge shadow affect over future generations. Discovering these secrets unexpectedly or by default as it were, for example, after a death, can be very unsettling. One of the hardest things to witness during enactments is the look on a person's face when they realize that their parents exploited and lied to them throughout their childhoods. Yet this realization, if followed by affirmation and human connection can, in itself, be reparative. The group provides the supportive witnessing, essential for participants to experience in order for them to be able to accept the reality of what occurred. As the community of witnesses accepts them, so they can then accept themselves.

Rehabilitating Honour

Shame and honour are intertwined. Honour is conferred by the group (family, profession, society) and the individual accepts the identity of self as an honourable person in the eyes and judgment of the group. Honour is basically a public attribute. When individuals believe that their inner self has been seen by the group, whether it is a family or a society, and been judged as not-good-enough, then they feel dishonoured. For many people, the choices imposed by codes of honour are inescapable and are linked to the pressure exerted on them by their group, usually by arousing shame. The focus is on their character, which lies close to their very core. That is why the effects of shaming are so painful and long lasting.

It is for precisely this reason that allowing the group to see the "lived tragedy" is a major risk and a test of the safety of the group. The content of both the enactments and the debriefs appears to have an "honour" thread. The lead is both surprised and relieved to see that the group does honour them in spite of what happened. Risking exposure in the group, and being honoured for it, is an antidote for shame. When participants say "I honour you" to a lead, as they often do, they typically mean that they respectfully affirm that they have seen the individual behaving courageously, sincerely, and lovingly. In this way, the groups are rehabilitating honour from the family's perversion of it. Honour is related to resolve and integrity. Moreover, the ritual of honouring calls forth the deepest emotional resources of the participants. When the role players told Darren in the classroom that they respected both his fortitude for surviving his childhood catastrophe and also the fact that he did not become violent in return, Darren felt vindicated and affirmed.

Feedback from the group often differs from the lead's usual ways of thinking about what happened to them. Shame is a thought disorder, says Kaufman (1985), and we have heard many examples of this in the groups. One man who killed an animal thought he was a monster. Another man, whose "transitional object" was his computer (that is, his most important, primary relationship) and who had no social circle, thought he had been "abandoned in the tide of history" and was useless, when in fact he had been responsible when younger for raising his sister. Many people who were physically abused believe that the abuse was their fault; they were "bad". Darren believed that he was a violent person even though he had never physically abused or tormented anyone. Thought disorder means that as a result of their shame, people beat themselves up, tormenting themselves with attributions such as "I did a terrible thing" or "I don't deserve to be happy" or "I don't deserve to live." Through Therapeutic Enactments they see that they did what they did in context, and they made it possible for themselves or their family or group to survive.

To return to the disaster and allow the feeling of shame often makes it possible to recover an honourable place. In the process, in the ashes we find a nugget of gold. As an example, one woman held herself in contempt because she stayed in an emotionally abusive relationship. She finally "cracked" one day and grabbed a knife, stabbing her own arm instead of killing her partner. This incident increased her self-contempt because part of her revenge fantasy was that she believed that he "deserved" to be hurt. However, it also freed her from the relationship because, after medical attention, she never returned to the apartment. During her enactment, she saw that the trauma had released her without her harming another human being. She reframed her role in the incident as honourable instead of as despicable.

One lead grew up with a sadistic parent who hanged her cat from a tree in their yard. She feared that she would be like him if she allowed herself to be intimate with anyone. As a way to balance the evil of her father, she made her mother out to be an angel. She idealized her mother, who had died when the lead was eighteen, and she longed for her daily. During her enactment she planned to speak to her imagined mother and ask her why she had married her father. As she did this, she realized that, in truth, her mother was not perfect and may have given up on her life early, unable to cope with her abusive marriage and leaving her children to cope with their father instead. She was able to accept this reality about her mother without feeling the need to protect her from the shame of her failure to be a good mother. She had been protecting her mother's—and her family's—honour at great cost to her own.

Sad to say, many people like Darren tell us that their treatment in school has left lasting wounds to their sense of self, which they have been unable to repair. Many injured people complain that it was their treatment in hospitals that really traumatized them. Many victims of crime report that it was their treatment by the criminal justice system that left them reeling. It aroused shame because they felt demeaned and dishonoured. Not surprisingly, many of the critical scenes that people choose to enact have to do with authority figures who have deeply shamed them. When honouring can replace shaming, participants experience this as reparative.

The ways of injury and dishonour can be subtle in groups. Injuries that arouse shame and rage, calling forth self-abasing feelings of our essential worthlessness, are called narcissistic wounds. They are experienced as an attack on the whole self. Even an abrupt "No!" from a therapist or group member can cause a narcissistic wound. When a person reveals an injury from someone in the group, there may be an underlying expectation that the person or persons "responsible" for the injury should respond appropriately, take the injury very seriously, and express remorse and contrition. However, the bottom line is that we express these injuries so that we will be free to move forward. It is the public expression that is key, rather than finding someone to take the responsibility. As the group moves into intimacy, we find that interpersonal responses containing apologies and concern are more commonplace. Remorse and contrition restore honour and the individual can relax back into the group.

This restoration is reparative not only for the lead but for the group as well. The witnesses in Therapeutic Enactment groups provide antidotes for the isolation and dishonour of shame. When the lead articulates shame in front of the group he or she bears witness, helping to pave the road back to connection. Witnesses do not censor, sabotage, criticize, make light of, or scapegoat. Their job is to be present, to hold the space, and often, in this work, to witness unfixable suffering. From an object relations point of view, witnesses become "good objects" for the lead. This has to do with the lead being truly seen by people who have value and, while outside the self, are experienced as part of the self. Witnesses therefore act as a social validation of acceptance and change. Witnesses have reported that when they return home after the workshop they notice they are experiencing life returning. When confronted with deadening shame, instead of falling back into depression, they are able to fight.

The group can repair the ravages of shame because it replaces the imaginary, historical, or invisible group that witnessed our shame. A real group, the present group, sees us clearly and, despite our shame, is affirming and loving. Moreover, this is not judgmental love that demands that we be on our best behaviour, lie about our true feelings, and put on an act. On the contrary, this group sees the worst, the degraded, and the shameful and is still able to keep in contact. When we acknowledge shame, we accept the truth that a disaster happened to us and we can speak of it in the group.

Reclaiming Authentic Voice

It is easy for people who suffer from toxic shame (Bradshaw, 1988) to create a projective identification (Klein, 1975) so that the group will attack and shame them. A projective identification can operate like a spell cast on the group. Projective identifications are unconscious processes whereby the individual manages to make another feel as they have been made to feel in the past. If one or more group members are in the throes of such a process, the group will have to wrestle with confusion and frustration as members attempt to bring this to awareness.

Many people, as a result of abuse or neglect, have had their spirit crushed. They bring this injury into the group. Only when the group is able to face this suffering realistically can it be repaired. For example, a member with a devastated spirit may come across in the group as cynical and sarcastic, questioning everything that is said and generally being a real pain. Darren, for example, had been accused by his fellow-students of being sarcastic. If group members were to respond sarcastically to him, then he would be confirmed in his fear that there really is no hope. Also, the group would have been forced into a projective identification response of anger and shaming, which would eat away at the integrity of the group. Reparation would mean that the group would have to stop and become aware of the individual's effect on them, mirror back the pain that they sensed, and ask for guidance about how they could be most helpful.

During the debriefing after an enactment, we often hear people say how grateful they are for having witnessed another's pain and humanity. They feel affirmed because the lead who planned to repudiate their tormentors in the enactment somehow, when they confronted these people truthfully and eloquently, found mercy instead of revenge. They are freed from the constraints of their past and from the people who delayed their development. For example, Darren firmly sent his grandparents and parents out of the room. He said that he was unable to forgive them but he did not want to rage at or injure them. When the yearning to be truly seen and heard is fully met in the group, when the group sees them warts and all, without the masks, arm and arm with their shadow, then the lead is free to act spontaneously and to move forward. We say that, in this way, the person has been redeemed. Honour and redemption, therefore, balance shame and degradation and bring the community back into harmony.

A common result of toxic shame is that the person believes that they have "lost their true voice". What often motivates people like Darren to undertake an enactment is a feeling of being stuck in current relationships, feeling dissatisfied with their superficiality, and having a sense that something important is incomplete or unresolved. They have lost their voice through an experience of shaming, an abusive relationship with a parent or other authority figure, or some kind of public humiliation or degradation. The result is that they have never been able to express feelings openly and clearly and hence they live a "silenced life". The original, strong, emotional, instinctual, child-voice has been exchanged for a workable and successful personality. Slowly the inner voice has been stifled and the values or social mores of the collectivity have taken over as "authorities" (Neumann, [1954] 1970, p. 350). The individual sacrifices depth and intensity for increased efficiency and group belonging. Frequently, this tension is reported as a physical symptom, for example: "I have an ache in my heart" or "a weight in my chest" or "I have a tightness or nagging pain in my stomach". Many people can point to exactly the place in their body where they carry the hurt or the weight. They have been oppressed and suffered depression as a result. The way out of this is through self-expression: they reveal their pain in the group. The Therapeutic Enactment group reorients individuals to the inner voice, this time in an environment that is hospitable to emotionality, intensity, and the expression of previously suppressed longing.

As an example of losing one's voice, one individual described his life as a split between two worlds. Literally, he was an immigrant in the "real" world. Symbolically he saw himself as a "stranger in a strange land". The experience of moving between the two worlds—old and new, mind and heart—was difficult. He felt the split as "a gap in his soul". He coped by enduring "a kind of longing that never left" him for "home" because he "never felt at home anywhere". In one world, characterized as the everyday life of family, work, and leisure, he was a highly functioning professional whose sense of responsibility tended toward perfectionism. On the inside, however, he held deep, emotional scars, blocked grief that held his feelings hostage, distancing him from the genuine connection and intimacy that he craved in his relationships. This situation caused him a great deal of torment. He was emotionally unexpressive, reserved, self-contained, and stoical. He had reached a point in his life at which he felt he could not continue like this. He wanted to find his voice.

One notably macho, athletic, commanding although soft-voiced lead who had been mercilessly bullied by his autocratic father, found it difficult to express this to the group. By the end of his enactment, however, he was roaring. Come to think it, we have had many soft-voiced individuals who have ended their enactments on powerful vocalizations. We had one lead whose rage was choking her and she wanted to let it out. She began by shouting, then screaming, but ended by singing at the top of her extremely impressive vocal range. In their guts, these people know that there is deadliness in being the naive or too-sweet self for too long, just as rage, over a lengthy period of time, also lays the land to waste and deadens everything. They realize that they have to find their voice and move.

One way to recover voice is to have the lead select a "young self" early on so they can re-meet their active, spontaneous self. This representation helps the lead know what it is they wish to go back and reclaim. Darren used his second double, an articulate and loud man, to express his "lost voice". When Darren stepped into the role after this double had confronted Darren's parents, he was able to shout loudly at his parents for the first time in his life. He commented later: "I surprised myself." He repeated some of the double's words but, as he got going, his own sentences came easily to his lips. During the debrief Darren reported that he felt gratified by the forceful way he had spoken to his parents. He also said that he was pleased about being able to make a vow about his children. He said that he would have been too ashamed to do such a thing before his enactment. He wept as he said that he realized that his relationship with his children was a sacred trust.

Darren keenly felt the shame of inherited trauma. He was the second-even third-generation adult child of alcoholics. Children of immigrants, survivors of torture, adoptees, descendants of perpetrators, children whose mother was a victim of spousal abuse, or whose parents survived racism, hatred, and oppression, carry a heavy shameful burden. It is important for these enactments to have a safe social setting and for the group members to be able to mirror the trauma as well as provide healing. The cultural differences between, for example, Chinese, Russian, First Nations, South American, and East Indian participants are real. Participants have to be encouraged to express these differences. Then they can be integrated into the process as the other members demonstrate empathy and respect. In addition, elderly, gay, and physically challenged participants, as well as those with nervous breakdowns in their histories, may feel particularly fragile in the groups. They have to be treated with sensitivity and not have their concerns minimized. We have directed enactments in the wonderful presence of tangible evidence of other cultures, including clothing, music, dancing, religious objects, and ancestral treasures. Many people believe that their pain or rage is so overwhelming that other people will be frightened and run away. Or they believe that they come from a culture so far away that nobody here can see it. Or they are ashamed of their culture for one reason or another. Reparation for them means finding out that not only does the group hang in there with them but people actually show them honour, respect, and, in so many cases, delight. Reparation often comes in surprising ways. Sometimes, the entire group is involved both at centre stage and as witnesses and willing participants in a potent, public, healing ceremony. Some of our enactments have involved, for example, spontaneously reprising parts of a Scottish wedding, a Jewish funeral, a First Nations talking circle and cleansing ritual, a Christian church service, an Argentinian dance, and a South African atonement court. All these activities serve as antidotes to shame and the memories of shame.

Summary

> *The past is never dead. It's never even past.*
> —William Faulkner, *Requiem for a Nun*

Most therapists who are seasoned as group leaders can tell stories of when, by ignoring the hidden presence of shame, their groups self-destructed. Due to the content of Therapeutic Enactments in which threads of shame are virtually omnipresent, therapists must pay particular attention, watching for secret shame as well as the rage that often is acted-out shame. The Therapeutic Enactment methodology handles this otherwise distressing or destructive group phenomenon most effectively because we are always on the watch for shame, bring it to group attention, and gently focus on the group itself as opposed to singling out individuals in their shame. We bring in the presence of the divine or transcendent meaning and this brings the group together in a way that offsets the potential isolating effects of shame, allowing members both to feel contained as well as in touch with something bigger than their separate pain. In the next chapter we shall describe our approach as used with common

themes such as death or separating from the parents.

Common Themes in Therapeutic Enactment

The books we need are the kind that act upon us
like as misfortune, that make us suffer like the death
of someone we love more than ourselves, that make us feel as
though we were on the verge of suicide, or lost
in a forest remote from human habitation.
A book should serve as an axe for the frozen sea
within us.

—Franz Kafka, in a letter to Oskar Pollak

The heart of the wise is in the house of mourning.

—Ecclesiastes 7:14

The primary focus of each enactment tends to fall into one of several common theme areas. Knowing these themes is diagnostically very helpful, for they help us assess the needs of the particular client in preparing their enactment. We have outlined two major themes in which individual tragedy reflects common experience: (1) death and (2) parents (father, mother, separation). They have their attendant sub-themes: shame, judgment, betrayal, abandonment, diminishment, and isolation.

Denial of Death

Of all the Therapeutic Enactments the ones featuring a death are the most universal and evocative. Death, for many of our participants, is indeed "the great catastrophe". Enactments involving unfinished business around a death are most common because the finality of death, and society's mishandling of the process of death and dying, can leave people with unresolved grief. Oddly enough, the means by which families often try to soften the blow of a death may actually harden the heart and foster a conspiracy of silence. Facing up to the reality of the death and the truth of its impact seems to free the person to fully grieve, accept, and integrate the death into their lives as a part of their identity that nurtures and sustains them. As Dayton (1994, p. 149) says: "In mourning we reach the parameters of our soul—we die an emotional death and are resuscitated. Deep pure grieving allows us to integrate the loss because nothing we have truly loved is ever really completely lost to us."

Many people who come to Therapeutic Enactment have suffered a loved one's death and feel distressed by the fact that the loved one "just disappeared" and there was no possibility of closure. Many, as children, were supposedly "protected" from the death, prevented from visiting their loved one in the hospital or attending the funeral. They were never allowed to grieve with proper acknowledgment and ceremony. Without saying goodbye, it is as though the loved one has not really died. In enactments planned around a death, the lead wants to experience the feelings and say the words that they believe are missing for them with regard to the death. Some may also want to hear the words the deceased person might have said (for example, "I love you" and "My life was better and richer because you were in it"). We have had a seventy-five-year-old woman who, for the very first time, was able to grieve the death of her sister when she was five. We have had forty- and fifty-year-old adults who were able to attend the funerals of parents, grandparents, or siblings who died when the lead was quite young. We have had a social worker in his fifties who was able to grieve the early deaths of dozens of his clients from alcohol and suicide. We have worked with a physician specialist in neonatology and a palliative care physician who were carrying the deaths of scores of their patients.

Sometimes an enactment will veer off into a death scene that was not planned in advance. For example, one lead was brought up by an unpredictable, narcissistic, and abusive father. He planned an enactment in which he and his father made model airplanes together and then later his father came into his bedroom and destroyed them. He told us he wanted to express his anger at his father. During the enactment, however, he became very sad. He continued the scene until the death of his father and included the funeral that in real life he had not attended. He spoke to his father and, in telling him about the lifelong impact of his destructive behaviour, the son was able to remember good things about his father. As an immigrant he had made a huge sacrifice for his future family and the son thanked him for that. Through a role reversal, he realized that his father had always felt dislocated and lonely. This empathic understanding of his father's situation allowed him to take some good out of his relationship with his father and so the pain in his heart was eased.

The grandmother of a young immigrant couple had died back in the old country and they were unable to be with her when she died. For them, not only had a grandmother died, but also their ties to their ancestors and their histories. They were left feeling completely isolated and bereft. By setting up the ceremonial funeral and involving the whole group, they not only got to move through a cultural ritual that was a part of their entire identity, but they experienced for the first time the power of their decision to emigrate as a good choice.

One man planned an enactment in which he confronted his elder brother, who had died when they both were children. He remembered his brother as both a "golden child" (the elder son and the parents' favourite) and as a "dark brother" whose idealized shadow had covered the man all his life. He felt that the death had left him all alone in his life to, as he said: "March or die!" He never talked about his brother outside the family, partly because there was so much nostalgia inside the family, but also because he felt he missed his brother so much that just thinking about him could send him into depression. He tried to keep these feelings at bay but, although he was enormously productive at work, his suppressed feelings turned him into a ghost, living a half-life emotionally. During the enactment he reclaimed his feelings of sadness and anger, not only about his brother's death and his parents' consequent abandonment and neglect, but about the half-life he currently was living with his family of choice.

One woman set up an enactment in which she moved through the deaths of twin infants who died immediately following birth. She was never allowed to see their bodies and there was no ceremony to mark their passing. Following her enactment, she set up a marker stone in her local cemetery so that they "would not be forgotten". She also gave a donation to the local children's hospital in their names. Another woman whose daughter had died at birth and never been mentioned again by the extended family introduced her beloved daughter to the group in a touching naming ceremony. She also set up a memorial scholarship in her daughter's name at a local hospital. Memorials for the beloved dead are extremely important because they honour the dead and ensure meaning and continuity for the living.

Repair of unresolved feelings around the death of a loved one may include saying goodbye, saying what was not said, and hearing what was not spoken. It also may include grieving, some kind of ceremony or ritual that honours the loss, or redoing what was in reality a negative experience. When people query us about the purpose of Therapeutic Enactment, we often respond by asking them to recall an unresolved incident in their lives that is played and replayed in their minds like a broken record. A couple of examples come to mind. A retired professor told us how he often ruminated over a scene in his mind from when, as a young boy, he witnessed soldiers coming to his family farm and taking away his father. He was haunted by the fact that he did not speak out or try to stop the attack although he was only seven. His daydreams were often filled with silent rehearsals of what he would have said to his mother back then as neither he nor his mother ever saw his father alive again.

A forty-year-old woman had not been allowed to attend the funeral of her father, who died when she was six years old. He had died young and tragically in an accident at work. We could hear the grief in her voice as she said: "I grew up thinking of him as my hero. I wanted him to be there so much. I thought about him every day." For her enactment she designed her father's funeral and burial. As she wanted to have his work colleagues attend, most of the group became involved in what developed into an elaborate funeral with a eulogy and music. It had a great deal of dignity and ritual power. However, when the lead got to the gravesite, one of the witnesses had brought in a container of earth from outside and poured it over the "coffin". At this point she broke down completely and wept for a long time. Afterward, she said that she felt great relief finally as if she could release her father into death and get on with the rest of her life. Such a visceral focus on experiencing, doing, and acting, rather than thinking and talking, typically promotes intense catharsis. It is a quick and efficient way for a person to repair an earlier wound, in this case, the loss of someone deeply loved. To prevent retraumatization, the group leaders have to be able to create an environment of safety, respect, and personal control in order to promote the healthy arousal of strong emotions.

Death enactments help to move the group to deeper levels of experiencing and expressing, and pave the way to communion. The rituals associated with public grieving provide one way to bring the group together for a common and meaningful purpose. Although these scenes tend to occur toward the end of workshops, on occasion they may be initiated at the beginning, helping the group to move ahead very quickly. Usually, though, safety and "realness" have to be built up before group members are ready to mourn their dead. The deaths that are mourned in the groups also include the losses and "little deaths" of parts of the self that have paralyzed movement and are finally being set aside. We have to find a way to integrate the reality of loss without denying, dissociating, or numbing and we do this in the Therapeutic Enactment group when people are given an opportunity to grieve, a process so often denied to people in their lives. Dayton (1997, p. 21) states: "Grieving actually allows reorganization and integration to happen because the pain is experienced rather than repressed, and so can be integrated into the self-system rather than split off."

The grieving process related to death may help with relief of pain, be an antidote to isolation, or free up long-standing but denied unhappiness and sorrow. Often, a traumatized person finds memories too overwhelming to feel or process, so they repress them, split off, or blurt them out in fragmented ways as symptoms. Leads suffering from unresolved grief may not be able to articulate a critical scene, hence the therapist needs to assist them in articulating and forming the scenes.

The death may not be of a person or relationship; perhaps the death was symbolic, as in death of innocence, a dream, or the true self. One man, who was deaf, could not pinpoint a specific scenario when he had been injured because there had been so many: his parents rejected him; he was badly bullied at school; he was treated badly by medical and educational personnel; he was covered in shame when he went out in public. In this case, we agreed to an enactment that depicted this man's journey of sorrow through several different developmental stages in his life because he insisted that these had contributed to "the death of his soul".

Parents and the Family Romance

We have had many clients who have been too ashamed of parental abuse to mention it during the planning for their first enactment. The sense of it for many people is that they have been betrayed by those who were supposed to love them the most. Abuse takes many forms, including not having been kept safe, being used, or having a sacred trust broken. This is so hurtful that the person, trying to make sense of the betrayal, blames themselves: "There must be something wrong with me. I'm defective."

Parent enactments chip away at the "family romance". When damage is inflicted in the early developmental stages, one way of coping is for the individual to idealize the parents and family of origin, thus remaking reality and factoring out the pain. Some have called the family romance a quest for lost paradise. The fact that most of our clients have not had a safe and secure upbringing does not prevent them from seeking a lost paradise, even one never experienced in the first place. The family romance is essentially the fantasy bond that a person can perpetuate long into adulthood and that prevents the possibility of intimate relationships with peers, partners, or both. People who are still entranced by the notion of the lost paradise may be unable to turn their faces toward adult peer relationships because they may be prone to constantly recreate scenarios of betrayal and rejection.

We find that many of our clients buy into the family romance because it seems easier for them than acknowledging that they were misplaced and mistreated in their early families. Many abused children cling to the abusing parent and will not hear a word said against them. Many grown-up children of alcoholics deny their parent's drinking or at least minimize the adverse affects. We had a lead whose mother was an incorrigible, narcissistic, out-of-control, sexually inappropriate, and abusive alcoholic. Yet this lead offered to take care of her mother and let her live in her new house with her new partner. We have had several leads confront their parent during an enactment for the first time and realize that they have been totally repressing their true feelings and living in a fantasy. During an enactment a lead who had idolized her father spoke to him in her bedroom. She realized that when she was a young teenager he used to come into her bedroom nightly and tell her how dissatisfied he was with her mother and how much he loved her. She had thought this was a sign of his devotion but, as she was speaking, she realized that he had exploited her devotion to him.

In addition, we have worked with people who suffered emotional abuse in their childhoods through neglect. Van der Kolk (2002) has shown that the highest incidence of trauma in the population is due to neglect and breaks in the primary attachment. One woman whose parents were both university professors was locked out of her house every Saturday for the entire day although she was only five years old. Every summer between the ages of eight and fourteen she spent with complete strangers, minders who were hired to look after her while her parents travelled in Europe. One lead, an accomplished physician, stated that his parents were remote, never attending any of his school or leisure functions, and never expressing strong emotions. As soon as he and his twin sister reached eighteen, they were asked to leave and find another place to live. Some people describe their childhoods as "bland", when "nothing happened" and "there was no connection". They say that their parents were interested only in how things looked, in the facade of a happy family. The parents made sure that no strong feelings were expressed about anything but that the children had "good manners", were "well behaved", "did them credit", and kept themselves very quiet, undemanding, and verbally appreciative. Our clients from backgrounds like this tend to be compulsive, depressed, anxious, and conciliatory.

If the psychological process is working well, the individual can individuate from the good-enough family with grace. The person may even internalize the parents as good objects and this allows the creative growth process to continue. The person may have children of their own or their creativity may be manifested through their work or vocation. If the process does not work well, then one of the consequences may be that the individual cannot trust the objects or people in their lives to be good. Thus they have difficulties with attachment and trust. The person keeps their distance from their families, partners, children, friends, and colleagues. Or they may constantly test and attack them. Their work may become a burden to them and they may respond by doing more and more with less and less return in terms of satisfaction. They are out of touch.

Soul Destruction

There is an extreme form of parent-child damage and we refer to this as "soul destruction". We have conducted several enactments with leads whose parents were so damaged themselves that they ended up trying to destroy any signs of life in their own children. We have worked with children of trauma survivors whose childhoods were stereotypes of loneliness and lack of warmth. They grew up feeling that they were unreal and that the world of intimacy and connection was, if not unreal too, at least forever shut off from them. Many of these adults are extremely cerebral, accomplished, achievement-oriented, and competitive. Our view is that parents who have not faced up to their own grief and pain create a two-dimensional family for their offspring. There is no depth and, in fact, no room for the child to experience and express their own sorrows and pain. When they grow up, they may be cordial and tolerant but they are fundamentally unreachable in intimate circumstances. We find that these men and women avoid relaxed roles and are rigid and exacting. Restoration needs to include exploration of their gender roles because people from backgrounds like this are not good at playing husband or wife, father or mother, and lover or beloved roles, as they have not seen these roles modelled.

Given that enactments often focus on early family disasters involving fathers and mothers, it is important to explore the family relationship in leads coming into Therapeutic Enachtment.

Separating from the Parents

Some of the enactments that begin with a death scene segue into another universal theme of separation from the parents. In psychological terms, healthy childhood development is promoted when a primary caretaker (usually a mother) acts as a good object, allowing herself to be used as a function of the child's development. She is able to tolerate all of her child's emotions from temper tantrums to sobbing. A child who is able to make use of her mother's emotional nourishment gradually develops a healthy sense of self as separate and alive. She is able to feel anger, grief, rage, or sadness without making her mother insecure or anxious. In other words, the child comes to know her own feelings and is certain that they are a part of her. This contact with her own feelings and needs gives her self-esteem and strength.

This means, symbolically and in practical terms, accepting our identity as the child of our parents. It also means accepting integrity in the face of authority and with regard to reality itself. According to Campbell ([1949] 1968) acceptance is an essential step toward maturity and individuation whereby the adult child is autonomous from the parent and not neurotically attached. This changes our relationship to authority figures in society in general. It means that we must come to terms with our own strengths and limits. We have realized the potency of those early wounds through the enactments we have seen. Since participants often feel guilty about their negative feelings for their parents who they insist are "good-enough" or "did the best they could", we have to work very carefully to preserve honour and not retraumatize or shame. We accomplish this by taking them seriously, including their ambivalence and caution. We believe that their stance is linked to Shapiro's (2001) responsibility (defect) category of belief clusters; that is, they think they are responsible for the failures of their parents. Because we are born dependent, it is completely overwhelming for a small person to come to the understanding that their caretakers are incompetent or dangerous. So they come to the conclusion: "It must be me. It can't be them. I have to do better, be better." This is the beginning of striving and overfunctioning.

Fathers

One variation on the parental theme is an emerging desire for separation from and atonement with the father. To illustrate the impact of the parent on the formation of the child we recall that one lead's plan for her enactment was to "get real about everything". In her family, speaking the unspeakable would have meant to confirm that they were in the presence of evil in the person of her father and nobody would do that. She refused to use a double because she was asserting her ability to confront evil for herself. In this unusual case, it was important to the lead not to have a double. The family story in this case was that the lead's father was brutal and tyrannical. He was a survivor of the concentration camps who treated his family sadistically. The lead suffered because of her belief that, if she truly accepted who he was and what he did, it would kill her. She believed that the father's descent into darkness had already killed her mother. During the enactment she repudiated her father by telling him that she rejected him as a father and had no love for him. The words were no sooner out of her mouth than she realized that her father, who had attempted to stamp out his family's religious background, was actually the conduit to a rich heritage for her. She became determined, for the first time, to find out about her family's background and to learn about Jewish history and culture. In addition, she was able to drop the idealization of her mother in favour of seeing and accepting her as a flawed person who did the best she could under the circumstances of her life. This was a remarkably freeing experience for the lead. She was the first lead to bring God into one of our enactments because she wanted to be sure that someone had really "seen" the profound depth of her isolation and despair. In speaking to God about her father, she was able to affirm her reality and redeem her inheritance as a child of God. Thus it was possible for her to know and believe that, although something important was lost (something that, in fact, could not be restored), all was not lost.

In another enactment we were unsure whether it was about "killing the father" or "atonement with the father". Certainly we began with "killing". In the enactment the lead was determined to kill his father, who the lead described as "a hard-hearted man. He had no tender side at all. He controlled everything." The lead himself had veered between being hard-hearted and being compliant and passive. Then, for many years, he had "gone into a shell". He said that he "withered out there". Shame for this lead lay in his belief that his father did not love him and neither did his mother. Therefore he believed that he was unlovable. While he understood cognitively that it was not his fault that his parents were unable to love him, he had continued to blame himself throughout his life.

Some kind of peace, absolution, or atonement is helpful in cases like this. The therapist might reasonably ask the question to the lead: "How would you want 'pay back' for this?" When doing set-up for an enactment, therapists should remember the possible themes and watch for the direction in which the lead needs to move, thus opening up the possibility of repair. In this case, his mother sided with his father and this betrayal of the children bled all the life and trust out of the family, sadly, a common theme in Therapeutic Enactments. He couldn't even call his mother "Mom" but addressed her by her given name. His steps toward repudiation of his parents were not clear because he believed that, in effect, he was the one who had been so bad that he deserved what they did to him. He was torn between the reality of his actual parents and his yearning for the loving parenting he had never received. He had three children of his own and he was strongly motivated to be a different kind of parent to them. His question to himself, and the group, was "How shall I know what to do?" In this enactment, and in many others, members of the group in the roles of the "good-enough" parents had to come in and show the lead's parents how to parent with tenderness.

In many families where parents have behaved like monsters, the monsters may not be monsters all the time. In fairytales, sometimes the beast becomes a man for part of the day and the witch is always able to don disguises. This situation makes it harder and more troubling for the child. It keeps the person stuck and holds up the possibility of repair. However, despite uncertainty in some enactments, the lead's need for repudiation is clear. They have to say "Stop!" firmly and out loud. Once this is accepted, without blame or judgment in the group, the lead may discover that, in truth, even here where they thought there was no hope, some may be found. A father might have shown a lead how to work with his hands, how to work hard, or feel safe in the outdoors. These fragments, when remembered under the intense emotional circumstances of the enactment, can help the lead restore a sense of balance.

During the enactment in which the lead told us that he was determined to kill his father, he remembered the useful things that his father had given him, including his skill at carpentry and building. In the end, instead of killing him, he publicly acknowledged the bad and the useful things, introduced his father to his grandchildren from whom he was cut off, and then banished his father from his sight. He wept then, as, for the first time, he was able to allow himself to feel the loss of a "real" father, knowing that he had not had one, and now never would. He felt that banishing his father was better for his own soul than killing him because he did not want to be violent like his father. Also, he realized his father had suffered the great loss of the companionship of his grandchildren and for him that was enough payback. It was the grieving that led this man back to himself and not the activity of revenge or punishment.

We had one lead whose mother had run away and left her and her younger sister with her father when both girls were very young. The father subsequently had a schizophrenic breakdown and was hospitalized, but only after he had thoroughly confused and frightened his daughters, who were isolated with him for many months. Although the woman was now a helping professional, she had a very low tolerance for emotional expressions, especially anger. Every time there was anything close to conflict in the group she would freeze and later start to weep. Her enactment contained a scene in which her father behaved in a bizarre manner in public, an event she remembered as extremely shaming. She enacted the scene twice, in the second version having people actually come to help her family. This lead realized that it was true that her father in his illness had isolated the three of them and that she had lived in dread of exposure and shame, which had become second nature to her. This realization dissolved the terror for her as she accepted that for him it was a reasonable coping measure from his perspective and she and her sister really were helpless at that time. She saw that she was not helpless now at this period in her life and moreover she was helping others. This affirmed that her choice of career was true. She had worked hard at it and could be proud of her achievements. She could relax and allow herself to be competent without having to control the emotions of others.

In another enactment, the lead was unable to individuate from her real parents because she felt that they were not strong enough. Actually, she described her father as wishy-washy and clinging. She said he had "no boundaries". She described her mother as "missing in action". At the same time, she experienced both parents as intrusive and dependent. When she became a wife and then a parent herself, she had a strong desire to enforce some reasonable emotional distance with her parents. When individuals have this sense of readiness, as well as a sense of urgency, enactments tend to go smoothly. For her, the timing was connected to her sense that she had not been parented properly, and as she tried to parent, she was smothering herself. Also, she saw herself slipping into slavery as a wife and mother by trying, through her perfectionism, to make up for her own losses. The lead was seeking, in her marriage, the nurturing that she had not received from her parents. This dream of nurturing, idealized because never actually felt, is hard to let go. The partnership will be unable to bear such a burden. The result will be disappointment and resentment for both partners.

In situations like these, we often have the father role split into two parts: (1) the good parts and (2) the bad parts, so that the lead can speak to each separately and thereby take in or identify with the good parts of the parent, which had previously been repudiated.

Mothers

Since the mother is such a critical player in the development of the child (for better or for worse), negative and cruel actions by mother have particularly long-term damaging effects on the psyche and personal development.

We have conducted several Therapeutic Enactments where the leads were literally almost killed by their own mother when they were infants. As one of our leads pointed out when she confronted her family in the enactment, this really did kill something vital in her. Her soul was in jeopardy and her capacity to love and trust was shattered. In addition, if the surrounding people blame, or ignore, then this may traumatize the child and later prevent them from moving on with their lives. Certainly this was the case in the following situation.

The lead's mother had been involuntarily incarcerated in a mental institution after she had attempted to kill her infant (the lead). This mother may well have had postpartum depression; however, in the 1950s, she was diagnosed as schizophrenic and subjected to a frontal lobotomy. This possible misdiagnosis allowed the lead to fret all her life about "tainted blood", and also about why her mother picked only her to kill and not her little sister, who was nearby. Understanding postpartum depression clarifies this because the mother, in her distress, would only want to take the present infant with her because, in her illness, the previous one had ceased to exist. This was important information since the lead's life was affected by her fear that her mother chose to murder her because of who she was, rather than as a result of her illness.

The therapists helped set up the scene in the house where the attempted murder occurred, and the lead chose to have members of the group role-play the rest of the family as witnesses. At the outset of the enactment, she reported that she felt "numb". The body has its own wisdom (Van der Kolk, 1994) and obviously her numbness deadened pain. Later, she said she felt very sick and nauseous. In our groups we have had several reports of such a nature and, is some cases, actual vomitings. These are survival defence mechanisms that may later become habits when any strong feeling is called for. In this case, the pre-trauma, vital, screaming, yelling, endangered infant did not survive the onslaught psychologically. How can we attempt to reclaim a very early vital self who was murdered? More than one enactment may be required to go back with leads to very early, pre-verbal experiencing.

The lead described her mother as creative and artistic. Behaviourally, she was really different from the norm then, as now. The problem was that, given subsequent events, forever after creativity and vitality became associated with mayhem in the lead's psyche. This was enough to shut down her emerging self in early adolescence. She thought that if she allowed herself full rein to her outrageousness and spontaneity, she would become like her "psychotic" mother. She ended up numbing herself in defence.

This was another enactment in which the lead did not want to use a double. When working with abuse survivors, the survivors themselves often have to begin by speaking the unspeakable out loud. The rest of the group, including other survivors who may be present, have to hear and witness this process very intently. Our experience shows that when others can do that for us, it makes us real, sometimes for the first time. Repair of the wound to the self is then possible.

This lead's enactment really began the week before she came into the group, when she confronted the therapists about the preparations, the set-up, the roles, and so on. She began to test the trust between her and the therapists, a crucial part of the work that she needed to do. The more anxiety-provoking the anticipation of the enactment is, the greater the lead's need to develop ways to enhance more feelings of personal control. Given this lead's story, safety and trust were crucial. In this case, the lead spent considerable time on her car phone the night before, talking to her role players to make sure they understood their roles. Many leads have difficulty taking in that the group really is there for them and members will follow their instructions to the letter. In this case, in a moment of deep empathic immersion, the lead experienced, just for a few moments, somebody else recognizing and holding her horror and anguish. Later she said that they "had mercy on me". This kind of experience tends to increase self-acceptance.

Another enactment illustrates again that, for reparation to be possible, the lead's true story needs to be seen and heard by affirming others. The woman who dreamed of her mother wearing a witch's hat set up a scene that enacted the dream that recurred when she was between three and five years old. In the dream, her mother entered her bedroom in full "witch" regalia, pointy black hat and all. As the set-up unfolded, it became apparent that the bedroom was, in fact, the "scene of the crime". The lead's mother tyrannized her and she had to watch the abuse of her younger sister. This engendered rage and helplessness, two potent forces that were turned against her self. She became her own tormentor, thinking: "Because you didn't love me, I was unable to love myself." Also, she had ended up tormenting the person she was unable to protect—her sister—out of rage at their dependency. In her present life, any signs of dependency in the lead's significant others aroused contempt.

Abused children may be neglected or diminished by the non-abusing parent, who in a very real psychological way refuses to see them. One lead's mother had a true malignant power that was covered up when the father was present (the witch became a queen again). The father promised safety by his presence but was unable to deliver. He did not allow himself to see so it was impossible for her to trust him. A major part of the work of Therapeutic Enactment is expressing the truth of a situation, relationship, or process that was hidden or denied in the individual's past experience and prevented them from moving forward emotionally. They are stuck back in the pain, the lack of clarity, and the humiliation of the original situation. They are not sure what's real and what's not. Repair involves enacting a scenario in order to expose and experience the emotional truth of the experience in front of witnesses. As a result, leads find that their feelings about events, now that they are no longer fantasies, are smaller, thereby lessening the threat of being overwhelmed by them. Their feelings are validated and therefore manageable.

One lead began by commenting that her mother was "a completely different woman now" (from the woman who had burned her as an infant) and so she felt "guilty about doing this piece of work" about her. These feelings are common in Therapeutic Enactments and in therapy generally. They are related to shame and to preventing ourselves from accepting that a disaster has occurred. This lead was still "struggling with the torment of what she did to me back then". This is exactly right. Her mother was able to move on because her children's complete dependency on her was no longer an issue. The lead, however, was not able to move on. She had scars from the burning that were often red and inflamed. The lead could not or would not force her mother to become again the person she was once. However, for the sake of her own repair, she had to squarely face the reality of what kind of mother she did, and does, have. This meant facing her "false cheer" about her childhood and the reality of the mothering she received. This lead woke up the morning after her enactment feeling ashamed and exposed and wanting to leave. She expressed these feelings to the group during the check-in and explained that this was an enormous breakthrough for her: to stay and to express her shame. She wept and this signalled the beginning of self-acceptance.

Someone in a group mentioned "misguided loyalty" with regard to participants saying that they feel squeamish about exposing their parents' shortcomings in the group. However, not to tell the truth would be to maintain the pretence, the facade of okayness over the starkness of the reality. As a lead said to his mother in his enactment: "I forgive you but things will never be the same. What you took from me can never be made right." What these parents took from their children can never be restored. However, both these leads became parents themselves within a year of their enactments. Through expressing their grief about the way their parents treated them, by accepting that this was not right and was a disaster for them as children, they were free to be better parents.

We have directed several Therapeutic Enactments with women whose mothers beat them. Being physically beaten by one's own mother is a terrible violation of one's dignity and personhood. It adversely affects both the development of a sense of personal agency and also the ability to read correctly the intentions of others. What these women shared was an inability to recognize the presence or absence of safety. They coped by keeping their relationships superficial. They may have developed only a half-formed or half-informed sense of danger, of intrigue, and of politics. Unfortunately, some people who have been physically abused may continue to have relationships with people who do it to them again. These women tend to have a deep-seated need to keep control of themselves and others. In addition, because there exists a political taboo about blaming the mother, their isolation, disorientation, self-blame, and despair are increased.

In many enactments, leads have had to extricate themselves from the parent or parents who held them and the whole family captive. In an enactment about the archetypal cruel witch mother, the mother was out-of-control and brutalized her daughter and, by extension, the whole family. The lead had lived in an idyllic real place during her childhood but said her mother was "the serpent in the garden". One of the tragic things about the lead's situation was that she didn't have to do anything to precipitate the violence; she just had to be. This mother deeply envied her eldest daughter simply because she was a child who was growing up in a better situation than she had as a child thus the daughter was "spoiled". This mother nearly killed her daughter through physical abuse and her daughter grew up wanting to destroy herself. To compound the problem, this lead's father sacrificed her in order to save himself. He was terrified of his own anger so he projected it outward and married a woman whose anger was out of control. These parents failed in their "moral responsibility to their children", a sentence that this lead had used earlier about another participant's parents. In a very deep way, her mother and her family dishonoured this lead. In order to redeem her honour, she instinctively had to, in public, do an honourable thing. She accomplished this task when she repudiated her mother but did not fall off into evil herself by killing or punishing her mother. Bypassing revenge, without propitiating or grovelling, restored her honour.

It is crucial for the lead to be reminded not to drift back. This is a necessary admonition to people after their enactments since the pull or lure of the unconscious to go back down into the darkness is so strong. In another enactment where the mother was the abuser, the lead's mother was "a force of nature" and, as we know, natural disasters can exert an almost hypnotic fascination over humans. The individual who was role-playing her mother came on so strong that the lead momentarily became frozen in her own enactment. She recovered quickly but this was important information for her. She had to keep warning herself that, in her present-day relations with her mother, "the archetypal witch" still possessed the poisoned apple and was able to hypnotize her into eating it, just as she had hypnotized her into the negativity and abuse that she dealt out in the past. In reality, humans can become immobilized in the face of curses or spells and die. For this lead, her task was not to try and save (or change) her mother but to free herself from her mother's malignant spell.

The Impact of Role Confusion in the Family of Origin

Another parental theme is the damage that is done when children are forced to act as adults or parents to their parents. Role confusion or role diffusion in childhood accounts for much of the distress we see in clients and is a major cause of trauma in their lives. Many participants have experienced what it is like to be a child forced to act as an adult, a confidant, or as a substitute spouse. Professional women relate how it feels to go about in disguise pretending that they are not female. Professional men, like Michael, have felt what it is like to be completely out of balance, suppressing their emotional expressiveness. Unmothered girls have grown up to be mothers themselves and feel bewildered and assailed. Unfathered boys grow up and have difficulties becoming lovers, husbands, and fathers. We are not just describing a simple one-to-one correlation between a developmental lack of opportunities for role modelling and role distress and incompetence. The participants in the groups often struggle with huge loss, grief, and resentment in their inner lives because of the "unreasonable" role demands in their homes and work. They suffer from "divided loyalties", learned through their exposure to narcissistic parenting. One lead who described his mother as "opportunistic and instrumental" gave us an example of his mother's mixed messages: "Come for brunch and fix my computer." He had never been sure whether she loved him for himself alone or for what he represented and could do for her.

Moving from ambiguity to clarity about our social and psychological roles helps people feel differently about their situations. For example, many adult children of alcoholic, mentally ill, or narcissistic parents had to act as caretakers in the family throughout their childhoods: "where the parents in a healthy family system attempt to provide for the emotional needs of the children, in a narcissistic family system, it becomes the responsibility of the children to meet the emotional needs of the parents" (Pressman & Pressman, 1997, p. 12), what might be described as emotional incest.

This is an example of role abomination. Much of the therapeutic repair in groups is related to mending the effects of role abominations. This pertains both to individuals and to the group as a whole. For those who were robbed of childhood, an enactment that revisits a childhood experience can facilitate moving the person away from the earlier role confusion. Such role confusion may paradoxically result in a child psyche existing in an adult's body. Many leads, when they see their little child "double" having to act as an adult and say or do inappropriate things with adults in the family, are really struck with the impact of it, often for the first time. They may have to express clearly what this took away from them, lose the faint hope that they could ever have different childhoods, and feel the resulting grief and anger. The woman who was unable to feel felt compelled to dash into the circle and grab her father when he yelled at her child self. She screamed at him and ordered him out of the room. Then she went down on the floor, held the child double in her arms, and wept for a long time. (This is another example of the need for safety alertness in enactments. The child double role player must be supported by another witness who can stand or sit behind them throughout. Also the child double may need to be debriefed separately and carefully.)

One of several enactments we directed on a similar theme was with a woman whose grandparents and mother had survived the displaced persons camps after the Second World War in Europe. The family was isolated. Ever since she was a very little girl she had taken care of the adults, speaking English, shopping, and dealing with schools and government. As an adult she was a gifted administrator in her work life but was alone in her private life except for a string of unsuitable and distressing liaisons with cold men. She constructed a scene in which her family of origin bound her with ropes, held on to her, sat on top of her, and yelled unceasing demands at her at the top of their voices. She had to tear herself away from them and free herself while they tried with all their strength to prevent her from leaving. She realized that while she had moved from one end of the country to the other to get away, she had carried them with her. Her shame, guilt, rage, and grief were so forceful that she prevented herself from forming close relationships in case they slipped out. She had literally shut herself down. At the close of her enactment she screamed "I am … [name]. I am free" so forcefully and loudly that one participant ran out of the room covering her ears. (A senior group member followed her to check that all was well. It was.)

Another enactment, again with a woman who had moved across country to escape, involved her confronting her drunken parents while her grandparents and brothers looked on. She realized that the whole family had conspired to exploit her caretaking behaviours, not just her parents. She said she had been "served up as a sacrifice to their needs". In a role reversal with her brothers, she saw that they had looked to her to provide the parenting none of them was receiving from the parents. Her rage at her brothers had generalized to all relationships with men and, while she looked after them both at home and in her work life, she felt self-righteous in her contempt for them. Now she was able to feel compassion for her brothers and, while weeping for them all as "little lost children", she reclaimed her sense of herself as a loving and good person.

We are not saying here that there shouldn't be flexibility in roles. Our work is about restoring a sense of balance, comfort, and identity, not about whether mother or father is masculine or feminine enough. We examine the consequences of one parent over-compensating for the other, of martyrdom, keeping secrets, and lying. Examples that come to mind are when mother says to child: "Wait till your father hears about this" or when father says to child: "Your mother didn't really mean that." We do not want to replace the problems of role rigidity and role abomination with rigid ideas about what a man or a woman should do. We encourage people to relax and be who they are. Some women will develop an interest in what has been designated as a typically "male" activity; for example, one participant loved her motor bike. She could assemble and disassemble it. We have had several males who stayed at home with small children while their spouses went out to work.

When we speak of the roles of the parents, we don't mean gender roles. In symbolic terms, both father and mother play necessarily different roles in the family that can assist or hinder the psychological development of the youngster. The symbolic father influences the ways in which individuals interact with the "world outside". The symbolic mother keeps the person in touch with the inner self. People learn these symbolic meanings just as they learn about their "real" parents and they are common aspects of Therapeutic Enactments in which the group itself can stand in for "the mother" (Malcus, 1995). Symbolic parent complexes can prevent the individual from growing up. The struggle against such complexes is a struggle against being swallowed up by the unconscious. Enactments are helpful in jump-starting blocked growth and social development because they bring the unconscious shadow concretely out into the consciousness of the group. This allows individuals both to recognize parental complexes and practise new behaviours.

Summary

> Love, any love, is made up of time, and no love can avoid
> the great catastrophe. Love does not defeat death but through love
> we catch a glimpse, in this life, of Life itself. Not of eternal life
> but of pure vitality. Love is a heartbeat of time.
> —Octavio Paz

Jung (1931) once commented that neurosis began with the avoidance of legitimate suffering. Therapeutic Enactments can be used as reparative tools to work through the paralysis and fragmentation of blocked grief and trauma, toward wholeness again. When archetypal themes are present, group members are fully engaged and the isolation of trauma is mended. These themes arise in all therapeutic groups. Being able to identify the main theme helps to focus the enactment on the essential processes required for the client to achieve their goal of resolution and reintegration. Further, the themes are recognized as universal by the other group members, which adds to the depth of their experience in the group. Some people come to do enactments to repair abuse that was so terrible that it calls forth the deepest possible resources of the group. Planning for these enactments needs to be done with great care, attending to every last detail. Our next chapter describes such an enactment. Marion had suffered severe injuries that had resulted in Post-Traumatic Stress Disorder (PTSD). Enactments to repair PTSD are difficult and for this reason we have devoted an entire chapter to this example.

A Therapeutic Enactment to Repair Complex Post-Traumatic Stress Disorder: Marion's Story

Oh you have been leading me beside strange waters
Streams of beautiful light in the night
But where is my pastureland in these dark valleys?
If I loose my grip will I take flight?

—Bruce Cockburn, "Strange Waters"

I was ready to tell the story of my life
But the ripple of tears and the agony of my heart
Wouldn't let me.

I began to stutter saying a word here and there
And all along I felt as tender as a crystal
Ready to be shattered.

—Jalal al-Din Rumi, "I Was Ready to Tell" (Fragment #1419)

We had been trained to believe that Therapeutic Enactments should not be used with people who suffer from dissociation and Post-Traumatic Stress Disorder (PTSD) (Herman 1992, p. 121) for two reasons. First, such an approach involving performance, feelings, and memories will be unsuccessful and therefore promote retraumatization. In short, it will make the person worse. Second, these people are so fragile that any group method will injure them and destroy the group. So this begs the question, Why do it? The clients with PTSD who we include in our groups have stable personal lives on the dimensions of work/career and social life. Therefore, taking the risk to encourage enactments with our clients does not run the risk of destabilizing fragile individuals who do not have jobs, relationships, or grounded lives. However, very careful pre-planning is essential.

This chapter outlines what goes on when therapists facilitate a difficult enactment with a PTSD client. Protecting the group is absolutely crucial as group members who act as witnesses may be retraumatized; they may regress back to anxiety or fear or go into trance, numb out, or dissociate—a common response to overwhelming pain or threat. In fact, witnesses in one complex enactment were asked to wear masks because the lead wanted them to be protected from the reactions of the witnesses to her enactment. In another, witnesses were asked to turn their backs so they would be protected from a potentially injurious enactment and also because the lead was ashamed. In both these enactments, witnesses required greater support for debriefing. Our experience with PTSD clients tells us that it is important to use a carefully chosen smaller group that includes the lead's therapists or at least supportive friends and colleagues.

Building the Group into a Safe Container

The groups must be safe for both the PTSD lead and the witnesses. Enactments about sexual abuse in particular need careful planning because the content arouses strong feelings and group members need to believe that the container can hold them.

Once, in our early days of working together, we had a participant who acted as a witness for most of the workshop. On the last day, she asked to do an enactment disclosing her early sexual abuse to her current partner. Sadly, we agreed. We had done no assessment or advance preparation with her but she was a fellow professional and we thought she had the skills and awareness to engage therapeutically. Later, we realized that she showed many of the signs of a borderline personality disorder in that she was impulsive, hostile, intrusive, sexually inappropriate, and verbally incontinent, often telling lies and making up stories. From the beginning of her enactment she vigorously resisted facilitation and direction. She was determined not to let the therapists or group members help her. The group process became a vivid projective identification of the ways in which she had experienced her family and others as treating her. Although we managed to bring this process to awareness without shaming or blaming, this woman's enactment of sexual abuse was an exceptionally prolonged experience and very hard on the group.

We are more careful now about whether we will go spontaneously with an impulsive enactment. Today we would not conduct any enactment about sexual abuse impulsively. Generally in our work we appoint someone to the role of "safety monitor". The person chosen for this task is an experienced group member who has completed their own enactment and is familiar with groups and with people who dissociate. The safety monitor looks for dissociation not abreaction (intense expressions of emotion). Compared with dissociation, abreaction is easier to deal with in groups even though it is the worst fear of most therapists as group leaders (it's loud, messy, and looks uncontrollable). Senior group members can deal with emotional outbursts from witnesses; providing empathy, support, and sensitivity in order to make the witness feel safe and contained. Senior group members can be helpful to the enactment process, cueing the therapists, providing input to role players, and supporting people who are playing difficult roles. In contrast, safety monitors focus specifically on possible breaks in the group that result from members who may experience retraumatization and dissociation.

From experience with other intense enactments we knew that Marion's enactment of the sexual abuse she experienced as a child would be upsetting for the group. However, we had faith in our method, we trusted one another, and we both had experience with counselling clients who had survived sexual abuse. We had learned the hard way what not to do. We decided to respond to this potential lead's call for help but to proceed with caution and care in order to reduce trauma and dissociation.

Trauma and Dissociation

Trauma is associated with shame, vigilance, and numbing. Dissociation is common. Turkus (1992) describes dissociation as follows:

> The essential feature of dissociative disorders is a disturbance or alteration in the normally integrative functions of identity, memory, or consciousness . . . In PTSD, recall/re-experiencing of the trauma (flashbacks) alternates with numbing (detachment or dissociation), and avoidance. Atypical dissociative disorders are classified as Dissociative Disorders Not Otherwise Specified (DDNOS).

Dissociation is a psychological defence mechanism in which our identity, memories, ideas, feelings, or perceptions are separated from conscious awareness and cannot be recalled or experienced voluntarily (*The Merck Manual*, 1997, p. 430). It is a self-soothing technique used to manage intense fear. It often occurs with flashbacks and triggers such as words, smells, something seen or heard on the radio or television, or a sudden or unexpected touch. Also individuals can be triggered by witnessing the emotional reactions of others and tuning in to the other person's dissociation and trance state. Dissociation happens very fast. Individuals learn to dissociate early in childhood in order to "disappear" from traumatizing situations in which they are trapped. After years of practice the response is practically automatic. They barely feel the fear and—bang!—they're gone. Therapists understand that dissociative individuals are difficult to work with. Braun (1988) incorporates the four dimensions of dissociation as behaviour, affect, sensation, and knowledge. If the person is unable to stay conscious of any one of them, then they are dissociating. Say, for example, during an assessment a person tells a terrible story with tears pouring down her face. The therapist gently says: "I know this must be very hard for you. I notice that you are weeping." The individual replies: "I don't know what you are talking about. I am not upset." What aspect is missing here? The answer is both affect and sensation. The person is not feeling her feelings of sorrow nor the tears against her skin. Would this kind of dissociation be Marion's method of coping with her trauma?

Marion's Story

Marion, a woman in her late thirties, had a childhood history of repeated sexual abuse committed by her mother, grandfather, and several of her mother's boyfriends. Some of the abuse incorporated ritualistic elements. Marion worked as a counsellor in the alcohol and drug field and had recently completed her master's degree in counselling. She was bisexual and had endured a long series of abusive relationships with short-term partners of both genders. She was currently in a stable relationship of several years standing with a woman. Marion was a recovering alcoholic who suffered from depression, panic attacks, and flashbacks. She reported that she dissociated for self-protection. Sometimes, Marion ended up in places and didn't know how she had got there. Once she found herself, on foot, in a public phone booth out on the highway.

Marion had many triggers. Sometimes she cut herself as a tension release. This is important information because therapists have to be alert to the possibility of the urge to cut returning after the enactment. Briere (1996) calls cutting an affect-regulation strategy to cope with insupportable intense emotion. The result of cutting is a physical sensation of release rather than an emotion. Therapists have to be cognizant of these possible reactions because, in enactments, the tension builds slowly at the beginning as the lead and therapist walk around the circle and tell the story.

We shall illustrate Marion's enactment by moving through the six stages: (1) assessment, (2) preparation including setting up, (3) resource installation, (4) enacting, (5) debrief, and (6) follow-up.

Assessment: Assessing Client Needs and Developing an Enactment Plan

We do much more pre-planning with especially vulnerable individuals who have suffered abuse and may suffer from post-traumatic stress. From the therapist's point of view, the goal during assessment is two-fold: (1) to assess readiness, urgency, or appropriateness of leads and/or their issues and (2) to collaborate with the lead in identifying the key critical scenes to be re-created. Readiness requires therapists to exercise a level of clinical judgment; for example, we screen out people who are not ready or those whose defences preclude them from fully participating in the group process. If the person cannot be made safe in a group then an enactment must be postponed.

The therapist may judge that an individual is not ready for Therapeutic Enactment if any of the following characteristics are evident:

- they are too fragile—weepy and emotionally labile;
- they have no impulse control;

- they have no boundaries;
- they cannot focus;
- they are too raw—filled with rage or hyper-aroused; and
- the trauma is too recent and they need individual therapy first.

Our method demands readiness, which is the dependent variable, not the client's level of psychopathology. Readiness is apparent when the client demonstrates the following characteristics:

- they have survived the traumatic events for a considerable number of years;
- they have created a stable personal life;
- they have a job, career, or school goals that are established and long-standing;
- they have a clear scenario that they can communicate to us; and
- they can state reasons for wanting to free themselves from the traumatic events and make them into "ancient history".

Assessment and preparation is particularly crucial for participants who have been sexually abused in order to ascertain that all these conditions are met.

A colleague at Marion's work referred her to us. She attended two previous enactment weekends as a witness; then she approached us about doing an enactment. She told us in advance of our interview that her issue was incest and ritual abuse. We decided to interview her while making no promises about actually conducting an enactment with her. Marion was very nervous but, then, so were we. We heard her history and realized that, while she had managed to create a high-level career and stable life for herself, she was in pain daily as a result of the toll of her sexual abuse. Marion had been an excellent student in her graduate program, which included a practicum where she worked with traumatized women and children. She was able to tell her story clearly and so we decided to help her do an enactment.

The DSM-IV Criteria for a Diagnosis of Post-Traumatic Stress Disorder

Marion exhibited classic symptoms of Post-Traumatic Stress Disorder. *The Diagnostic and Statistical Manual of Mental Disorders*, 4th edition (DSM-IV) describes Post-Traumatic Stress Disorder as follows:

A. The person has experienced, witnessed or was confronted with an event/events that involved actual or threatened death or serious injury, or threat to the physical integrity of self or others AND the person's responses involved fear, helplessness or horror.

B. The traumatic event is persistently re-experienced in at least one of the following ways:

- Recurrent and intrusive distressing recollections of the event.
- Recurrent distressing dreams of the event.
- Acting or feeling as though the event were recurring (including flashbacks when waking or intoxicated).
- Intense psychological stress at exposure to events that symbolize or resemble an aspect of the event.

C. Persistent avoidance of stimuli associated with the trauma or numbing of general responsiveness (not present before the event) as indicated by at least three of the following:

- Effort to avoid thoughts or feelings associated with the event.
- Efforts to avoid activities or situations which arouse recollections of the event.
- Inability to recall an important aspect of the event (psychogenic amnesia).
- Markedly diminished interest in significant activities, such as hobby or leisure time activity.
- Feeling of detachment or estrangement from others.
- Restricted range of affect; e.g., inability to experience emotions such as feelings of love.
- Sense of a foreshortened future such as not expecting to have a career, relationships, children or a long life.

D. Persistent symptoms of increased arousal (not present before the event) as indicated by at least two of the following:

- Difficulty in falling or staying asleep.
- Irritability or outbursts of anger.
- Difficulty concentrating.
- Hyper-vigilance.
- Exaggerated startle response.
- Physiological reactivity on exposure to events that resemble an aspect of the event, e.g., breaking into a sweat or palpitations.

B, C, and D must be present for at least one month after the traumatic event.

The traumatic event caused clinically significant distress or dysfunction in the individual's social, occupational, and family functioning or in other important areas of functioning.

The definition refers to a "sense of a foreshortened future" and we are often struck by the many variations of this symptom that we see in our clients. Many survivors, even professionals with substantial incomes, have difficulty thinking of the future. They do not visit a physician or dentist on a regular basis. Their houses or apartments are temporary or look temporary. They drive ramshackle cars. They do not contribute to retirement savings plans. They do not have wills. Many clients will come right out and say that they do not expect to live until retirement so it is reasonable to not prepare for it. In Marion's case, her partner wanted to buy a house with her but she was uninterested.

Herman (1992, p. 119) has added her own definition to the DSM-IV definition of Post-Traumatic Stress Disorder. She calls it:

Complex Post-Traumatic Stress Disorder
1. A history of subjection to totalitarian control over a prolonged period (months to years).
       This includes survivors of sexual and physical abuse in their own homes.
2. Alterations in affect regulation.
       This includes self-injury.
3. Alterations in consciousness.
       This includes dissociation.
4. Alterations in self-perception.
       This includes helplessness and shame.
5. Alterations in perceptions of the perpetrator.
       This includes idealization of the offender.
6. Alterations in relations with others.
       This includes isolation and/or perpetual search for a rescuer.
7. Alterations in systems of meaning.
       This includes despair.

Although Marion had never been formally diagnosed as suffering from complex PTSD, as she told us her story we went through the checklist with her. We realized that she was coping with many of the symptoms on a regular basis. She described a childhood of unrelenting disorganization and abuse. Her mother was a drug addict, her grandfather was an alcoholic, and her father left before she was two. Her mother had a series of fellow-traveller boyfriends for twenty years and then died when Marion was twenty-eight. Marion left home and went on the streets when she was sixteen. She was rescued by a church group and joined Alcoholics Anonymous. She went back to school at twenty-five and finally to university.

Marion was a quiet person and said to us that shame was her bane. She had a tendency to flush when speaking in the group and this caused her much distress. She felt overwhelmed by relationship and career demands. She and her partner, who was an-adult-child-of-alcoholics, kept themselves to themselves and had no social circle.

During our initial interview, which was about a week before the workshop, we asked Marion which "scenario" she wanted to enact. What was the core issue or critical event she was committed to healing? In listening to her reply, we looked for pivotal scenes that she remembered with strong feelings, confusion, questioning, and ambivalence. For example, in shame enactments, many leads will remember a scene in which they felt themselves to be completely at the mercy of their parents. They remember feeling dismissed, demeaned, or repudiated. As Harry Stack Sullivan ([1953] 1968) once commented, by the time we are fifteen we have received ten thousand looks that could kill. This may be the core issue of shame, helplessness, and isolation. Marion suffered lifelong shame as a result of sexual abuse by her family. Marion described her core issue as "I hate myself because I am worthless." Later, during the enactment it emerged that her negative cognition was: "I deserve to be abused because I am dirty."

At this point, our aim is to help the lead construct a "concrete representation" of an internalized image or state. Many people like Marion will say that they do not remember their childhoods. One woman who was in her mid forties and had a long childhood history of repeated sexual abuse by her alcoholic father and several of his cronies had huge gaps in her memory of ordinary events in her past like birthdays or her first day at school. Marion's abuse had some ritualistic elements and her mother, also an alcoholic, was a participant in several of the incidents. As we often do, we asked Marion about a physical reaction or sensation and we helped her describe it. We said: "Tell us where you feel it in your body." We asked Marion to point to the sensation or to place her hand on that part of her body. Sometimes we encourage the client to reflect on an "event" (a death, funeral, journey, or party); an "image" (grandmother lying in her coffin); a "feeling" (feeling sick and nauseated); "sensation" (the leather seats in parents' car); or a "dream". Frequently, a clear memory is provided, but for many clients it is not easy to recall, especially for dissociative individuals.

It is not surprising that leads, especially those suffering from trauma, may not be able to "see" or conceptualize a critical scene. Freyd (1996) makes it clear that memory in the traumatized does not work in the usual ways. When we dissociate, the traumatic scene is never encoded in memory so it cannot be retrieved normally. Dissociative individuals do not perceive things clearly. They see things through a fog; the lights might appear to be flickering, or the colours in the rug might appear to be moving. These perceptual differences occur because the person was accustomed to trying to change the traumatizing environment to make-it-not-happen. It is this focusing on the affective, physical, and imaginal self, rather than the cognitive self, that helps the therapists and lead co-construct a scene. During both the assessment and the enactment, having present a person who has expertise in dissociation is enormously helpful.

Another lead in her late twenties or early thirties was the child of immigrants to Canada. She had a childhood history of repeated sexual abuse by her older brother and several of his neighbourhood friends. The rest of the family had never been told of these incidents. The family went about meeting with one another, holding family dinners and celebrations, without this truth ever being expressed. This woman had never discussed it with her brother and he had not admitted the abuse to her. She was married with no children. Her husband knew nothing of her early history. She found ordinary encounters in family gatherings to border on the surreal. The starting point for her enactment was the strips of carpet on the basement steps and the wallpaper. Similarly Marion was able to focus on her bedroom in her childhood home—the scene of the abuse. She was five years old.

Preparation: Setting Up, Initiating, Identifying, and Co-Constructing Scene

As therapists, we don't always know exactly how a scene will unfold. We agreed at the end of the assessment that Marion needed to be able to say some things to her mother. She also wanted to hear some things back; for example, that her mother knew that what she did was unforgivable. Marion was clear that this was not just about the sexual abuse. Her mother also had been sexually abused by her father, the grandfather who was now abusing Marion. The fact that Marion's mother had failed to protect her child from a repeat of her own trauma was evil in Marion's eyes. Her lack of action had come close to ruining her daughter's life. Marion told us that she wanted to rage at her family so we designed the scene to reflect that. However, as usual, we were open to reshaping it at her direction.

During preparation, the therapists helped Marion to gradually construct, or reconstruct, the nuclear script or pivotal scene for enactment. By the time we got into the workshop we simply had to put the structure in place. Hers was the last enactment of the workshop so everyone was familiar with the format and was prepared to witness a new enactment. We were concerned, however, that some members of the group would be highly affected as they witnessed Marion's enactment. Because it is our job as therapists to always keep one eye on the development and climate of the group and the other eye on the process of the individual who serves as the lead, we decided to take extra time at the beginning of Marion's enactment to prepare the group. We told them: "We are asked now to witness terrible events. We know that you can do this for Marion. We know that you can support each other through this enactment. Please watch over one another and, if you see someone faltering, go and sit beside them. Don't leave the room until we're done." Each participant stood and declared something like this: "I am here. I will do this." (People put their own words to the declaration.) At this point, cued by the therapist, participants could choose to leave the room if they believed that they could not be present for the lead. The therapist made it clear that no shame or blame would be attached to the choice to leave the room. A senior group member would usually go with anyone who needed to leave.

Setting up the Enactment

Marion had to construct actual physical entities of space, time, shape, and form. Sometimes people bring props but Marion wanted nothing to do with real objects from her past so we helped her create a bedroom with found objects. She wanted a blanket so we brought a beautiful, soft woollen one. We also helped Marion find her role players. In fact, we took a more directive role than we normally do and called upon experienced group members to assume the critical roles as they were so negative and intense. We always tell witnesses they can refuse to accept a role if it is not a good time for them or if the role is too close to one of their own experiences. In this case, three senior group members were chosen for the key roles and another witness played Marion's partner. They were apprised of their roles prior to the enactment so there were no surprises.

Sometimes leads may choose for roles witnesses who have never been to a Therapeutic Enactment group before. In these circumstances, the individual chosen, even though willing, may experience a sense of discomfort and confusion about what is required. They may need some direction in the moment from the therapist so they can be true to the roles ascribed. In Marion's case, we prepared the role players thoroughly a short time before the enactment. We told them, directed by Marion, how the perpetrators walked and talked and the words they typically used. This kind of advance preparation provides safety for the role players and adds to the potency of the group. In Marion's case, before the enactment began, we held a little circle for Marion and her helpers in an adjoining room so that all the players could physically come in touch with each other. This is crucial both to emphasize the delicacy of the work about to be done and to offset dissociation in lead and role players. We had people stand shoulder to shoulder, hold hands, and breathe together. People said whatever they were moved to say. In this way we installed the relationship between the lead and the role players as another resource. Marion prayed for strength and guidance and expressed her determination to see the work through.

Resource Installation

We asked Marion to choose resources that might include her partner, church group, or other friends but not her immediate family. Marion had decided not to have her absent father present and because she was an only child she had no need to consider whether siblings should be present. Marion chose her resources from within the group. She chose an adult double to be with her during the enactment. This woman stuck very close to her throughout, even keeping her hand on Marion's shoulder during the early part of the enactment.

Because we increasingly are asking people to choose a child double as well as their adult double, particularly in situations where the scene is set in childhood, we also asked Marion to choose a child double.

During assessment Marion had great difficulty thinking of a "safe place" from her childhood. In fact, there was no such place for her and she felt ashamed. To soothe this shame, we pointed out to Marion something we have found helpful through our experiences in cases like this: the most important resource is the "precious, undamaged self". In response Marion told a happy memory of herself as a little girl sitting with her grandmother (who had died when Marion was five) in the garden, digging in the dirt. To enact this safe place Marion chose a witness to be her grandmother and to play out that scene with her child double. Marion was surprised at the strength of her emotion as she watched this scene because she had almost forgotten that she had a grandmother. To protect her grandmother and little child from the horror, she decided to have them sit just inside the circle during the enactment and turn their backs until it was over.

The feelings that arose in Marion in the presence of the grandmother were intense. As therapists we had to walk a fine line at this point. We didn't want to get stuck in an abreaction this early, yet we didn't wish to reinforce the defence of suppressing emotions either because it would hamper the catharsis that is important to enactments. We paused for a few minutes with Marion installing her child double in the garden with her grandmother before moving on so that Marion could really take in the loss—as well as the presence—of such loving support.

As she watched the scene with her little child double, Marion suddenly was struck by the realization that she had almost died as a result of her abuse and that, in fact, it was a miracle she had survived. Marion said that her "soul had been in jeopardy". She spontaneously decided to choose "an angel" to sit at the side of the bed as the sexual abuses were portrayed. Marion told us that this angel had saved her life even though she had not known it at the time. In this way Marion as a lead had changed the action of the enactment based on an emerging need. As therapists we remained flexible and ready to spontaneously shift the focus of the action accordingly in response to the lead's implied or direct communication. We recognized the symbolic value of installing the angel as a resource.

In our culture we have a tendency to think that symbolic and ceremonial things aren't important. Yet, in real life, many people do all sorts of ceremonial things, such as keeping photographs of their ancestors, writing in journals, remembering anniversaries, or having china passed down from grandparent to grandchild. These objects or experiences are viewed as meaningful and supportive. Leads come up with their own ceremonies that are experienced as resources. For Marion, introducing her "angel" was one such ceremony.

We asked Marion to stand aside for a moment and look at the scene as it has been set up. We asked her what she saw and what negative belief about herself she had as a result of observing the scene. When she looked at her bedroom she responded: "I think I am weak and helpless." "I think I am an idiot." "I am ashamed because what happened was all my fault." I deserved it." However, when she looked at her little child playing with her grandmother she answered: "It wasn't my fault. I was just a little girl. I did the best I could." "I am OK." "Somebody in my family loved me." "I am not bad. I am good." When she looked at the angel she said: "I love her."

This was a very moving part of the enactment for the two therapists leading the enactment and we found ourselves in tears. We were open and comfortable in expressing our feelings, and, as therapists and leaders of the group, we demonstrated authenticity, which allowed the group to relax. Group members could see that the therapists were in charge and were not dissociating. It was important for the group members to observe the therapists take this difficult work seriously and yet not be destroyed by it.

Co-leading a group can be fraught with peril, as some of the literature testifies, and therefore as the therapists co-leading an enactment, we must "do our inner homework" by constantly checking in and connecting with each other. We have to build in constant debrief space for self-care after each group and sometimes after each enactment. After Marion's enactment, for example, we spent over an hour debriefing, mainly talking through our grief and anger about what her family had done to her. During the actual enactment, however, admittedly we had to put most of these feelings aside. We have found, though, that as co-leaders, if we constantly suppress our feelings, particularly grief, envy, or dominance and submission, then group safety will be in jeopardy. It is important also that the therapists as co-leaders not withhold reactions from one another. We have to be able to tolerate chaos and uncertainty, open ourselves to feedback, and address worries, hurts, or slights.

Enacting: Moving through and Experiencing the Chosen Scenario

Many deeply distressed people have survived by putting their emotions away and Marion was no exception. She was used to minimizing and controlling her feelings. She was accustomed to dissociating. At the beginning, as she stepped into the circle, she seemed quite calm, perhaps even remote. This most likely is a sign that she was dissociating. It's not just that people who dissociate cannot feel their feelings. They are not "in" their bodies. How did we get her back? During the assessment we learned that Marion's safe place or object was the scene in the garden with the grandmother and we established a way to cue her to this place if needed. During the enactment we could then use grounding strategies such as saying to her: "Marion, are you with us? Now look at the garden. Notice your breathing." We might also use aromatic oils by placing a drop in the palm of the lead's hands, and have her rub her hands together. Frequently we will ask: "What are you feeling in your body right now?" "Point to where the feeling is." We may ask a witness to do bilateral tapping on the person's shoulders while we go through these checks.

In some cases, the catharsis or early arousal of blocked grief or anger is the pivotal moment of the whole enactment; therefore, it is important that therapists attend very close to the lead and keep the reparative goal or goals in mind. For example, we planned a Therapeutic Enactment with a man who wished to say goodbye to his dead brother. The scene was to be in the car where the death took place, which meant the lead was going to move toward the car. However, as soon as the in-role brother entered the circle and began to speak as the real brother the lead released his full grief. This was the core part of the enactment. In this we never actually moved to the scene of the car. In Marion's case, she had expressly said that she wanted to enact a specific scene in her bedroom where she could get angry. Since this was the primary and pivotal scene to be enacted we agreed to begin the enactment there.

Marion and the therapists moved to action in the group. The events she had described, imagined, or visualized were set into motion. We did not want the events of the story fleshed out in as much detail as we usually do. The co-therapist was able to move the timing along while the "inside" therapist elicited the story. The therapists worked together as a team, one performing the directing role and the other very attentively observing the lead's and the group's actions and reactions. Together, the therapists observed and consulted about the interactive process going on in the group, but our primary focus was on Marion, the lead. While she was walking around the circle and telling her story, the "observing" therapist was forming a gestalt of Marion's esprit de corps. She was paying close attention to what Marion actually said as well as her body language and emotional arousal, at the same time looking for dissociation. A therapist who has experience with dissociative clients recognizes movements of the eyes and head, which goes down and to the side when a person is "disappearing". She notices changes in the client's breathing (rapid breathing, rapid heart rate). Thus with Marion the observing therapist was able to assist the "inside" therapist to change direction, bring in new elements, and finally make a ceremony to symbolize the actions. Again, we did not want Marion to go into too much detail here as we thought it important for her to get into the action as soon as possible. This was similarly the case when she brought up the key players, her resources.

When the role players were inside the circle, the therapist led Marion over to the bed and helped her get onto it. The impact of having a male therapist in a sex abuse enactment is not to be underestimated. The group held their breath as Marion tucked herself into her little bed. Again, we checked for possible dissociation. Then the grandfather entered the room and stood silently over Marion. At this point she screamed a cry of terror at the top of her lungs and flung herself into the arms of the therapist, who was standing slightly off to the side. We were now no longer enacting but reliving. This meant we had to watch for signs of retraumatization—dissociation, sweating, coldness, and paralysis. The safety monitor watched the group carefully as well. The male therapist turned Marion away from the scene and held her until she stopped yelling. Then he asked her to come back into the scene. He said he would go with her. He would not leave her side. They went back to the bed and the therapist called in the mother and boyfriend as well as the grandfather. They came in slowly and all three stood over the lead. Again, she sprang up and screamed at the top of her voice. The therapist and her double stood on either side of her. The angel came and stood between her and the perpetrators. The therapist sent the three perpetrators away to the other side of the large room and said to the lead: "Okay. Let's go very slowly now. We are not going to leave your side."

Marion went back to the bed and lay down. The therapist instructed the grandfather to walk very, very slowly toward the bed. At every step the therapist stopped him and asked Marion: "Is this okay?" As is recommended in these kinds of enactments, the therapist and Marion had agreed previously that she would use a signal to notify him if he were going too fast or she felt unsafe and he would call a halt. The therapist responded to the lead's verbal signals to "Stop!" "Help!" or "Wait!" Hand signals were also used. Guided by Marion, and with many long waits, the therapist slowly positioned the grandfather at a safe distance from the bed at about five meters. The therapist positioned each of the other two perpetrators in the same way. This took a long time but Marion, although trembling with anxiety and hanging onto her double for dear life, was able to look at them without screaming or running away. Finally, all three were standing about seven or eight meters from Marion and off to one side so that she was not blocked or crowded. Then the therapist had the double step forward to confront them. One experienced group member was asked to stand behind the double in support, lightly touching her shoulders, for the duration.

At this point, the observing therapist took the double's place at Marion's side. The angel was standing close by on a low chair so that Marion could see her at all times. Other members stood behind the three people playing the perpetrators, as by this time they were also struggling with their own feelings coming from the role taken and they needed support. As therapists dealing with complex abuse situations such as this, however, we needed to be extra careful about limiting spontaneous contributions and abrupt movements from group members. Some of the witnesses, out of their own anxiety and distress, felt a need to "rescue" the lead by offering their services as doubles. In anticipation of this need the therapists had told the group at the beginning that doubling, in this enactment, was permitted only if directed by the therapist. As Marion screamed in terror when the role players approached her bed, the person in the role of the double was overwhelmed and couldn't speak. She was probably either dissociated or retraumatized. At a signal from the observing therapist, several members of the group came up, one by one, and helped the double find the right things to say. Anger, a signal emotion in situations like this, is just the first stage in confronting the reality of the abuse. It has to be expressed and clears the way for more complex expressions. The double said something like this: "What you did was unforgivable. You completely failed in your duty to me when I was a small child. What you took from me can never be restored and that is all on your consciences." Other members stepped forward and said similar things, often with a great deal of forcefulness. Then the double said: "In spite of what you did to my body you could not take my soul from me. You left me feeling dirty. But I know now that this was not my fault." At this point Marion leapt forward, jumped up on the bed, and expressed the full force of the pent-up rage and grief that had been held frozen for so long.

Following this emotional release, members of the group quickly assembled the next scene. Marion sat flanked by her support. The judge sat on a chair on top of a table. The perpetrators stood in front of him. The rest of the group stood behind Marion. The judge spoke sternly and eloquently of the reprehensible deeds done by the three. Marion's double testified about the long-standing effects of their actions on her. The judge pronounced them guilty. He said that they did not deserve Marion, who was a good person, loved and respected in her community. Their sentence given by the judge was that they would never be allowed near her or any other child. In addition, their community condemned them. The group responded: "We agree."

Marion told the judge that while she was thankful for his actions, she felt that she also had to speak to God. Because of the abuse she experienced as a child Marion believed she was dirty and irredeemable. She wanted to hear otherwise from God's lips as it were. We had not planned for this part of the enactment but Marion was completely in charge by this time. We could see that she was deeply in touch with her experience and resonating with a felt sense of what she needed to create a sense of completion. So we set up an enactment in which Marion could hear the voice of God.

In other enactments, we have had a witness play God. This time, we simply had the voice of the observing therapist (as chosen by Marion) come from behind a screen. Marion then asked her angel to take her to speak to God. She told God what had happened to her at the hands of her own mother and family. She said: "How could you have let this happen? How could you have let me think for years that I was dirty? What were you thinking?!" God replied that she was very sorry that Marion had suffered so. She said that while she had been unable to prevent bad things from happening to Marion, she had sent her an angel to watch over her. God said that Marion was not dirty but beautiful. She asked Marion to hold out her hands. She said that she had given Marion very beautiful hands to remind her, every time she looked at them, that in spite of everything bad that had happened to her, God had loved her from the start and loved her even more now. Marion wept as God told her that from now on she could look at her own hands, a gift from God, and see how beautiful and alive she was.

The directing therapist then stepped forward and said to Marion gently: "We have to go now. Is there anything else you want to say to God before you go?" Other than expressing gratitude and love, Marion was ready to move into closure and debrief. The therapist called for a short break before we moved on.

Debrief: Sharing Reactions to the Enactment Experience

In Marion's enactment the group was too devastated by grief to either go for a break or come back together without help. At the completion of the final scene, we stopped for a long moment, took a look around the group, and realized that they could not get back into their seats without first coming into the centre of the room to hold onto one another. We led a grieving circle for about five minutes, during which people breathed and wept together. Then we sent everyone outside to breathe beside the lake. The two therapists took additional time to de-role the players while we were outside. This was not a normal de-roleing because this group of role players was very upset. We had them stand close together and breathe. For grounding we drew attention to the light on the water and the trees. Someone had a little vial of lavender oil and it was sent round the group for people to rub a drop into their palms of their hands. The safety of this group was paramount. These witnesses and role players had been involved in very intense emotional scenes. Their own personal material may have been evoked and they needed affirmation and support. The therapists had to facilitate the debrief, make sure that all were present (not dissociating), all were heard, that grief was discharged, and that the group came back into balance.

When we came back into the circle, Marion wanted to hear from each player what effect assuming their roles had on them. She also wanted to hear from each group member. Participants were able to convey to Marion the horror they had experienced as they witnessed her story. They described what she had endured as "evil". The man who played Marion's grandfather wept as he described his feelings of terror and disbelief as he approached her bed. The witnesses were grateful for Marion's survival, courage, and essential goodness. One person described Marion as "a walking miracle".

To conclude the debrief, Marion—still a practising Christian—asked us to sing a hymn. Another woman sang a beautiful song as well. Marion, although she wept and even laughed at one point, was in charge about what she wanted done throughout the debrief. At the end, she said she felt tired but relieved and relaxed. We had to be mindful of the possibility that this was a manifestation of another layer of dissociation. Relaxation can actually be endorphin-induced euphoria often caused by cutting or some other similarly extreme action. People who cut themselves can look relaxed immediately afterward; they can look blissed out. We also checked for dissociation because John Hartung and Michael Galvin (2003) has pointed out that some people can flip quickly between hyper-arousal (as in the enactment) to numbing. This is another reason why we moved very, very slowly through the stages of the enactment. We were containing Marion's arousal so that she did not become overwhelmed.

Follow-up: Checking in with the Client Post Enactment

During the first twenty-four hours following the enactment, Marion said that she felt completely cleansed after her work. She did not fall into the depression or shame that often follows successful enactments. Instead she felt revitalized. Nevertheless checking for dissociation was key as leads and/or other specifically identified participants must be followed up within twenty-four hours after the end of the group. As therapists we touched base and had an expert in dissociation from the group do so as well. With leads who tend to dissociate or may harm themselves, such follow-up is particularly crucial. Individuals who were sexually abused like Marion may have been subjected to commands to keep silent with threats of harm to self or others and can take these on like powerful hypnotic suggestions.

We met with Marion a few days after the workshop debrief and recommended EMDR sessions to finish up the aftermath of the enactment. She met with an EMDR therapist for about ten sessions. She told us that her negative belief: "I am dirty" had been replaced by "I'm stuck. I can never get to achieve what I want. I'm damaged inside." She wanted to change this to a positive belief: "I'm free. I can be happy."

When we saw Marion six weeks later at the workshop debrief, she looked great. She was working through the aftermath with her own therapist and said that she felt as if a "huge dark shadow had been lifted off her heart". However, several of the group members were still struggling with what they had witnessed and their need to be heard in the follow-up meeting was important. We discussed dissociation and retraumatization during a lengthy debrief, which, in the case of workshops containing enactments such as Marion's, may take three or four hours to complete. Debriefs cannot be cut short so therapists need to warn the group in advance of coming together that we will be meeting for a long time.

It turned out that Marion did have a delayed reaction to the enormity of the public airing of what happened to her in her childhood. She called us three months after the debrief and told us she was depressed. This is a common reaction after the release felt during the enactment. We use a Frozen North analogy to describe this experience for participants. If you come into a warm cabin after being out in the frozen wilderness, your fingers and toes will be frozen. As the warmth comes back into them, your fingers and toes begin to burn. It will be very painful.

Marion changed her job shortly after this individual work. She decided that she did not want to work alone in private practice. Instead she took a position in a team that included one member who had been through our program. One year later she was still working there and feeling that she had found her niche. Five years later when we met up with Marion at a conference, she had moved to another resource team of which she was the administrative head. She and her partner had separated. However, Marion said that they were still friends. She was involved with a church and sang in a choir. Marion reported that the path she was on pleased and satisfied her.

Summary

What though the field be lost?
All is not lost ...
—John Milton, "Paradise Lost"

In Marion's enactment, she was able to internalize a sense of self as good and clean. A new positive core belief about the self appeared to replace the earlier negative one. Her childhood had lost the power to constantly hurt or enrage her. In a fundamental way, she was able to have mercy on herself and remove any sense of importance from her perpetrators. She felt that justice had been seen to be done. Her "angel" had been for a moment a physical being who was then taken away from the enactment, as Marion put it, "in my soul". She was able to accept the reality of her family without feeling trapped by it. In fact, she had even retrieved her grandmother as a good object because, hitherto, her grandmother had been lost to her. Marion felt free to move forward in her life, make choices, and not feel constantly dragged down by the undertow of unrealized needs and feelings.

We are particularly grateful to EMDR practitioners for helping us to incorporate safety, resources, core beliefs, and body awareness into the groups. We taught Marion the Butterfly Hug for self-soothing before the enactment began and we incorporated this into the beginning of her enactment so that group members also could use it as necessary. Everybody in our assessments is asked to identify a safe place for ongoing regulation. Yet neither our approach nor EMDR is a "quick fix". They both share intense emotional arousal, cognitive or behavioural change, freedom from distressing or retraumatizing material, and a goal of calm and self-efficacy. Just because a therapist is trained in EMDR does not make them an expert in dissociation. When referring an enactment client to an EMDR practitioner therapists should be sure to find one experienced in working with dissociation. This is part of our emphasis on safety that has made it possible to accomplish reparative work at a very deep level for both leads and, in many cases, witnesses too.

Now that you have followed the treatment for Marion's distress, you can see that our belief is that people don't need to be frozen in their wounds no matter how gigantic the injury. Although we cannot undo the injury, as a result of the public affirmation in the group, these people can feel vindicated in their suffering so that they can drop an assumed identity like "I am a victim." They feel free to go beyond victimization and coping to reclaim a vital life—tending instead to move toward a sense of wholeness versus fragmentation. Some people are actually empowered to help others after being released from their prison cell of pain. They feel a sense of gratitude for life and a generosity toward others returns—the essence of reparation. Although the term "reparation" was used by Melanie Klein (as quoted in Hinshelwood 1991), our emphasis on reparation as an approach to group work is unique. Our groups become an arena where a person can be free to really practise whatever it is they want to learn; they can also practise expressing themselves in different ways. In our next and final chapter, we will illustrate our methodology of reparation.

Reparation: Tears Are Not Enough

People change, and smile: but the agony abides.
You cannot face it steadily, but this thing is sure,
That time is no healer ...

—T.S. Eliot, "Four Quartets: The Dry Salvages"

Tho' much is taken, much abides; and tho'
We are not now that strength which in old days
Moved earth and heaven, that which we are, we are ...

—Tennyson, "Ulysses"

The concept of reparation is the thread that runs through our Therapeutic Enactment work and the purpose behind all enactments. Each lead comes to Therapeutic Enactment in near desperation, thirsty for relief and release of anxiety, immobilization, and emotional deadness. Through Therapeutic Enactment they experience strong emotion, which is the beginning of reparation but only the beginning. Unlike traditional psychodrama, which focuses on catharsis—the release of strong emotion—Therapeutic Enactment stresses that other elements: safety, grieving, and group communion are essential additional components that contribute to renewed vigour and a new sense of self.

What Is Reparation?

The *Oxford English Dictionary* defines "reparation" as "spiritual restoration of a person, renewal, reconciliation, make amends for, compensate for, remedy a loss, set right, revive, salvation, to heal, to return". Similarly, "reconciliation" means "to restore to harmony, to restore to the sacred". These excellent definitions encapsulate the reparation we seek through Therapeutic Enactment. Reparation has other meanings for other cultures and professions. For some it means receiving just desserts, justice, and fairness. Many see reparation as linked to financial compensation for losses. For others, it means going back to the beginning and making everything right again. The South African Truth Commission uses the word "reparation" to mean that victims' stories are heard and they get a chance to confront their accusers.

What does reparation mean for us as we conduct Therapeutic Enactments? Our purpose is to help people restore meaning to their lives, regain parts of the self that were lost, and become free of the trauma that brought them into the group. As you have learned throughout this book, we assist with repairing the self of those who were damaged in childhood or later injured as adults. In groups we bring spiritual restoration for wounded souls and provide opportunities for the setting right of wrongs through witnessing the enactment of the wrong followed by communion in the group.

Reparation after a disastrous injury is not simply about time passing or "getting over it". Even just talking or weeping about it won't be enough. Reparation goes far beyond coping to a sense of renewal. We restore an important part of the self to the "sacred", a task not taken lightly, but an increasingly vivid component in reparation.

Reparation is not symptom reduction, the teaching of coping techniques, or the learning of new behaviours as is often the case using single system approaches to therapy. Rather reparation involves helping the person return to a sense of "wholeness". Following a Therapeutic Enactment participants tend not to see themselves as "victims" or "survivors" because there is usually a significant shift across a number of dimensions, leading to a change in identity that tends to be about the whole person rather than one aspect of the person.

Reparation does not mean restoring that which was lost since we cannot pretend that our injuries have not changed us irreparably. We might think of reparation after a break or a loss in similar terms to repairing a precious vase. Afterward, the vase is still with us but, if we know where to look, we can see the tiny cracks where it was repaired.

Melanie Klein (as quoted in Hinshelwood 1991) states: "The experience of reparation is a tolerance of the loss, and guilt, and responsibility for the loss, while at the same time feeling that not all is lost. The possibility of retrieving the disaster remains a hope." The experiencing and then release in the groups of "taboo" and "shadow" emotions like grief, shame, and rage means that people are able to discharge unwanted feelings and beliefs that have frozen their emotional expressiveness and liveliness. In recognizing their grief about what happened to them, these individuals finally admit to themselves that something dear to them, something important—even irreplaceable—has been lost. Retrieving the disaster means to restore to a damaged sense of self a sense of self-control and forward movement after trauma. In this way, all is not lost. The person can say: "A terrible thing happened to me. Yet I am still alive. I can love and be loved."

Reparation is an important concept because it speaks to the purpose of psychotherapy. Can therapy undo the past? Can it bring back the dead? Can therapy wipe our memories clean of past hurts? Can therapy give us back our innocence? Can it restore us to the way we were before we were injured? Can therapy bring back our youth? The answer to all of the above is: No! Therefore what can we hope for? This is where the idea of reparation is so commanding. Reparation means to repair a break, to accept a loss, to carry on but not to carry on as a ghost. Reparation means to return to a relationship with the self that is uncontaminated by compulsive anxieties attached to past injuries. If a bad thing has happened to us even the thought of it is retraumatizing, so wounding in fact, that we suppress both thoughts of it and feelings of pain. This defensiveness narrows our responsiveness in present encounters as we are always guarding ourselves against further loss and pain. Thus we feel chronically dissatisfied in our interactions with others. Our lives have lost meaning and we feel vulnerable a lot of the time. Therefore what can be repaired? Not the past but its malignant influence on the present. What can be repaired is the hole we sense at our centre where all our energy and hope for the future drains away. What can be repaired is our belief that we are of no worth. What can be repaired is our fractured self, driven relentlessly on to perfectionism in a vain attempt to make up for the sins of our past. Reparation is an accomplishment, however, that cannot be achieved alone. For this we need help and this is where the communal processes involved in Therapeutic Enactment are key.

Five Steps in Individual Reparation: Coming to the Group

Individual reparation follows a path of five steps: (1) coming to the group, (2) accepting, (3) relinquishing faint hope, (4) grieving, and (5) returning to self by reconnecting to the group and extended community.

The first step is coming to prepare for an enactment as this means that the individual has decided to accept that an injury has occurred to them. This is a very big step and actually signifies the beginning of the enactment (even though they are not yet in the group) because the person has stepped away from isolation and despair toward a therapeutic commitment to their own healing. Participants may still be minimizing their pain, denying the extent of the injury, and protecting their parents or others involved right up to the time they step into the circle. However, they have set in motion a process that includes a readiness for acceptance and this is a very positive component of the change process. This acceptance does not fuel despair but leads into the second step.

Accepting the Reality of the Disaster

The second step in reparation is about publicly accepting that things were as bad as they really were. As the enactment proceeds this acceptance becomes real and participants accept that they never got something very important that they wanted and needed when they were little children and they are never going to get it. Bion (1961) uses the expression "the catastrophe of childhood", capturing the fact that the traumas normal people are called upon to integrate in infancy and childhood are truly intolerable. For many people, the disaster began at birth, in the very fact that they were born into this family. The particular family or these parents have never managed to accept or love the individual as they are, in the way that was wanted. For others, a major break with the family developed at adolescence or in youth as the individual chose a path that offended the family value system. Some people come to do enactments because, when very young, they had to cope with the aftermath of the death of a loved one and were prevented from grieving that loss or perhaps even acknowledging it. Many children were not allowed to attend hospitals, funerals, or the deathbeds of parents. This attempt to spare them pain ultimately can hurt them.

For example, one lead had her twin sister knocked down in the street and killed in front of her at three years old. Her sister was taken to the hospital and the child never saw her again. Her parents would not allow her name to be mentioned. The lead "forgot" that she had a twin and suffered all her life from an acute sense of dislocation and grief that she was unable to locate in what she "knew" about her early experience. She felt cut off from her own soul. She thought that there was something terribly important missing in her family but she could not get anyone to tell her the truth. As a result she was distrustful and overly cautious in relationships. It was only in her late fifties when a dying relative reminded her of her twin that she began to understand. Reparation includes the notion of acceptance of the reality of what happened, no matter how painful. The lead believed that her family had never accepted the death of her sister and so pretended that it had never happened; that is, that her sister had never lived. This coping strategy had backfired and left the lead feeling bereft. It is only when the reality of the depleting effects of suffering is fully accepted that reparation is possible. This is difficult for most of us to accept as we are averse to feeling vulnerable, yet the possibility and necessity of reparation is the basic belief behind Therapeutic Enactment.

Some professionals, particularly soldiers and police, are trained to be in charge, respond quickly, and move on to the next crisis immediately. Most professionals have difficulty accepting themselves as "suffering". Treatment for vicarious trauma is a fairly new area of expertise because many professionals have resisted this idea of "suffering". Unwillingness to accept that they were wounded is compounded by "refusal to mourn" and this hardens the heart and takes away resilience. They can be successful at work but depleted emotionally and spiritually. Livingston (1991, p. 42) describes "refusal to mourn" as an attempt to hold onto an illusion by pretending that whatever was lost or died was not lost. If they do not grieve for it then it never happened. These people masochistically make the same mistakes again and again in a fruitless search for the perfect relationship (without mistakes, aging, or dying), or the perfect job or transitional objects such as cars, clothes, houses, or furniture—a concrete and tangible something to hold onto that can be controlled and never changes.

This is also what Alice Miller (1981) means when she refers to many people as "prisoners of childhood". Many people hold themselves back from close relationships because they are afraid of loss, as was the family of the woman who lost her twin. However, a major loss has already happened to them. This loss can never be replaced nor the reality of it ever set aside. Many injured people believe that facing up to these feelings will destroy them. They would rather lick their wounds in private and risk the loneliness that might result.

For example, one lead was the head of his department and a person of notable dignity, learning, and tolerance. He was the only son of immigrants and grew up in poverty with a drunken, abusive father and a sedative-addicted mother. He was a fine-boned, self-contained boy who by the time he was in high school realized that he was homosexual. He was almost completely split off from his earlier family life and led a secret life of addiction and self-destructive sexual encounters with strangers. One year after a suicide attempt he came to do a Therapeutic Enactment. He set up the enactment, choosing group members to play his parents, siblings, and high school buddies. He had them meet with one another and talk about him: what kind of a person he really was, what happened to him, what they knew about him, and what they had done to him. He observed these scenes and saw that he was, in fact, a gifted individual who would have been exceptional no matter what his background. For him the repair was in letting the group see the nightmare of his early life and then discovering that the members accepted and respected him. He was able to recover a sense of personal direction and renewed energy to achieve his life goals.

In addition to their own distress, many people are reluctant to face the fact that a disaster has happened to someone they care about or even someone they do not know but whose story has touched their hearts. We have worked with people who experienced horror in childhood. Unlike terror, horror is not a feeling but a stuck, impaled reaction to something unwatchable. These people witnessed something so dreadful that they were frozen in shock and disbelief. They were unable to call for help. Their minds were paralyzed. They dissociated. Many later describe it as "evil". Often, the horror was about being forced to watch an attack on someone else. After such an experience, the very world of feeling itself may seem unreal and they carry dissociation into their present adult lives as a friendly coping method.

The same dynamics of avoiding acceptance are seen with clients whose injuries did not originate in childhood but result from an assault on the self, a trauma occurring in adulthood. Whether it is people who have been sexually or physically assaulted, soldiers who have been exposed to horror or had their life threatened, or someone on their death bed, the response is the same. People generally move to denial, avoidance, and isolation. The common response is: "Carry on and try to forget." Of course this exacerbates the effect of the trauma even further.

These people want to shield themselves from facing feelings, especially grief. They are ashamed of the fact that they could not control events or they believe they should have been more able or less weak. This is particularly evident in the social conditioning that engenders a "suck it up" attitude in professions like soldiering, policing, or medicine. These people risk putting themselves out of touch emotionally, making intimacy with others impossible. We have had many clients who throw themselves completely into their work, giving it most of their time and skill, but they are not available interpersonally either to their colleagues or to those at home. They are unable to relate to themselves let alone others.

What is important at this second step of reparation is that participants put aside denial and secret shame. They have to accept, during the assessment phase (and later an acknowledgment must happen in the group), that a disaster has occurred to them. This disaster may result from war, the Holocaust, an earthquake, accident, crime, illness, distressing assault, or abusive or damaging relationships. The death or disappearance of a parent, or suicide, depression, and alcoholism may have the same effect, as can a history of slavery, colonialism, or forced emigration for a group of people. To state that they were traumatized is to reveal the self-contempt they harbour in private. To express this in groups is not easy because it brings up dishonour for many people. People are ashamed of their "weakness". They think: "I must be weak or I could not have been hurt like that." Or they believe they deserved to be injured because they were "bad".

Common enactments portray situations in which the self is physically assaulted, or even "damn near killed" by the person or people who are supposed to be nurturing and protecting it. These are experienced as deep betrayals of the natural order of life; that is, life is unfair and there is no justice. Such violations are felt as a profanity and an annihilation of the sacred in life itself. Consequently the inner landscape of the person is laid bare. There is no new growth and a sense of hopelessness is pervasive. Unfortunately, many people are stuck in this landscape, fruitlessly searching for what eluded them in the past.

Relinquishing "Faint Hope"

The third step in reparation takes place when participants begin to relinquish the faint hope that it can be made not to have happened; that is, if they try harder or act better they can change what happened. The witnesses in the group are able to hold the story of the person so that it is no longer theirs alone. This facilitates a true acceptance of what happened without the previous distortion, denial, or rationalization.

Many of us still carry the illusion or "faint hope" that we will wake up one day and realize that we had a better childhood than we actually had. Thus we prevent ourselves from leaving childishness behind. For example, one participant, when asked how she was spending the Thanksgiving holiday, replied that she was having dinner with her (exceptionally abusive) parents. A group member, in a very quiet voice, asked "Why?" The woman burst into tears. For a moment she saw the hopelessness of her quest to have different parents than the ones she actually had. We told her the story of the poisoned well: no matter how many times you change the bucket or rope, no matter how many hopes you have, or how thirsty you are, the water will always make you sick.

Many people continue to place themselves in distressing family situations, often through weekly dinners, phone calls, or meetings, in the "faint hope" that one day the abuse will magically change to nurturing and appreciation. This faint hope can result in surreal events. For example, one lead told how she had invited her estranged mother for Christmas holidays against her own "red flag" feelings that the visit would be another disaster. Her mother arrived and instantly began criticizing the lead for being a bad housekeeper, home decorator, wife, and parent. Her faint hope that things would be different faded quickly in their first hour together; then she felt trapped. She began to accept extra shifts at work to get out of the house during her mother's visit. One day the lead was sitting at work in despair when she suddenly realized that her mother was at home alone with the lead's toddler daughter. She got out of work and went home to confront her mother, realizing that she could get out of the trap for her daughter but not for herself. This lead knew that the abuse she suffered in childhood as well as currently made a relationship with her mother impossible. However, until her daughter was born she had behaved as if this reality was not real.

Hanging on to "faint hope" means a "refusal to mourn". Many adults do not realize that they are yearning for the ability to accept and nurture the vulnerable or shamed parts of the self. They have projected this desire outward and tried to find a partner or someone else to do it. They suffer from terminal disappointment and resentment because their unaware significant others are unable to replace what was taken from them. In one of the enactments a woman, who had been treated very badly by her mother and wanted to be angry with her, found herself weeping and asking her mother why she was unable to love her. Afterward, she commented that she was surprised by the compassionate conclusion to her enactment, as she did not really want to forgive her mother. She realized finally during the debriefing that it was her own little child spirit inside that she was forgiving and embracing. She had been hooked by her belief that she had to get that (impossible) nurturing from her mother or several unsatisfactory mother substitutes in her adult life.

Paradoxically, real hope for the future returns when "faint hope" is discarded. When a lead is able to accept reality, then they are free from the trap of guilt, helplessness, and shame. They are able to understand that a disaster happened but they themselves are not a disaster. The individual's essential wholeness in the face of suffering is the goodness that survives. Often, this realization leads the person into grieving for what was taken from them.

Grieving

Grieving is the fourth step in the reparation process. Complete acceptance of what happened enables two very important processes to occur: the first process is the urge or freedom to move forward into action—no longer frozen or stuck—and to begin the enactment by speaking, doing, and showing. Leads report that it feels as if a momentum has been building up in the earlier three steps and a sense of urgency now propels them into enactment. The second process, so crucial to the therapeutic endeavour, is the release of emotional expression (catharsis), a letting go of what has been held inside for so long. There are many forms of this, including raging, yelling, screaming in agony, keening, moaning, or wailing. The dominant expression is that of grieving.

High levels of self-disclosure and expression clear the way to reparation. The very act of public grieving can release the individual from helplessness. The group also is released from the immobilization that the contemplation of unfixable suffering evokes. The enactment may arouse anger, disappointment, humiliation, rage, or desire for revenge. The lead may begin to express these feelings and yet give over to cleansing grief. It is possible actually to see the turn toward the "reparative moment" as the individual stops and almost simultaneously moves in different, more productive directions. A reparative moment for one woman whose mother was a lifelong alcoholic came as she was in the middle of pleading with her mother, asking her to stop drinking and pay attention to her daughter. Suddenly, she stopped and said: "I'm doing it again! I'm begging for love." At this she wept and was able to let go of her need to have a different past than the one she had.

We worked with one man who wanted to exact revenge on a sadistic bully at his workplace. He enacted a scenario in which he forced the person to endure what he had endured: poking fun, belittling, and throwing things at him. He said he felt released as soon as that was done and felt no need to prolong the revenge or gloat over it. His next move in the enactment was to go over and speak to the person in the role of his estranged wife in a very gentle way even though he had been very angry with her. At this he broke down and said he finally understood how much his sadistic father's treatment of him influenced his relationships with others. He often felt at the mercy of others when they tried to hold him, however mildly, to account. He would feel vulnerable and attacked and respond sadistically. Then, when people would either attack back or run away in return, he felt hurt and misunderstood. This behaviour pattern had broken up his marriage and contributed to many other unsatisfactory relationships.

The goal in reparation therefore is not just emotional expression or catharsis. Reparation means a change in the relationship to the self. Many people are stuck in self-contempt because of the enormity of their vengeful desires toward the ones who wounded them. They are surprised that, in speaking the truth about what happened to them, they are not moved to seek revenge or even justice.

A woman in one of our groups had been in a foster home and been scapegoated and tormented by the foster mother. In planning her enactment she said she wanted to enact the abusive scenarios and then force the foster mother to eat the unpalatable food and be locked in a dark closet for twenty-four hours, just as she had been treated. As part of her enactment, she was able to choose "good-enough parents" from the group to replace her real parents, who had consigned her to the foster home. She asked these symbolic "good-enough parents" to come with her and support her as she went to punish her foster mother. When she got into the scenario, she told her foster mother what she was going to do to her. As she said the words, she realized that she was finally free of the woman. Instead of punishing her she had her stand in front of the group and the members, one by one, came up to face her. They told the foster mother what she had done to a helpless little child and they expressed their outrage. When the lead heard this, she felt vindicated and wept. Speaking in a role reversal with her "good-enough" mother she heard herself utter the sentence: "You are a good person." This was reparative for her because, as she said in the debrief, she had never felt she was a good person. Now she believed herself to be good.

In this example, reparation restored to the imagination the idea of the good-enough, nurturing parent. With reparation one retrieves the sense that one is at home in the universe, that the universe is nurturing, that one can love and be loved, that one is in the right place, and that one's life has intrinsic meaning. As a result, the person can feel tenderness instead of self-contempt.

In fact, we believe that a large part of establishing the safety necessary for reparation to occur in Therapeutic Enactment groups is to install the therapists as the "good-enough" parents (Winnicott 1965) from whom the group members, and particularly the leads, can separate safely and with mutual respect. Bion (1961) believed that this individuation was a necessary step in evolving from dependency, which perpetuates feelings of guilt about greed because the individual is being greedy in demanding more than his or her fair share of parental care. If members get stuck in "dependency", then the group will be unable to fulfill its purpose.

Another example of the way in which angry confrontation can turn to insight and ultimately self-regard if grieving returns is seen in a lead who was engaged to be married but was suddenly dumped by her fiancé when he left a message on her answering machine. He quickly married someone else and she never heard from him again. The group referred to him as the "Daemon Lover". This lead began her enactment planning to take her fiancé to task. Her emerging sense of outrage served as an antidote to her humiliation. She had felt annihilated by him. His actions had shamed her, causing her to withdraw from her community. Consequently, repair had to be done in public. She wanted to "stand up to him", and began by saying: "You betrayed me. You humiliated me and broke my heart. How could you say you loved me and do such awful things?" She stopped then and the therapist stood next to her, asking: "What's happening now?" She wept and replied: "I realize that I was never really in this relationship. I never let him get close to me. I was pretending to be the daughter my mother wanted who has a big white wedding to a handsome man." The therapist said: "Okay. Say that to him now." Eventually, she was able to say to her former fiancé that, even though she had been unfair to him, the way he had ended the relationship was wrong and he had no right to do that. Then she went to speak to her mother. The enactment ended after she told her mother that she was finished being a little girl living out her mother's dreams. She was going to live her own life on her own terms from that moment on. She was no longer hooked into her impossible desire to undo the past (we call it "trying to get juice out of a dry orange"). The freeing of her blocked grief allowed her to have compassion on herself at the same time as resurrecting her clarity and decisiveness.

Enactments with angry confrontations re-emphasize for us the necessity of taking care of the safety of the group as a whole. As the leads grieve, so do the members of the group. "Toxic grief" (Bradshaw 1988) occurs when the process is blocked or diverted into rage or blaming. Sometimes in the middle of an enactment the lead may be furiously raging at someone whom others in the group might want to "protect". These witnesses have momentarily stepped out of the symbolic or imaginary reality where everyday concerns are set aside for the purposes of ultimate reparation. Or some witnesses, after difficult enactments when they come back to the "real" from the "symbolic" or "imaginary" modality, remember that they have views, beliefs, and values about certain controversial topics and this has to be handled in the groups with open discussion. The grieving cannot be blocked by the interference of members' anger, politics, or attributions.

Many enactment participants for years have carried emotional pain linked to some past dishonourable act. They are worn down by their attempts to appease the guilt gods within, the ones whose despicable voices are heard every day: "You're not good enough." "No one will ever love you." "You will always be alone."

A woman who came to see us was in terrible spiritual despair because of an abortion she had had some years previously. She was a skilled and loved professional. Her colleagues consulted her with respect. She was much admired as a member of her ethnic community and as a role model for young women. Regardless, she thought she was a fraud. She was uncertain that what she had done could ever be forgiven (by God). Certainly, she was unable to forgive herself. She was sinking into depression and her relationship with her current partner was in jeopardy. She asked us if we had ever performed an enactment that dealt with a worse sin.

Clearly this kind of enactment involved subject matter that was extremely difficult and complex. Such enactments should be attempted only with extreme caution, by highly skilled therapists, in well-established, cohesive groups as some therapists and group members will have difficulty with confrontational topics like abortion, torture, and so on. However when pursuing the relief of suffering, therapists focus on the suffering, not on judgments about the rightness or wrongness of the topic of the suffering.

In the assessment, we asked her what reparation would look like to her? She said that if God would forgive her she would be able to go on. However, she said that she deserved to be punished for what she had done and this should be part of the enactment too. We were drawn into her suffering and dismayed by her longing for punishment. She designed the scenario so that she would give up her child and then she would be taken to speak to God. She chose a double and people to play a close friend and the baby's father, who was a married colleague. We also had roles for a doctor and a nurse. We kept the assessment short because this was such a highly charged scene and we did not want the catharsis to happen during our planning session. The lead chose to do her enactment a week later on the last (third) day of a workshop. Her resources were two close friends, a man and a woman, who attended with her, an object from her childhood, her prayer book, and her belief in a compassionate God.

We co-created the scene in a clinic room where the abortion was to take place. We had her get up on the table ready for the procedure. Then the doctor and the nurse came in. The father was standing off to one side while the double stood at the head of the table. We noticed again, as we have in many of our extremely intense enactments, that this lead did not use her double to enact the scene first. She wanted to do it for herself. As soon as the medical personnel approached she froze and then burst into loud sobs. The therapist asked her if there was anything she wanted to say to them. She said she wanted to go directly to speak to God.

This lead carried a huge burden of guilt and grief that was blocked from expression by frozen feelings. Her negative cognition was: "I don't deserve to live." Because of her spiritual beliefs she could not commit suicide so she cut off her life energy instead. She needed to stand in front of her family or church and tell them what she had done. Since that was impossible, she chose a setting where she could express the truth in safety. The positive cognition she wanted was: "I have suffered enough. I can live again."

She addressed God who relieved her of her "sin". Then she wanted to speak to her baby. She chose a person from the group to play the role and sat on the floor holding her while telling her what had happened and saying goodbye.

Reparation in this case was like lancing a boil. After the infection of guilt was lanced in public, this lead's grief was released. She experienced this release as agonizing and her suffering evoked many mirroring responses in the group. Yet afterward she felt a great deal of pressure had been lifted from her. She said she felt tired but free of pain for the first time in years. However, the group had to be debriefed, as many participants were sobbing or frozen in place. We came together in a grieving circle before going to debrief. After debriefing, there was a spontaneous release of joy among the group.

When difficult painful truths are confronted and grief is experienced and acknowledged in the group, participants experience a form of bonding that is characterized by intense feelings of affection and connection with others. When the process involves confronting social taboos the resulting reparation is truly cathartic. It is always amazing in groups how the pain of grieving, once experienced and expressed, is followed by joy and laughter, even singing and dancing. When others witness our experience with respect, it causes us to change how we view our own experience and ourselves. Reparation is accompanied by a sense in people that there is something bigger than expected here, a spiritual component that illuminates and guides the life and the therapeutic work. Many people comment that they believe that they were spared "for a purpose". They feel a desire to tell their stories and help others. Shame and self-torment change to self-acceptance and relief.

When grieving is unblocked it can be released into mourning. In Therapeutic Enactment groups members learn to do "wu kei" (eat bitterness), a concept that we borrowed from one of our Chinese clients. "Eating bitterness" means to have the strength to truly accept the pain of existence deep inside oneself. This gives meaning to suffering and makes room for mourning. It is similar to Herman's discussion of "tasting fear" (1992, p. 198). To taste fear means to understand (not minimize, deny, or dissociate from) the difficulties of life's tasks but to feel strong enough to master them. In addition, Herman stresses that recovery is never complete. Traumatized people are serving life sentences in a sense. They cannot go back to being people who have never been traumatized. But they can heal and retrieve the lost joy in living.

It is important to distinguish between grieving and mourning. Grieving is difficult since grieving contains anger and resistance and appears to produce helplessness. However, it must be done and once the grief is released, people find that in reality, they feel better, stronger, more relaxed. They have accepted what happened to them and are ready to move into mourning. Mourning includes an acceptance of the reality of the loss and also a commitment to get on with living. Grief is a reaction to an outside blow. Mourning is an internal state affirming continued life in spite of sorrow.

The role of mourning is to convey dignity to death and to affirm life. Mourning is developmental. It requires the passage of time. Grieving precedes mourning because grief is not about acceptance. It is about loss, rage, hatred, struggle, and agony. Mourning is an acceptance of the reality of life itself as both tragedy and survival. We cannot heal without going through a period of mourning. Time passes and loved ones die. Dreams die. However, new life grows and we go on. We take our losses deeply inside and we accept that, although we have lost something important, all is not lost. Mourning allows concern to return after the narcissism and emptying out of grief. The person who mourns has re-established their bond with the external world and therefore with life itself. We hear leads give big sighs at the end of their enactment and say: "Yes, that's the way it was." A short time later we see them laughing and being playful with others.

Many people who come to do enactments appear depressed. They say they are mourning because they never had the childhood they wanted or the parents they deserved. Some mourn because they never had a childhood at all. Many people mourn because they have never been loved for who they really are. In order to survive in their particular families, they have developed a "false self" (Kohut 1977). This false self may have been so successful that now they do

not know if anyone can see them truly. Others have ⎡
mourning as their lifetime's reality: "I mourn because I e:
help them retrace their steps to the point of the disaster
They can return to acceptance and mourning without bl
necessary vitality from the rest of their lives.

Thus the individual moves to the fifth step, coming ba
a changed relationship to self and with the members. In 1 ......ng to oneself
and restoring contact with others the participant comes back into their body,
allows feelings to happen, sets boundaries, takes charge, and faces reality. Life
energy returns and relationships with other people are no longer felt as extra
burdens in already overburdened lives. The individual is able to reconnect with
others in the group and, by extension, with self, family, colleagues, and society.
At this point the change process begins to include the cognitive self-reflective
component, not present to any extent during the experiencing and doing part
of the enactment. The three components of experience, emotion, and thought
begin to integrate at this point. Often, as a result of having done the enactment
in the group, people feel more connected to something larger than themselves,
or larger than the group, a divine spirit or sense of meaningfulness in life.

Returning to Self and Moving Out into the World

The final stage of returning to self and moving out into the world is a major piece
of the process of Therapeutic Enactment in groups that can be very demanding.
During the closure phase, the enactment groups assist the individual to focus
on the relationships in their "real" lives. They carry the learning, insights, and
intentionality with them. It is important to reinforce that participants are not
exchanging the immobilization of trauma for that of dependence on the group.
All relationships must entertain the notion, in fact, the reality, of separation, loss,
and grief. In the groups, members are learning to allow this truth to revitalize
their relationships rather than kill them emotionally. When the participants
return to the world, they want to go with energy and anticipation.

The transition between the intensity of the group and the familiar habits of
the workaday world can be tricky. We try to normalize some of the emotional
reactions often encountered and prepare participants for misunderstandings,
loss, emotional ups and downs, and sometimes even chaos and "positive
disintegration". Many group members suffer from reactive depressions in the
days after the group ends. Some report feeling disoriented or anxious. Some,
like Marion, have delayed reactions. Others, like Darren, make major changes
in their lives. Most people report that the journey back to their "real" lives is
demanding. We have heard stories from participants who attend the residential
weekend and experience social contacts on the outside as troublingly superficial
and false. We alert participants to be aware of these possibilities and to look
after themselves. We encourage group members not to travel to and from the
workshop alone but to car pool so that everyone has company on the journey
home. Participants are given a list of possible reactions or questions that they

anticipate from others following the workshop upon going home. We include possible ways to respond effectively to these reactions to help ease the re-entry experience so common after such intense personal work. Finally, if group members agree, we provide a list of participants so that people can contact each other as part of their own follow up.

Reparation continues during the time following the group. Insight and awareness is triggered by reactions outside in the "real" world, as significant others such as family, friends, or colleagues respond to the different ways in which participants present themselves. Reparation is consolidated when the client checks in with an individual therapist following the enactment, an essential step for most participants as Therapeutic Enactment is viewed as an adjunct to ongoing therapy and not as a substitute for it.

Herman (1992) describes four steps in recovery from trauma: (1) safety, (2) remembering, (3) grieving, and (4) reconnecting. Reconnecting is a psychological, political, ethical, and social process. It is about reconditioning and mastery. Herman calls it restoring "desire and initiative". This includes a renewed ability to play and use one's imagination. Reconnection includes accepting reality and speaking the truth.

The feelings of separation and guilt that trouble people who have suffered unresolved psychological injuries are difficult to integrate personally, socially, and professionally, because they are not talked about openly. To admit to suffering is an attempt to bring oneself back to a shared sense of reality with others, a necessary step in the repair of traumatization. Herman (1992) states: "As each survivor shares her unique story, the group provides a profound experience of universality. The group bears witness to the survivor's testimony, giving it social as well as personal meaning" (p. 221).

We have read about the work of Archbishop Tutu and the South African Truth and Reconciliation Commission (Krog 1998), which has encouraged acts of peace and reparation in their traumatized community. Their process squarely confronts denial and minimization and puts truth above other virtues. The public hearings promote confession, atonement, and forgiveness. They call this process restorative justice, which focuses on restoring the personhood that was damaged or lost. Tutu emphasizes that healing means restoring memory and a public validation that "You are not crazy. Something seriously evil happened to you."

Addressing one's injuries in public means wrestling with the implications of trust and intimacy when really all that wounded people tend to do is helplessly isolate themselves. Just as reparation includes reclaiming one's world in terms of meaning, reconnection means that one has to learn, or at least remember, how to communicate. Many injured people have become phobic about discussing personal hurts or admitting to pain. Highly functioning people come to the groups to "help others" but deny that they are in pain. They say that their childhoods were happy and they were never abused. Yet these same people, when they see that they are in a safe group, begin to talk of events back home. They describe being disciplined with wooden spoons, leather belts, garden tools, soap in the mouth, enemas, two-by-fours, and even guns. Their coping strategies have involved putting these disturbing memories out of their consciousness and minimizing their long-term impact and importance.

In order to survive they had to be strong and so anything that makes them feel weak comes close to annihilation in their minds. They take a false pride in their own ability to tolerate injury. Many individuals have enshrined independence as a high value. They fear dependency, and believe that it is better to keep their worries to themselves and get used to being alone. They may have grown up in households where the family members were unable to express their feelings. Or, simply, they may never have learned the positive consequences in terms of delight in intimacy that result from relationships in which the participants share their innermost natures with each other and do not seek to wound. Sadly, they may believe that emotional loneliness is just the way things are.

These people have become "ghosts". In fact, some people in the groups initially appear so drawn and ephemeral that their presence is hardly felt. The transformation in the face, body, voice, and expression in these people after an enactment is so dramatic that group members will comment in astonishment and appreciation. One man, a driven, high-achieving professional, realized during his enactment that he was, to all intents and purposes, an orphan. His parents had not planned for him. They adored his elder brother. He believed that his parents neither understood nor approved of him. In his enactment, he was assigned good-enough alternative parents with whom he bonded immediately. He said that his dream was to go swimming with his new parents. The three of them went to the lake outside the group room and jumped in! When they had dried off and rejoined the group, the change in this person was so remarkable that the group was dumbstruck. Six weeks later, at the workshop debriefing, the change was still noteworthy. Someone had taken photographs while the three were swimming in the lake. These photos were compared later with previous photos from the lead's workplace. He looked like a different person.

Havens (1986), while describing ways in which humans protect themselves from potential predators, comments: "Many productive, apparently normal people do not have much interest in others, not even their spouses and children. The contacts they form . . . are polite, intellectual, or manipulative, but without fire and blood" (p. 12). These people are invisible or "absent". In a very fundamental way, they have lost their past, present, and future and thus their vitality. They are unable to respond to others in ways that promote intimacy. Yet the Latin roots of "respond" are "to pledge or promise". Responsibility is linked to the spiritual, the serious, and the sacred. The one who is unable to respond, therefore, is cut off from both their own depth and connection with the other, and from communion with life itself. Reparation for them includes reclaiming the meaning of their lives in a way that validates the reality and substance of their suffering. For this connection to occur, the group has to form what Hinshelwood called "reflective space", "that aspect of the group in which members link emotionally and from which the personalities can emerge" (1994, p. 96).

As mentioned earlier, forming a safe space means that group members can be protected from attack and the group, from self-destruction. Members have to be seen and heard, both nurtured and challenged in the group. For example, the therapists must be skilled at gently encouraging group members to speak into the group. People can begin with one word—their name perhaps—then one short sentence or acknowledgment. Group members can "pass" when they are not ready or able to speak yet. However, they need to be supported to "show up" and take their place in the group as continued "absence" would raise the group's anxiety about their possible judgments, contempt, or ability to attack.

The existential psychotherapists, including Fromm (1956) and Rollo May (1967), stress connection as a basic human need. As Fromm puts it: "The experience of separateness arouses anxiety; it is, indeed, the source of all anxiety. Being separate means being cut off, without any capacity to use my human powers" (p. 7). This kind of separateness brings up fears of being separated from a sense of the meaning of life. Group members have to feel connected not just to one another but to a universal humanity and transcendental spirit in the groups.

Closure of the group and going "back to the world" is the trickiest part of this therapeutic work, as leaving the group is like experiencing another death. In this sense, all successful therapeutic processes are leave-taking rituals because it is important to prevent retraumatization as a reaction to grief and loss. Separating from the group as it closes may bring up inchoate fears of separation and disconnection that will prevent members from leaving cleanly. No matter what illumination and communion has been experienced in the group, whatever learning has taken place, people still have to be able to adjust to their home circumstances when the group ends.

Group members who return from the highly charged communion of the group to their personal and work worlds have to become, as Campbell ([1949] 1968) named it, the "Master of the Two Worlds" and this allows them "freedom to live". The two worlds are (1) the divine/symbolic and (2) the human/real. Campbell states: "This brings us to the final crisis of the round, to which the whole miraculous excursion has been but a prelude—that, namely, of the paradoxical, supremely difficult threshold-crossing of the hero's return from the mystic realm into the land of common day. He has yet to . . . take the return blow of reasonable queries, hard resentment, and good people at a loss to comprehend" (p. 216). The Master-of-the-Two-Worlds is able to use the wisdom of the depths to transform their work-in-the-world. They are not separated from their own soul. Their ability to make contact with the sacred has not been drained away by their contact with daily, practical concerns.

Those who are trying to speak the truth, find the meaning of what happened to them, and heal are working in the symbolic realm. To literalize their memories, or confuse this with attempting to change the past, or even to assume that there will be an exact transition from the enactment to their "real" lives would be to reinforce a completely erroneous, narrow, superficial, black-or-white polarized conceptualization of their psychological being. Traumatized individuals tend to go over and over the original hurt. Therefore, there has to be a sense of moving through and not becoming trapped in constant retraumatization. In order not to be trapped as either victim or revenge-perpetrator in an endless tit-for-tat, participants need to move to a middle way in which they are free to live their lives fully without tormenting themselves endlessly with fantasies of rage and revenge. Individuals have to wake up and grow up. Some people refer to the return of concern for others as "awakening from a spell". In order to break the spell, someone has to come who can move in and out of the spell, or move "between the two worlds" without becoming frozen.

The groups have to be hospitable to members' journeying through their own darkness in order to reclaim liveliness through integrating their instincts and the shadow into their everyday responsiveness. However, to complete the adventure, the individual must "survive the impact of the world". Two things typically occur following repair work. Group members have experienced a sense of mastery and they want to begin to build confidence on this. The world and the people in it look different now because group members have been in an altered state of consciousness, the fall-out of which changes perceptions of self in a positive direction and makes others less contradictory and difficult to deal with. By acting and believing differently in the world, people find that others respond differently as well. If reparation is to be more than a mist, people must have the flexibility to perform the demands of their various roles in the lives they have made for themselves. However, they also have to be able to stay in touch with their own feelings as well as maintaining deeper connections with valued others.

Summary

So we beat on, boats against the current,
borne back ceaselessly into the past.
—Francis Scott Fitzgerald, *The Great Gatsby*

What, now, is the result of the miraculous passage and return?
—Joseph Campbell

In this our final chapter we have discussed our key concept of reparation—the goal of Therapeutic Enactments. Enactments are designed to assist people through the steps toward reparation—acceptance of injury, relinquishing faint hope, facing reality, grieving, and moving on with life. Our hopes of designing a method that would fill the gap in group therapeutic approaches have been realized tenfold thanks to the courage and integrity of our participants. We are grateful to all of them.

The model that we have developed allows participants to risk embodying the fullness of their life experiences, regenerate their healing capacities, support their natural desire for wholeness, and experience being witnessed and unconditionally honoured by the group members. Therapeutic Enactment is fundamentally about creating the optimal conditions in which healing of the individual can occur in community, with community, and ultimately for community.

References

Adler, Alfred. 1925. *Individual Psychology*. Tatowa, NJ: Littlefield, Adams and Co.

Adler, Alfred. 1938. *Social Interest: A Challenge to Mankind*. John Linton and Richard Vaughan, trans. London: Faber and Faber.

Amundson, Norman E., William A. Borgen, Marvin J. Westwood, and Diane E. Pollard. 1989. *Employment Groups: The Counselling Connection*. Toronto: Lugus Press.

Bandura, A. 1986. *Social Foundations of Thought and Action: A Social Cognitive Theory*. Upper Saddle River, NJ: Prentice Hall.

Baum, S. 1994. Change processes in psychodrama. Unpublished master's thesis, University of British Columbia, Vancouver, BC, Canada

Bion, Wilfred R. 1961. *Experiences in Groups and Other Papers*. London: Tavistock.

Black, Timothy. 2003. Individual narratives of change in therapeutic enactment. Unpublished doctoral thesis, University of British Columbia, Vancouver, BC, Canada

Blatner, Adam. 1996. *Acting-in: Practical Applications of Psychodramatic Methods*, 3rd ed. New York: Springer.

Bly, Robert. 1981. *The Man in the Black Coat Turns*. New York: Viking Penguin.

Bly, Robert. 1988. *A Little Book on the Human Shadow*. San Francisco: Harper

Bly, Robert, and Marion Woodman. 1998. *The Maiden King: The Reunion of Masculine and Feminine*. New York: Henry Holt.

Bradshaw, John. 1988. *Healing the Shame that Binds You*. Deerfield Beach, FA: Health Communications.

Bragan, Kenneth. 1996. *Self and Spirit in the Therapeutic Relationship*. London: Routledge.

Braun, Bennett G. 1988. The BASK model of dissociation. *Dissociation* 1(1): 4–23. Annotated by Noel Clark.

Briere, John. 1996. *Therapy for Adults Molested as Children: Beyond Survival*. New York: Springer.

Brooks, Dale T. 1998. The Meaning of Change through Therapeutic Enactment in Psychodrama. Ph.D. dissertation, University of British Columbia.

Bruning, Roger, Gregg Schraw, and Royce Ronning. 1999. *Cognitive Psychology and Instruction*, 3rd ed. Upper Saddle River, NJ: Prentice Hall.

Buber, Martin. 1965. *The Knowledge of Man: Selected Essays*. Edited by Maurice Friedman. London: George Allen and Unwin.

Buell, A. 1995. Experience of significant change for psychodrama audience members. Unpublished master's thesis, University of British Columbia.

Campbell, Joseph. [1949] 1968. *The Hero with a Thousand Faces*. Bollingen series. Reprinted Princeton University Press.

Dabrowski, Kazimierz. 1964. *Positive Disintegration*. Boston: Little Brown.

Davis, Madeleine, and David Wallbridge, eds. [1981] 1987. *Boundary and Space: An Introduction to the Work of D.W. Winnicott*. Reprinted New York: Brunner/Mazel.

Dayton, Tian. 1994. *The Drama Within: Psychodrama and Experiential Therapy*. Deerfield Beach, FA: Health Communications.

Dayton, Tian. 1997. *Heartwounds: The Impact of Unresolved Trauma and Grief on Relationships*. Deerfield Beach, FA: Health Communications.

Diagnostic and Statistical Manual of Mental Disorders, 4th ed. (DSM-IV). 1994. Washington: American Psychiatric Association.

Donigan, Jeremiah, and Richard Malnati. 1987. *Critical Incidents in Group Therapy*. Monterey, CA: Brooks/Cole Pub.

Edelson, Marshall, and David N. Berg. 1999. *Rediscovering Groups*. London and Philadelphia: Jessica Kingsley Publications.

EMDR Advanced Training Manual. 2003. British Columbia School of Professional Psychology.

Femi, Isoke, and Donald Rothberg. 1997. Unlearning oppression: healing racism, healing violence. *ReVision* 20(2): 18–24.

Figley, Charles R. 1995. *Compassion Fatigue: Coping with Secondary Traumatic Stress Disorder in Those Who Treat the Traumatized*. New York: Brunner/Mazel.

Firestone, Robert W. 1985. *The Fantasy Bond: Structure of Psychological Defenses*. New York: Human Sciences Press.

Ford, Donald H., and Hugh B. Urban. 1998. *Contemporary Models of Psychotherapy: A Comparative Analysis*, 2nd ed. New York: John Wiley and Sons.

Freyd, Jennifer J. 1996. *Betrayal Trauma: The Logic of Forgetting Childhood Abuse*. Cambridge, MA: Harvard University Press.

Fromm, Erich. 1956. *The Art of Loving*. New York: Harper and Row.

Gilligan, Carol, Rogers, Annie G. and Tolman, Deborah L. eds. 1991. *Women, Girls, and Psychotherapy: Reframing Resistance*. Binghamton, NY: Harrington Park Press.

Gilligan, Stephen. 1997. *The Courage to Love*. New York and London: W.W. Norton and Co.

Gladding, Samuel T. 1999. *Group Work: A Counselling Specialty*, 3rd ed. Upper Saddle River, NJ: Prentice Hall.

Gladding, Samuel T. 2002. *Group Work: A Counselling Specialty*, 4th ed. Upper Saddle River, NJ: Prentice Hall.

Grotstein, James S. 2000. Some considerations of "hate" and a reconsideration of the death instinct. *Psychoanalytic Inquiry* 20(3): 463–80.

Hahn, William K. 1994. Resolving shame in group psychotherapy. *International Journal of Group Psychotherapy* 44(4): 449–61.

Hammerschlag, Carl A., and Howard D. Silverman. 1998. *Healing Ceremonies: Creating Personal Rituals for Spiritual, Emotional, Physical, and Mental Health*. New York: Perigee Books.

Hartung, John G., and Michael D. Galvin. 2003. *Energy, Psychology and EMDR: Combining Forces to Optimize Treatment*. New York: W.W. Norton and Co.

Havens, Leston. 1986. *Making Contact: Use of Language in Psychotherapy*. Cambridge, MA: Harvard University Press.

Herman, Judith. 1992. *Trauma and Recovery: The Aftermath of Violence from Domestic Abuse to Political Terror*. New York: Basic Books.

Hillman, James. 1972. *The Myth of Analysis: Three Essays in Archetypal Psychology*. New York: Harper Torchbooks.

Hinshelwood, Robert D. 1991. *A Dictionary of Kleinian Thought*, 2nd ed. Northvale, NJ: J. Aronson.

Hollis, James. 1994. *Under Saturn's Shadow: The Wounding and Healing of Men*. Toronto: Inner City Books.

Janoff-Bulman, Ronnie. 1985. The aftermath of victimization: Rebuilding shattered assumptions. In *Trauma and Its Wake*. C.R. Figley, ed. New York: Brunner/Mazel, pp. 15–33.

Jarero, Ignacio, Lucy Artigas, Magaly Mauer, Tere Lopez Cano, and Nicte Alcala. 1999. *Children's Post Traumatic Stress after Natural Disasters: Integrative Treatment Protocols*. Poster presented at the annual meeting of the International Society for Traumatic Stress Studies, Miami, FL. Also available at www.emdrportal.com.

Jilek, Wolfgang G. 1982. *Indian Healing: Shamanic Ceremonialism in the Pacific Northwest Today*. Surrey, BC: Hancock House.

Jung, Carl G. 1931. *The Practice of Psychotherapy*. Princeton University Press.

Kaufman, Gershon. 1985. *Shame: The Power of Caring*. Cambridge, MA: Schenkman Books.

Kearney, Michael. 1996. *Mortally Wounded: Stories of Soul Pain, Death, and Healing*. New York: Scribner.

Keats, Patrice. 2000. Using masks for trauma recovery: A self-narrative. Unpublished master's thesis, University of British Columbia., Vancouver, BC, Canada

Keats, Patrice. 2003. Vicariously witnessing trauma: Narratives of meaning and experience. Unpublished doctoral thesis, University of British Columbia, Vancouver, BC, Canada

Kellerman, Peter J. 1987. Outcome research in classical psychodrama. *Small Group Behaviour* 18: 459–69.

Klein, Melanie. 1948. *Contributions to Psychoanalysis*, 1921–1945. London: Hogarth Press.

Knaster, Mirka. 1996. *Discovering the Body's Wisdom*. New York: Bantam Books.

Kohut, Heinz. 1971. *The Analysis of the Self*. New York: International Universities Press.

Kohut, Heinz. 1977. *The Restoration of the Self*. New York: International Universities Press.

Kohut, Heinz. 1984. *How Does Analysis Cure?* Arthur Goldberg, ed. University of Chicago Press.

Korn, Deborah L., and Andrew M. Leeds. 2002. Preliminary evidence of efficacy for EMDR resource development and installation in the stabilization phase of treatment of complex posttraumatic stress disorder. *Journal of Clinical Psychology* 58(12): 1465–87.

Krog, Antjie. 1998. *Country of My Skull: Guilt, Sorrow, and the Limits of Forgiveness in the New South Africa*. Johannesburg: Random House South Africa.

Lacan, Jacques. [1966] 1977. *Ecrits: A Selection*. A. Sheridan, trans. London: Tavistock.

Leveton, Eva. 1992. *A Clinician's Guide to Psychodrama*. New York: Springer.

Levine, Peter A., with Ann Frederick. 1997. *Waking the Tiger: Healing Trauma*. Berkeley, CA: North Atlantic Books.

Levine, Stephen K. 2000. *Mimetic Wounds: Trauma and Drama in Psychotherapy and the Arts*. University of Chicago Press.

Linehan, Marsha M. 1993. *Skills Training Manual for Treating Borderline Personality Disorder*. New York and London: Guilford Press.

Livingston, Martin S. 1991. *Near and Far: Closeness and Distance in Psychotherapy*. New York: Rivercross Publishing.

MacIntyre, Alasdair. 1984. *After Virtue: A Study in Moral Theory*, 2nd ed. Notre Dame, IN: University of Notre Dame Press.

Macmurray, John. 1995. *The Self as Agent*. Originally published as *The Form of the Personal*, vol. 1. Gifford lecture, 1953. London: Faber and Faber, 1957.

Malcus, Lawrence. 1995. Indirect scapegoating via projective identification and the mother group. *International Journal of Group Psychotherapy* 45(1): 55–71.

Mannoni, Maud. 1970. *The Child, His Illness, and Others*. New York: Penguin Books.

May, Rollo. 1967. *Psychology and the Human Dilemma*. New York: D. Van Nostrand.

Merck Manual of Medical Information, The. 1997. M.D. Berkow, Mark H. Beers, and Andrew J. Fletcher, eds. Whitehouse Station, NJ: Merck and Co. Ltd.

Miller, Alice. 1981. *The Drama of the Gifted Child and the Search for the True Self*. Ruth Ward, trans. Originally published as *Prisoners of Childhood*. New York: Basic Books, 1981. Revised and updated, 1996.

Mitchell, Stephen A., and Margaret J. Black. 1995. *Freud and Beyond*. New York: Basic Books.

Moore, Thomas. 1992. *Care of the Soul: A Guide for Cultivating Depth and Sacredness in Everyday Life*. New York: HarperCollins.

Moreno, Jacob L. 1947. *Theater of Spontaneity: An Introduction to Psychodrama*. New York: Beacon House.

Moreno, Jacob L. 1959. Psychodrama. In *American Handbook of Psychiatry*, vol. 2. Silvano Arieti, ed. New York: Basic Books, pp. 1375–96.

Moreno, Jacob L. 1971. Psychodrama. In *Comprehensive Group Psychotherapy*. H.I. Kaplan and B.J. Sadock, eds. Baltimore: Williams and Wilkins, pp. 460–500.

Morley, Jeffrey G. 2000. Trauma repair through therapeutic enactment: A protagonist's perspective. Unpublished master's thesis. University of British Columbia. Vancouver, BC, Canada.

Nathanson, Donald L. 1992. *Shame and Pride: Affect, Sex, and the Birth of the Self*. New York: W.W. Norton and Co.

Neumann, Erich. [1954] 1970. *The Origins and History of Consciousness*. R.F.C. Hull, trans. Bollingen series. Reprinted Princeton University Press.

Neumann, Erich. [1969] 1973. *Depth Psychology and a New Ethic*. Reprinted New York: Harper Torchbooks.

Perera, Sylvia Brinton. 1981. *Descent to the Goddess: A Way of Initiation for Women*. Toronto: Inner City Books.

Perls, Frederick S. 1969. *Gestalt Therapy Verbatim*. New York: Bantam.

Pert, Candace. 1999. *Molecules of Emotion: The Science behind Mind-Body Medicine*. New York: Scribner.

Pinkola Estes, Clarissa. 1992. *Women Who Run with the Wolves: Myths and Stories of the Wild Woman Archetype*. New York: Ballantine Books.

Plomp, Loralee Marie. 1998. Confronting Unfixable Suffering: The Lived Experience of Police Officers. Unpublished master's thesis, University of British Columbia, Vancouver, BC, Canada.

Pressman, Stephanie D., and Robert M. Pressman. 1997. *The Narcissistic Family: Diagnosis and Treatment*. New York: Jossey-Bass.

Rogers, Carl R. 1961. *On Becoming a Person*. Boston: Houghton Mifflin Co.

Rogers, Carl R. 1967. The process of the basic encounter group. In *Challenges of Humanistic Psychology*. J.F. Bugental, ed. New York: McGraw-Hill, p. 273. Also published in *New Directions in Client-Centered Therapy*. J.T. Hart and T.M. Tomlinson, eds. Boston: Houghton Mifflin, 1970.

Rogers, Carl R. 1985. In Charles J. Vanderkolk, *Introduction to Group Counseling and Psychotherapy*. Columbus, OH: Charles E. Merrill, pp. 88–96.

Rosen, Marion, with Susan Brenner. 2003. *Rosen Method Bodywork: Accessing the Unconscious through Touch*. Berkeley, CA: North Atlantic Books.

Rothschild, Babette. 2000. *The Body Remembers: The Psychophysiology of Trauma and Trauma Treatment*. New York: W.W. Norton and Co.

Schermer, Victor L., and Malcolm Pines, eds. 1994. *Ring of Fire: Primitive Affects and Object Relations in Group Psychotherapy*. London: Routledge.

Schieffelin, Edward L. 1976. *The Sorrow of the Lonely and the Burning of the Dancers*. New York: St. Martin's Press.

Schore, Allan N. 2002. Dysregulation of the right brain: A fundamental mechanism of traumatic attachment and the psychopathogenesis of posttraumatic stress disorder. *Australia and New Zealand Journal of Psychiatry* 36: 9–30.

Schutz, William C. 1958. *FIRO: A Three-dimensional Theory of Interpersonal Behavior*. New York: Holt, Rinehart and Winston.

Shapiro, Francine. 2001. *Eye Movement Desensitization and Reprocessing: Basic Principles, Protocols, and Procedures*, 2nd ed. New York and London: The Guilford Press.

Silverstein, Judith L. 1997. Acting out in group therapy: Avoiding authority struggles. *International Journal of Group Psychotherapy* 47(1): 31–45.

South African Truth and Reconciliation Commission. 1996. In *Country of My Skull: Guilt, Sorrow, and the Limits of Forgiveness in the New South Africa*, Antjie Krog, ed. Johannesburg: Random House South Africa, 1998.

Stanislavski, Constantin. 1936. *An Actor Prepares*. New York: Theatre Arts Books.

Stein, Robert. 1973. *Incest and Human Love: The Betrayal of the Soul in Psychotherapy*. New York: Penguin Books.

Stein, Robert. 1984. *Incest and Human Love: The Betrayal of the Soul in Psychotherapy*, 2nd ed. Putnam, CT: Spring Publications.

Stern, Daniel N. 1985. *The Interpersonal World of the Infant*. New York: Basic Books.

Sullivan, Barbara Stevens. 1989. *Psychotherapy Grounded in the Feminine Principle*. Wilmette, IL: Chiron Publications.

Sullivan, Harry Stack. [1953] 1968. *The Interpersonal Theory of Psychiatry*. Reprinted New York: W.W. Norton and Co.

Tomkins, Silvan S. 1962. Affect, imagery, consciousness. Volume IV of *Cognition: Duplication, and Transformation of Information*. New York: Springer.

Turkus, Joan A. 1992. The spectrum of dissociative disorders: An overview of diagnosis and treatment. *Moving Forward* 1(4).

Van der Hart, Onno. 1997. *Coping with Loss: The Therapeutic Use of Leave-Taking Rituals*. New York: Irvington Publishing.

Van der Kolk, Bessel A. 1994. The body keeps the score: memory and the evolving psychobiology of post-traumatic stress. *Harvard Review of Psychiatry* 1(5): 253–65.

van der Kolk, Bessel A. 2002. The assessment and treatment of complex PTSD. In *Treating Trauma Survivors with PTSD*, Rachel Yehuda, ed. Washington, DC: American Psychiatric Press.

Vanderkolk, Charles J. 1985. *Introduction to Group Counseling and Psychotherapy*. Columbus, OH: Charles E. Merrill.

Von Franz, Marie-Louise. 1972. *The Feminine in Fairytales*. New York: Spring Publications.

Watkins, John, and Helen Watkins. 1997. *Ego States, Theory, and Therapy*. New York: W.W. Norton and Co.

Watzlawick, Paul, Janet B. Bavelas, and Don D. Jackson. 1967. *Pragmatics of Human Communication: A Study of Interactional Patterns, Pathologies, and Paradoxes*. New York: W.W. Norton and Co.

Watzlawick, Paul. 1987. If you desire to see, learn how to act. In *The Evolution of Psychotherapy*. J.K. Zeig, ed. New York: Brunner/Mazel.

Webster, George C., and Francoise E. Baylis. 1999. Moral residue. In *Margin of Error: The Necessity, Inevitability, and Ethics of Mistakes in Medicine and Bioethics Consultation*, L. Zoloth-Dorfman and S.B. Rubin, eds. Frederick, MD: University Publishing Group, p. 3.

Wesselmann, Debra. 1998. *The Whole Parent: How to Become a Terrific Parent Even If You Didn't Have One*. New York: Da Capo Press.

Westwood, Marvin J., Patrice A. Keats, and Patricia Wilensky. 2003. Therapeutic enactment: integrating individual and group counselling models for change, *Journal for Specialists in Group Work* 28(2): 122–38.

Whitmont, Edward C. 1969. *The Symbolic Quest: Basic Concepts of Analytical Psychology*. Princeton University Press.

Winnicott, Donald W. 1965. *The Maturational Processes and the Facilitating Environment*. London: Hogarth Press and New York: International Universities Press.

Wolpe, Joseph, and Arnold Lazarus. 1966. *Behaviour Therapy Techniques*. New York: Pergamon.

Yalom, Irvin D. 1985. *The Theory and Practice of Group Psychotherapy*, 3rd ed. New York: Basic Books.

Yalom, Irvin D. 1998. *The Yalom Reader: Selections from the Work of Master Therapist and Storyteller*. New York: Basic Books.

Young, Jeffrey E. 1999. *Cognitive Therapy for Personality Disorders: A Schema-focused Approach*, 3rd ed. Sarasota, FA: Professional Resource Press.

Zweig, Connie, and Jeremiah Abrams, eds. 1991. *Meeting the Shadow: The Hidden Power of the Dark Side of Human Nature*. Los Angeles: Jeremy P. Tarcher.

About the Authors

How did two otherwise conservatively trained psychologists get into the soul-healing business? We both have been working with trauma for many years. Although coming from different backgrounds—and different countries—we had similar experiences and training.

Marvin Westwood is a professor in the Counselling Psychology Program and an Associate Member of the Faculty of Medicine (Family Practice) at the University of British Columbia. He graduated from the University of Alberta (Edmonton) and began teaching at St. Francis Xavier University in Nova Scotia. From there he moved to Montreal and was appointed to the Counsellor Education Program at McGill University before taking up his current position at UBC in 1980.

A major interest in both his teaching and research is in group counselling and psychotherapy with a commitment to finding out how group counselling can be a highly effective method for promoting personal change among clients. As a counselling psychologist, Marvin was always been drawn to the therapeutic approaches that offered opportunities for clients to act and express their experiences more fully. Marvin has been developing the Therapeutic Enactment model over a number of years and has endeavoured to extend the theory and expand application to diverse populations. The repair of trauma in a group context has been his most recent focus. Dr. Westwood maintains that complex client problems require complex interventions—hence the need for more multi-system approaches.

The treatment model he developed with Patricia Wilensky has been used with various client populations, including clients experiencing profound traumatic life events, soldiers, First Nations peoples, health care and counselling professionals, new immigrants, refugees, and during the training of graduate students. His work has been presented in Australia, Switzerland, Chile, Argentina, Malta, the United Kingdom, the United States, Japan, Hong Kong, and Indonesia. In recognition for his group-based work with soldiers recovering from trauma, he was awarded the Commemorative Medal for the Golden Jubilee of Her Majesty Queen Elizabeth II in 2002.

Patricia Wilensky left her childhood home in Belfast at the age of twenty-three when the most recent war began there in 1969. Belfast is where she began to learn, at an early age, about trauma and traumatizing circumstances. She grew up in a family and a culture where trauma, compounded by alcohol and its negative effects, was commonplace. Looking for answers led her to the study of psychology.

Moving to London, England, with a master's degree in child psychology, Patricia took a job as a school psychologist. All this took place before an understanding and a social context had developed in Britain for the widespread phenomenon of child abuse, particularly child sexual abuse. Patricia felt helpless and alone as she struggled to try to help her child and adolescent clients. There seemed to be no community or group support for them or for the professionals who worked with them. In the local education authority office where Patricia was based, she saw the psychologists, social workers, truant officers, psychiatrists, nurses, and police burn out quickly under the unremitting pressures of a job where very little could be done except uncover traumatizing situations and all without ever using the word "trauma". In 1970, realizing that she did not want to work alone, Patricia enrolled at the Tavistock Clinic in London for training in group work. Groups seemed an area where people could work with common purpose and support one another, and eventually groups became her professional area of expertise.

Patricia emigrated to Canada in 1973 and completed a doctorate in psychology. During this period Patricia worked as a school psychologist in Toronto and after that in the Ontario prisons. Again, she saw clients who had suffered through terrible childhoods and who were working with professionals who were miserable, ineffectual, and ashamed.

Patricia was exhorted by family and culture to "just get on with it" and she did. She became a successful psychologist with a large practice, married, and co-raised a family. While she had been drawn to psychology as a teenager and loved to study and read, she realized that the practice of psychology was soulless. Accepting a teaching position at the University of British Columbia in 1992, she met Marv for the first time.

Marv and Patricia decided to share a practice and co-lead groups. They found out quickly that the people who were drawn to our groups were interested in connection and spirit. Most of the group members had suffered trauma. At that time, they worked within the traditional methods of helping clients cope with trauma: empathy counselling, cognitive approaches, desensitization, and self-psychology. However, as group practitioners they were always searching for better ways to help participants reconnect and get past mental blocks and bad behavioural habits like addictions or aggression. They realized that group approaches that specifically dealt with trauma survivors were hard to find. Interprofessional groups for vicarious trauma were unheard of.

Marv and Patricia are committed to group work because they believe that interpersonal reconnection is an essential component in the repair of trauma. Yet it is missing in classical treatments. Therapeutic Enactment is designed so that both those who do enactments and those who witness them experience the process as nurturing, insightful, and helpful. They have found that this produces remarkable group commitment and opportunities for reparation of long-standing personal and cultural trauma. As a result of their own isolating professional experiences, they are particularly sensitive to the possibilities in group work of helping other professionals.

Acknowledgements

The pain of the world will sear and break our hearts
because we can no longer keep them closed.
We've seen too much now.
To some degree or other,
we have surrendered into service
and are willing to pay the price of compassion.

—Ram Dass

We wish to thank our students and colleagues who showed a keen interest in enactment work. Those who helped conceptualize the Therapeutic Enactment process and translate it into practice include the following: Hilary Pearson, David Kuhl, Tim Black, Lyn Martens, Patrice Keats, Douglas Cave, Paul Whitehead, Holly McLean, and George Passmore. Thank you. Our collaboration has been a source of inspiration and growth both personally and in the work. Two of Marv's colleagues at the University of British Columbia assisted in important ways. I am indebted to Marla Buchanan, who helped me with the theory development, and to Rod McCormick, for his input about using this approach with First Nations' people. Thank you to Brian Walker whose generosity and commitment is a major contribution in the instruction video showing Therapeutic Enactment in action.

For their devotion, we wish to thank students and clients of the Therapeutic Enactment reparation process, particularly the Soulcatchers Therapeutic Enactment Alumni Group, who continue to give so generously of their time and skill in spite of the heavy demands of their professions: David Bain, Joe Barnwell, Elana Brief, Janie Brown, Betty Calam, Elsie Devita, Ray Devries, Sharon Gretzinger, Susan Higginbottom, Eva Knell, Hilary Mackey, Deborah MacNamara, Belle McClure, Ed Peck, Lorne Prupas, Jamie Sork, Jenifer Thewalt, and Patrick Walker. Our work together continues. We have become a source of support and inspiration for each other and able to provide assistance to those who come to us for the relief of suffering. Thank you to the many others who have participated in our groups over the past twelve years and who still keep in touch. And in memory of John Cheetham.

Thank you to Sally Halliday whose assistance in the early stages of writing helped set the stage for this book; Shirarose Wilensky for her editing and videography; Dr. Olivia Scalzo for her input to the chapter on dissociation; Hilary Mackey, our body psychotherapist, for her help with the body process content; and Dr. Marshall Wilensky for his training and supervision in EMDR. Special thanks to Ann-Marie Metten for her tenacity throughout the editing process. Thank you also to Gray Poehnell for his layout of the book and design suggestions.

Patricia extends her thanks most of all to Marshall, Shirarose, and Eve, without whom this book would not have been possible.

Finally, to all of the many clients who trusted Marv with their lives: I have such gratitude. This book would not have been possible without you; your enacted stories are the basis of our work. Thank you to Dianne Westwood, my wife and confidante, who encouraged and supported me to pursue this work and who continues to influence both my thinking and practice.

From bitter searching of the heart, we rise to play a greater part.
—Leonard Cohen, "Villanelle for Our Time"

Index